European Free Trade Association (EFTA) and the European Economic Area (EEA)

European Free Trade Association (EFTA) and the European Economic Area (EEA)

Third Edition

Kyrre Isaksen
Michael Sánchez Rydelski
Carsten Zatschler

This book was originally published as a monograph in the International Encyclopaedia of Laws/Intergovernmental Organizations.

Founding Editor: Roger Blanpain
General Editor: Frank Hendrickx
Volume Editor: Jan Wouters

Wolters Kluwer

Published by:
Kluwer Law International B.V.
PO Box 316
2400 AH Alphen aan den Rijn
The Netherlands
E-mail: lrs-sales@wolterskluwer.com
Website: www.wolterskluwer.com/en/solutions/kluwerlawinternational

Sold and distributed by:
Wolters Kluwer Legal & Regulatory U.S.
920 Links Avenue
Landisville, PA 17538
United States of America
E-mail: customer.service@wolterskluwer.com

ISBN 978-94-035-3398-8

e-Book: ISBN 978-94-035-3408-4
web-PDF: ISBN 978-94-035-3418-3

This title is available on www.kluwerlawonline.com

The Authors

Mr Kyrre Isaksen was born on 19 June 1978 in Oslo. He graduated from the law faculty of the University of Oslo in 2005 and obtained an LLM from the University of Heidelberg in 2006. He has experience from the Legal Affairs Department of the Ministry of Foreign Affairs and from the Tax Law Department of the Ministry of Finance, as well as from the Secretariat-General of the European Commission. Between 2016 and 2019, he was Head of EEA Legal Coordination at the EFTA Secretariat in Brussels. In 2021, he joined the Legal and Executive Affairs (LEA) Department of the EFTA Surveillance Authority in Brussels.

Mr Michael Sánchez Rydelski was born on 30 May 1964 in Hamburg. He graduated from the law faculty of the University of Hamburg in 1990. In 1991, he also qualified as a lawyer in Spain. Between 1991 and 1994, he completed his German law training and worked during that time for the German Embassy in Paris, the European Commission in Brussels and the Office of the Legal Counsel of the United Nations in New York. Mr Sánchez Rydelski was admitted to the Hamburg and Brussels Bar in 1994. He practised international trade law and EU competition law in Brussels. In 1999, he joined the LEA Department of the EFTA Surveillance Authority in Brussels. Mr Sánchez Rydelski received his Doctorate from the University of Hamburg in 2001. In 2003, he was appointed Deputy Director of the LEA Department. Mr Sánchez Rydelski left the EFTA Surveillance Authority in 2007 and returned to private practice in Brussels. He has published several books on World Trade Organization (WTO)/European Union (EU) anti-subsidy laws and has written numerous articles on various topics of international trade law and EU competition law. Mr Sánchez Rydelski is guest lecturer at the Universities of Hamburg and Reykjavik. In October 2016, he returned to the LEA Department of the EFTA Surveillance Authority in Brussels. In December 2016, Mr Sánchez Rydelski was appointed Chairman of the Board of Appeal of the European Union Aviation Safety Agency (EASA).

The Authors

Mr Carsten Zatschler was born on 2 August 1974 in Brussels. He graduated from the University of Cambridge in 1996 and obtained master's degrees from the Université Panthéon-Assas (Paris II) and the Humboldt Universität zu Berlin before being called to the Bar of England & Wales by the Inner Temple in 1999. He was called to the Bar of Ireland in 2018 and became a Member of the Inner Bar (Senior Counsel) in 2021, specializing in EU and international trade law. His past roles include a decade in the cabinets of successive British Judges at the Court of Justice of the European Union, from 2003 to 2013 and two terms, from 2015 to 2021, as Legal and Executive Director of the EFTA Surveillance Authority in Brussels. Mr Zatschler sits on the Board of Appeal of the European Financial Supervisory Authorities (European Banking Authority (EBA), European Securities and Markets Authority (ESMA) and European Insurance and Occupational Pensions Authority (EIOPA)); is a Bencher of the Honourable Society of the Inner Temple; Adjunct Full Professor at the Sutherland School of Law, University College Dublin; and a member of the visiting faculty of the Wirtschaftsuniversität Wien and the Universidad Carlos III Madrid.

Table of Contents

List of Abbreviations

ACER	Agency for the Cooperation of Energy Regulators
CJEU	Court of Justice of the European Union
CSA	Competition and State Aid
EASA	European Union Aviation Safety Agency
EBA	European Banking Authority
EC	European Community
ECA	European Competition Authority
ECHR	European Convention on Human Rights
ECJ	European Court of Justice
ECN	European Competition Network
ECSC	European Coal and Steel Community
EEA	European Economic Area
EEC	European Economic Community
EESC	European Economic and Social Committee
EFTA	European Free Trade Association
EIOPA	European Insurance and Occupational Pensions Authority
ESA	European Supervisory Authority
ESMA	European Securities and Markets Authority
ETUC	European Trade Union Confederation
EU	European Union
FMO	Financial Mechanism Office
FTA	Free Trade Agreement
GATT	General Agreement on Tariffs and Trade
GBER	General Block Exemption Regulation
GCC	Gulf Cooperation Council
GDP	Gross Domestic Product
ICN	International Competition Network
ILO	International Labour Organization
LEA	Legal and Executive Affairs
MFN	Most-Favoured-Nation

List of Abbreviations

OECD	Organization for Economic Co-operation and Development
OEEC	Organization of European Economic Cooperation
SCA	Agreement between the EFTA States on the establishment of a Surveillance Authority and a Court of Justice
SGEI	Services of General Economic Interest
TBT	Technical Barriers to Trade
TEU	Treaty on European Union
TFEU	Treaty on the Functioning of the European Union
TRIPS	Trade-Related Aspects of Intellectual Property Rights
UN	United Nation
UNCTAD	United Nations Conference on Trade and Development
UNECE	United Nations Economic Commission for Europe
UNICE	Union of Industrial and Employers' Confederations of Europe

General Introduction to EFTA and EEA

1. The European Free Trade Association (EFTA) and the European Economic Area (EEA), while closely related, are appropriately dealt with in two separate parts here. The first part deals with the EFTA, which functions on the legal basis of the EFTA Convention.[1] The EFTA Convention promotes free trade between its four Member States: Iceland, Liechtenstein, Norway and Switzerland. EFTA is also a platform for an extensive network of free trade arrangements between the EFTA States and third countries.

2. The second part covers the Agreement on the EEA.[2] This is an agreement between the European Union (EU) and its Member States, on the one hand, and three EFTA States, namely Iceland, Liechtenstein and Norway, on the other hand. The EEA Agreement extends the EU's Internal Market[3] to these three EFTA States. Switzerland, the fourth EFTA State, is not a Contracting Party to the EEA Agreement. Therefore, with regard to the terminology, it needs to be noted that the notion 'EFTA States', when referred to in the first part, includes Switzerland, whereas when referred to in the second part it excludes Switzerland.[4]

1. A copy of the Convention establishing the EFTA can be retrieved from the website of the EFTA Secretariat at www.efta.int.
2. OJ L 1, 3.1.1994, 3.
3. Sometimes referred to interchangeably as the 'Single Market'. Here, 'Internal Market', which is the term used in the TEU and the TFEU is preferred.
4. *See also* Art. 2(b) of the EEA Agreement.

Part I. The European Free Trade Association

Chapter 1. Genesis and Historical Development

3. After the end of the Second World War, European countries began discussing the future economic order of their continent. These discussions were, to a large extent, held within the Organization of European Economic Cooperation (OEEC).[5] During these discussions two different concepts emerged. While a group of countries, led by France, considered it desirable to have not only a mere economic but also a political integration of Europe, another group of countries, led by the United Kingdom, was opposed to such political ambition. The latter group favoured a purely economic approach and advocated a free trade area for Europe. When it became apparent that the differences between these two camps were irreconcilable, the so-called inner six (Belgium, France, Germany, Italy, Luxemburg and the Netherlands) forged ahead and created a single European market with common supranational institutions. They established the European Coal and Steel Community (ECSC)[6] in 1952. Subsequently, in 1958, the European Atomic Energy Community (Euratom) and the European Economic Community (EEC) were established.[7]

4. This development left the so-called outer seven (Austria, Denmark, Norway, Portugal, Sweden, Switzerland and the United Kingdom) somewhat isolated. They reacted, in spring 1959, by taking the first steps in what was to become the EFTA. The negotiations on the establishment of EFTA were concluded with the signing of the EFTA Convention in Stockholm on 4 January 1960. Later, Iceland,[8] Finland[9] and Liechtenstein[10] acceded to the EFTA Convention. Most Member States would later leave when they became EC/EU Member States (*see infra*).

5. The OEEC was set up in 1948. It was the predecessor organization of today's OECD(Organization for Economic Cooperation and Development).
6. The ECSC Treaty (Treaty establishing the European Coal and Steel Community) was signed in Paris on 18 Apr. 1951 and entered into force on 25 Jul. 1952. The ECSC Treaty expired on 23 Jul. 2002.
7. The Euratom (Treaty establishing a European Atomic Energy Community) and EEC Treaties (Treaty establishing the European Economic Community) were both signed in Rome on 25 Mar. 1957 and entered into force on 1 Jan. 1958.
8. Iceland joined EFTA in 1970.
9. Finland was first associated with EFTA in 1961. Due to the special character of the association between Finland and EFTA, the position of Finland was for all practical purposes that of a member. Finland acceded formally on 1 Jan. 1986.
10. Liechtenstein was the latest country to join EFTA in 1991.

5. Unlike the EEC Treaty, the EFTA Convention did not envisage political integration. The EFTA States accepted neither the concept of a customs union nor the idea of supranational institutions. Instead, EFTA sought, in more narrow fields than the EEC, to achieve similar economic objectives through a substantially lower level of integration by way of intergovernmental cooperation.

6. The EFTA Convention contained provisions on the abolition and prohibition of import duties, quantitative restrictions, and equivalent measures on import and export of goods. It also contained provisions on the prohibition of certain forms of State aid and certain measures with regard to public undertakings, restrictive business practices, establishment, and dumped and subsidized imports. Special provisions meant that agricultural products and fish and other marine products were covered only to a very limited extent by the EFTA Convention. No formal and substantial coordination towards third parties was foreseen. Foreign trade policy remained at national level. The EFTA Convention entered into force on 3 May 1960 and a decision was taken to place the EFTA Secretariat in Geneva. With some exceptions, tariffs on industrial goods were finally abolished in 1966. Free trade in fish and other marine products was achieved in 1989.

7. The EFTA Convention had two other main purposes beyond the realization of free trade in industrial products among the EFTA States. First, from a more strategic point of view, the EFTA Convention was to counteract the negative impact on trade in the part of Europe not covered by the EEC's common market.[11] Second, it aimed to bolster the EFTA States' political weight in further negotiations for the establishment of a pan-European free trade area.

8. In this respect, the idea of creating a free trade area was a natural follow-up to the stalled attempts to establish a free trade area covering all European countries in the Organization for Economic Cooperation and Development (OECD) – an idea that was presented two years earlier but turned down by some of the EEC Member States, notably France.[12] Indeed, the EEC saw EFTA for a long time as some kind of rival organization in the process of shaping the economic order of the European continent. Especially for the first decade after the inception of EFTA, the relationship between the EEC and EFTA has been described as non-existent.[13]

9. Repeated offers by different EFTA States to the EEC to create a single European market were refused. Over time, EFTA stopped being an adversary to the EEC. The respective weight of the two organizations and the political atmosphere between them changed after the accession in 1973 of two of the EFTA States, namely Denmark and the United Kingdom, to the EEC, paving the way for the

11. J. Hettne & M. Fritz, *Sverige möter EG-rätten – EES-avtalet och dess införlivande med svensk rätt* 22 (Stockholm: Nerenius & Santérus 1994).
12. A brief description of the attempts to establish an OEEC FTA can be found in: S. Norberg et al., *The European Economic Area, EEA Law: A Commentary on the EEA Agreement* 39–40 (Stockholm: Fritzes 1993).
13. S. Norberg et al., *The European Economic Area, EEA Law: A Commentary on the EEA Agreement* 44 (Stockholm: Fritzes 1993).

remaining EFTA States to enter into bilateral Free Trade Agreements (FTAs) with the EEC. Norway also concluded negotiations for membership in the EEC but finally decided to remain outside after a negative referendum on membership. For some, the changes in 1972–1973 meant that EFTA became more of a platform for coordinating relations with the EEC.

10. The bilateral FTAs between EFTA States and the EEC, which were concluded in 1972 and entered into force in 1973,[14] were very similar in scope to the EFTA Convention. The bilateral FTAs provided for the elimination of customs duties and equivalent taxes. They thereby prevented the re-erection of tariff barriers between, on the one hand, Denmark and the United Kingdom and, on the other hand, the remaining EFTA States. The bilateral FTAs, however, went beyond previous agreements in that they extended the elimination of customs and tariff barriers to the EEC as a whole, thereby linking the two previous exclusive rival camps into a single preferential system. The bilateral FTAs also contained provisions on the elimination of quantitative restrictions on import and export of goods and of all discriminating measures having an equivalent effect. Derogations similar to those contained in the EEC Treaty were also provided for. Furthermore, the bilateral FTAs prohibited discriminatory internal taxes, prescribed that payments should be subject to free movement, and instituted a system regulating competition by means of rules governing undertakings, reminiscent of the competition rules in the EEC Treaty. Finally, the Agreements contained rules relating to 'distortive' State aid and included a reference to the General Agreement on Tariffs and Trade (GATT) dumping rules. The Agreements, together with the EEC Treaty, thereby provided a free trade area for goods between the EFTA States and the EEC.

11. In contrast to the EEC Treaty, but in line with the EFTA Convention, the bilateral FTAs did not cover agricultural products. Furthermore, they did not liberalize national rules concerning the free movement of persons, services and capital. They were also distinguished from the EEC Treaty by covering only goods that were produced in the EFTA or the EEC territories. Finally, although most of the rules in the bilateral FTAs were formulated in a manner broadly similar to the corresponding provisions in the EEC Treaty, their scope was not necessarily the same, as they had to be interpreted in a different context than their EEC counterparts. That being said, they did entail an expression of a possible future development parallel to that of the EEC. All but the Finnish Agreement contained a clause whereby the parties were ready to examine, in the light of developments in the EEC, the possibility of developing and deepening their relations where this would appear useful in the interests of their economies and to extend these to fields not covered by the Agreements.

12. After thirteen years of relatively stable membership in EFTA, the 1980s brought about some changes. On 1 January 1986, Portugal withdrew from the EFTA

14. The Agreements with Norway and Finland were concluded slightly later on 14 May 1973 and 5 Oct. 1973 respectively.

Convention and became a member of the EEC.[15] In 1986, Finland turned its associate membership of EFTA, which it held since 1961, into full membership. Most importantly, the EFTA States agreed to strengthen their already preferential relationship with the EEC by commencing negotiations on an EEA.[16] As a result of these negotiations, the EEA Agreement was established and entered into force in 1994. It was originally negotiated between all the EFTA States and the EEC and its Member States. However, Switzerland subsequently decided not to join this extensive arrangement.

13. Since the early 1990s, EFTA States have been expanding trade relations with partners in Central and Eastern Europe and the Mediterranean region.[17] Initially, the EFTA States focused on concluding FTAs with the countries of Central and Eastern Europe. Subsequently, they extended their network of FTAs beyond the confines of Europe.[18]

14. In 1995, three EFTA States, namely Austria, Finland and Sweden, left EFTA to join the European Community[19] (EC). An attempt by Norway to join this wave into EC membership was again turned down by way of a negative referendum on membership.

15. Another important development in the history of EFTA was the conclusion by Switzerland in 1999 of seven bilateral agreements with the EC covering a wide range of areas.[20] These included movement of persons, transport and Technical Barriers to Trade (TBT). The bilateral agreements entered into force on 1 June 2001. This development led to the situation that, in the fields covered by the seven bilateral agreements, the integration between the EC and the 'EEA-EFTA States' and between the EC and Switzerland were more advanced than the relations between Switzerland and its EFTA partners. In other words, the level of integration between the EFTA States lagged behind the level of integration that EFTA States had with the EC.

---

15. The EFTA Industrial Development Fund for Portugal continued to operate until the end of January 2002 in accordance with its statutes.
16. For a detailed history of the negotiation and implementation of the EEA Agreement, *see infra* Part II, Ch. 1.
17. Already back in 1979 EFTA signed its first FTA with Spain.
18. *See infra* Part I, Ch. 3, §2.
19. The Maastricht Treaty (TEU) changed the name EEC into EC.
20. Agreement between the EC and its Member States, of the one part, and the Swiss Confederation, of the other, on the free movement of persons (OJ L 114, 30.4.2002, 6); Agreement between the EC and the Swiss Confederation on Air Transport (OJ L 114, 30.4.2002, 73); Agreement between the EC and the Swiss Confederation on the Carriage of Goods and Passengers by Rail and Road (OJ L 114, 30.4.2002, 91); Agreement between the EC and the Swiss Confederation on trade in agricultural products (OJ L 114, 30.4.2002, 132); Agreement between the EC and the Swiss Confederation on mutual recognition in relation to conformity assessment (OJ L 114, 30.4.2002, 369); Agreement between the EC and the Swiss Confederation on certain aspects of government procurement (OJ L 114, 30.4.2002, 430); and Agreement on Scientific and Technological Cooperation between the European Communities and the Swiss Confederation (OJ L 114, 30.4.2002, 468).

16. This development, together with the fact that the multilateral trade agreements resulting from the Uruguay Round, as well as the FTAs between the EFTA States and third countries, went beyond the scope and coverage of the EFTA Convention, prompted the EFTA States to update the Convention. Upon invitation by Switzerland, they agreed to do so at the EFTA Ministerial Council in 1999. This brought the integration of their economies to the level of integration between the Swiss and EC economies.

17. The EFTA Convention was substantively modified and extended. The amendments to the EFTA Convention consisted, on the one hand, of modernization of the trade terminology used and, on the other hand, of an extension of its substantive scope and coverage. Although initially it was considered that the amendments to the EFTA Convention would mostly be of a technical nature, it took almost two years before a commonly acceptable text was presented for signature. The revised EFTA Convention (or so-called Vaduz Convention)[21] was signed in Vaduz on 21 June 2001 and entered into force on the same day as the Swiss-EC bilateral agreements, that is, on 1 June 2002.

18. The substantive fields newly covered by the EFTA Convention include trade in services and investment, mutual recognition of conformity assessments, free movement of persons, social security and mutual recognition of diplomas, land and air transport, public procurement and intellectual property rights.[22] In addition, the provisions governing agriculture were updated and were made more accessible while still maintaining the special considerations underlying the sector.[23]

19. It was also foreseen that certain Annexes to the EFTA Convention could be modified by a simplified procedure.[24] According to the Joint Declaration on the development of law, annexed to the EFTA Convention, the EFTA States endeavoured to update the EFTA Convention on a continuous basis. This would permit alignment of its content to the lowest common denominator between the content of the Swiss-EU bilateral agreements and the EEA Agreement.[25]

20. As a consequence of the global financial crisis in 2008 and its impact on the Icelandic economy, Iceland applied in 2009 for membership in the EU.[26] Accession negotiations between Iceland and the EU started in 2010. After a new government took over in May 2013, Iceland put the accession negotiations on hold. In March 2015, Iceland's government informed the EU that Iceland no longer wished to maintain its status as a candidate country for EU membership.

---

21. Convention establishing the EFTA: in the following the terminology EFTA Convention will be used.
22. For a description of the EFTA Convention, *see infra* Part I, Ch. 3, §1.
23. For a presentation of the changes brought about by the Vaduz Convention, *see* EFTA Bulletin, *The Updated EFTA Convention*, Issue 1-2001.
24. *See infra* Part I, Ch. 3, §1, II.
25. In 2005, Switzerland finalized the second series of bilateral agreements with the EU after the positive outcome in June 2005 of the Swiss referendum on the Schengen/Dublin Agreement.
26. The Lisbon Treaty transferred the legal personality of the EC to the EU.

Chapter 2. Institutional Framework

§1. Membership and Territorial Application

21. EFTA is an intergovernmental organization comprising four Member States, namely Iceland, Liechtenstein, Norway and Switzerland.[27] The EFTA Convention applies to the territories of these Member States except as provided for in Annex U thereto (Article 58 of the EFTA Convention). Annex U to the EFTA Convention states that Norway shall have the right to exempt the territory of Svalbard from the application of the EFTA Convention with the exception of trade in goods. Svalbard is Europe's northernmost territory, an archipelago close to the North Pole, which enjoys a special status under the Svalbard Treaty of 9 February 1920.

22. Membership of EFTA is open-ended. Article 56(1) of the EFTA Convention provides for the possibility of other States to accede to the EFTA Convention. The EFTA Convention does not contain any specific conditions for accession. The terms of accession would be determined in the negotiations with the applying State. Upon completion of these negotiations, the EFTA Council[28] would take a decision approving the accession setting out the terms and conditions thereof. The EFTA Convention would enter into force in relation to an acceding State on the date stipulated in an EFTA Council Decision (Article 56(1), third sentence, of the EFTA Convention). Any new membership would entail the acceding State applying to also become a party to the FTAs[29] between the Member States and third countries, unions of States or international organizations (Article 56(3) of the EFTA Convention).

23. Withdrawal from the EFTA Convention is also possible. Article 57(1) of the EFTA Convention allows any Member State to withdraw from the EFTA Convention with twelve months' notice (Article 57(2) of the EFTA Convention). Before such withdrawal takes effect, the Member States have to agree on appropriate arrangements and equitable cost sharing relating to the withdrawal.

§2. Institutions

I. The EFTA Council

24. The EFTA Council is the highest governing body of EFTA with responsibility for all matters concerning the relations between the EFTA States and between EFTA and third countries. The EFTA Council is the forum in which the EFTA States consult, act together and negotiate. The responsibilities of the EFTA Council are

27. EFTA enjoys privileges and immunities on the basis of headquarters agreements it concluded with Switzerland, Belgium and Luxembourg respectively. In the EFTA States it moreover enjoys similar privileges and immunities in accordance with the Protocol on the legal capacity, privileges and immunities of the EFTA.
28. *See infra* Part I, Ch. 2, §2, I.
29. Concerning the FTAs, *see infra* Part I, Ch. 3, §2, II.

listed in Article 43(1) of the EFTA Convention. They comprise, *inter alia*, management of the relations between the EFTA States under the EFTA Convention. In that function, the Council supervises the application of the Convention and keeps its operation under review. The Council also decides on amendments to the Convention.[30] In principle, any decision of the EFTA Council to amend the Convention is to be submitted to the EFTA States for their acceptance in accordance with the respective internal legal requirements. It is only where the EFTA Convention foresees another (simplified) procedure that the Council may actually take the decision concerning an amendment.[31]

25. The Council also has a broad mandate to decide on policies to promote the overall objectives of EFTA and to facilitate the development of links with other States, unions of States or international organizations. The EFTA States discuss and decide in the EFTA Council on the development of EFTA's relations with third countries, negotiate trade and cooperation agreements and manage existing trade and cooperation agreements. These last competences, which are set out in Article 43(1)(e), (f) and (g) of the EFTA Convention, relate to EFTA's extensive third-country activities. Finally, the Council endeavours to resolve disputes that may arise regarding the interpretation or application of the EFTA Convention and considers any other matter that may affect the operation of the EFTA Convention.

26. The EFTA Council usually meets once a month at the level of Heads of Permanent Mission to EFTA in Geneva and twice a year at Ministerial level. Each EFTA State is represented and has one vote (Article 43(2) of the EFTA Convention). Decisions and recommendations of the Council are taken by unanimous vote, except insofar as the Convention provides otherwise. According to Article 43(5) of the EFTA Convention, decisions or recommendations are regarded as unanimous unless a Member State casts a negative vote. Decisions and recommendations, which are to be made by majority vote, require the affirmative vote of three Member States. Article 44(a) of the EFTA Convention empowers the EFTA Council to lay down the Rules of Procedure, which may include a provision that procedural questions be decided by majority vote. The EFTA Council has adopted Rules of Procedure which allow majority votes for procedural issues, including for the agreement on the time and place of its meetings and for the adoption of its agendas. However, decisions tend to be reached by consensus.

27. On 9 November 2017, the Council consolidated its decision on public access to EFTA documents.[32] According to this decision, the EFTA Secretariat makes available to the public by placement on its website the documents listed in the Annex to

30. All Council Decisions amending the EFTA Convention since 2001 are available on the EFTA Secretariat's website: www.efta.int/legal-texts/efta-convention/council-decisions-amending-the-convention.
31. Regarding the field of application of the simplified procedure *see infra* Part I, Ch. 3, §1, II.
32. Council Decision No. 6 of 2007 (as amended). Access to EEA-related documents is regulated by Standing Committee Decision No. 3 of 2007. The Decisions are available on the EFTA Secretariat's website: www.efta.int/legal-texts/public-access-archives.

the decision. In addition, any person may request, subject to some exceptions, access to documents drawn up or received by the EFTA Secretariat that are in the EFTA Secretariat's possession.

28. The Council is responsible for administrative and budgetary matters in EFTA (Article 44 of the EFTA Convention).[33] The Budget Committee[34] assists the Council on EFTA budgetary matters.

II. Organs, Committees and Other Bodies Assisting the EFTA Council

29. According to Article 43(3) of the EFTA Convention, the Council has the power to set up organs, committees and other bodies, as it considers necessary to assist it in accomplishing its tasks. On the basis of this provision, a large number of Committees and expert groups have been established to assist the EFTA Council. These organs, committees and other bodies are listed in Annex S of the EFTA Convention.[35] They all enjoy similar status vis-à-vis the EFTA Council. For example, the expert groups[36] do not operate under the authority of the committees; they report directly to the EFTA Council.

A. *Vaduz Committees Entrusted with the Updating of the EFTA Convention*

30. Certain committees play an active role in the context of the regular updating of the EFTA Convention. It is the EFTA Convention itself that provides that these committees are to be set up. The committees are responsible for air transport, land transport, movement of persons, conformity assessment, organic agriculture, public procurement and seeds.[37]

31. A common feature of these committees is that they are all responsible for, *inter alia*, recommending that the Council amends certain provisions of the annexes to the EFTA Convention under which the committees operate. Only the Committee on Mutual Recognition in Relation to Conformity Assessment has wider ranging powers. That Committee is entitled to decide itself on certain amendments to the

33. *See infra* Part I, Ch. 5.
34. *See infra* Part I, Ch. 2, §2, II, D.
35. By Council Decision No. 2/2010 of 17 May 2010, the following Committees were deleted from Annex S: the Committee of Trade Experts, the Committee on Agriculture and Fisheries and the Committee on Economic Development.
36. There are, for example, the following expert groups: Group of State aid experts; Group of experts on public procurement; Group of experts on intellectual property; Group of experts on price compensation; Group of experts on services, investment and establishment; Group of experts on efficient trade procedures; and Group of legal experts.
37. *See respectively* Council Decision Nos 5/2002, 6/2002, 7/2002, 8/2002, 9/2002, 10/2002 and 11/2002 of 18 Jun. 2002 (copies of these decisions can be requested at the EFTA Secretariat in Geneva).

annex to the EFTA Convention under which it is set up (Annex I on Mutual recognition in relation to conformity assessment). Nevertheless, it has to notify the Council of all its decisions without delay.

B. Pre-Vaduz Committees Entrusted with Specific Tasks

32. Other committees have specific tasks, which are not related to the updating of the EFTA Convention. They include: the Committee on TBT,[38] the Committee of Origin and Customs Experts,[39] and the Committee on Trade Facilitation.[40] The functions of these committees are to make reports and proposals to the Council on matters falling in their respective fields of competence or on any other matter referred to the Committee by the Council.

33. The Economic Committee[41] can also be placed in this category. It is responsible for a limited number of subject matters (economic and monetary problems and policies). However, instead of making reports and concrete proposals to the Council, its function consists almost exclusively in exchanging information and views.

C. Pre-Vaduz Committees with Horizontal Mandates

34. A third category of committees includes those that have a more horizontal mandate. The most typical and best known of these committees are the Consultative Committee,[42] the Committee of Members of Parliament[43] and the EEA-EFTA Forum.

35. Representatives of industry and labour in the EFTA States exchange views among themselves and with the Council in the Consultative Committee. The Consultative Committee is a forum for social partner organizations (trade unions and employers' organizations) in the four EFTA States. Through its cooperation with social partners in the EU and in the countries acceding to the EU, the Committee also serves as a link between social partners in EFTA and in the current and future EU countries.

---

38. Council Decision No. 10/84, as amended by Council Decision Nos 8/88 and 4/94. The Committee on TBT discusses standardization and conformity assessment policies.
39. Council Decision No. 8/74, as amended by Council Decision No. 4/92. The Committee on Customs and Origin Matters oversees cooperation in the customs field, particularly in relation to the FTAs. It discusses questions in relation to rules of origin. It also addresses unresolved technical customs issues among EFTA States.
40. By Council Decision No. 1/2010.
41. Council Decision No. 16/64, as amended by Council Decision No. 11/73 and replaced by EFTA/C.SR 9/95 (EFTA/EC 1/95). The Economic Committee exchanges views on economic policy in the EFTA States and conducts a dialogue on such matters with the EU.
42. The Terms of Reference of the Consultative Committee were adopted by Council Decision No. 5/61, as amended by Council Decision Nos 10/68, 11/88, 1/94, 2/94 and Council Report EFTA/C.SR 9/95 of 1995.
43. Council Decision No. 11/77.

36. The Consultative Committee is a vital platform for dialogue and consultation. The members of the Consultative Committee are designated by the Member States and chosen from the social partner organizations in the four EFTA States. Normally, six members each from Norway and Switzerland, four members from Iceland and two from Liechtenstein participate in meetings of the Committee. The Consultative Committee elects a Chairman and two Vice-Chairmen, chosen from among its members, with a term of office of two years. The European organizations European Trade Union Confederation (ETUC) and Union of Industrial and Employers' Confederations of Europe (UNICE) may send one observer each. The Consultative Committee adopted its own Rules of Procedure.[44]

37. The Consultative Committee usually holds three to four internal meetings per year, in addition to the annual joint meeting with the Standing Committee of the EFTA States.[45] Biannually, the EFTA Social Partners meet with the EFTA Council at Ministerial level: in the spring with Ministers from all four EFTA States and in the autumn with the 'Ministerial Chair'. Annual meetings with the Committee of Members of Parliament ensure exchange of views between Social Partners and Parliamentarians of the EFTA States.

38. The entry into force of the EEA Agreement has meant that two EFTA Parliamentary Committees now exist: the Committee of Members of Parliament of the EFTA States, which deals with EEA-related matters and forms the EFTA side of the EEA Joint Parliamentary Committee,[46] and the Committee of Members of Parliament of the EFTA Countries, which deals with all other matters, including relations with third countries.

39. Although being two distinct bodies, the two Committees hold their meetings jointly and function practically as one, with Switzerland switching to observer status when EEA issues are discussed.

40. Members of Parliaments of the EFTA States debate among themselves and with the EFTA Council in the Committee of Members of Parliament of the EFTA Countries. Occasionally, they meet with their counterparts in countries with which EFTA has trade relations in connection with Joint Committee meetings between EFTA and partner countries. The Committee of Members of Parliament of the EFTA Countries normally holds around seven meetings per year, in addition to the two customary joint meetings with EFTA Ministers.[47] The Committee also meets on a regular basis with the Consultative Committee.

44. The Rules of Procedure are available on the EFTA Secretariat's website: www.efta.int/advisory-bodies/consultative-committee.
45. The meeting schedules of the Consultative Committee are available on the EFTA Secretariat's website: www.efta.int/advisory-bodies/consultative-committee.
46. *See infra* Part II, Ch. 3, §3.
47. The work schedule of the Parliamentary Committee is available on the EFTA Secretariat's website: www.efta.int/Advisory-Bodies/Parliamentary-Committee-1273.

41. The Committee of Members of Parliament of the EFTA Countries has five members from the national parliament of Iceland, two members from Liechtenstein, six members from Norway and five members from Switzerland. Together they elect their chairperson from among themselves to serve a term of one year. For a chairperson to be elected he/she needs to be elected by a simple majority of the members present.

42. The Committee on Third-Country Relations[48] has a rather horizontal mandate. The Committee on Third-Country Relations is involved in the negotiation of FTAs and matters related to their functioning; preparation of Joint Committee meetings under Declarations of Cooperation; preparation of recommendations on other third-country matters and other issues as referred to the Committee by the EFTA Council. The Committee meets on a regular basis.

43. The EEA-EFTA Forum was set up by a decision of the Standing Committee of the EFTA States as an informal body to involve elected representatives from local and regional authorities in EEA matters.[49] The Forum works closely with other EEA-EFTA bodies and has established links with the Committee of the Regions of the EU.[50] The Forum has twelve full members, six from Iceland and six from Norway. Switzerland observes the meetings and Liechtenstein has decided not to take part for the time being.

D. *Pre-Vaduz Committees with Technical Mandates*

44. The Board of Auditors[51] and the Budget Committee[52] are not as much concerned with the political process within EFTA as with the good operation of the bodies and institutions of EFTA. They are bodies of a more technical nature.

45. The Board of Auditors acts as the supreme auditing authority of EFTA and reports directly to the EFTA Council. It is responsible for the audit of the accounts of the EFTA Secretariat, the EFTA Surveillance Authority[53] and the EFTA Court.[54] It also serves as the EFTA contact point for the Court of Auditors of the EU for the control and auditing of the 'EEA-EFTA contributions' to the EU budget.[55]

48. Council Decision No. 2/96. The Committee on Third-Country Relations oversees the functioning and development of free trade and cooperation agreements with third countries.
49. Decision of the Standing Committee of the EFTA No. 10/2009/SC of 3 Dec. 2009 establishing a Forum of Elected Representatives of Local and Regional Authorities of the EEA EFTA States.
50. *See infra* Part II, Ch. 3, §8.
51. EFTA/C.SR 14/92 (EFTA/EEA 46/92 para. 14) and Council Decision No. 6/98.
52. Council Decision No. 10/60.
53. *See infra* Part II, Ch. 3, §6.
54. *See infra* Part II, Ch. 3, §7.
55. *See infra* Part II, Ch. 7, §1.

46. The composition of the Board of Auditors varies depending on the body to be audited. If that body is the EFTA Secretariat, all the EFTA States will be represented on the board. If it is the EFTA Surveillance Authority or the EFTA Court that is audited, only the 'EEA-EFTA States' are represented. This being said, the Members of the Board are independent in the performance of their duties.

47. The terms of reference governing the audits also change with the body to be audited. Indeed, each of the bodies in question has its own Financial Regulations, which apply to the audits.

48. The Budget Committee carries out the tasks allotted to it by the Financial Regulations as well as any additional tasks that might be conferred upon it by the EFTA Council. In particular, it is involved in the establishment of the annual budget of the EFTA Secretariat.[56] Each EFTA State is represented on the Budget Committee.

III. The EFTA Secretariat

49. Article 44 of the EFTA Convention provides that the EFTA Council is to make arrangements for the secretariat services required by the association. Accordingly, an EFTA Secretariat has been established. Its headquarters are located in Geneva, with branch offices in Brussels and Luxembourg. It has an annual budget of around CHF 23 million and approximately one hundred staff members. A Secretary-General, assisted by one Deputy in Geneva and two Deputies in Brussels, heads the Secretariat.

50. The headquarters in Geneva are responsible for the provision of the Secretariat services concerning the EFTA Convention and the EFTA States' third-country relations. In Brussels, the Secretariat provides support for the management of the EEA Agreement and assists the EFTA States in preparation of new legislation for incorporation into the EEA Agreement. The Secretariat also assists the EFTA States in the preparation of input to the EU decision-making. The Statistical Adviser's Office in Luxembourg handles statistical cooperation in the context of the EEA Agreement. It is also involved in technical cooperation programmes in the Central and Eastern European Countries and in the Mediterranean Countries. Only one division, the Administration Division, is divided between two duty stations. Both the Statistical Adviser's Office and the Administration Division operate directly under the authority of the Secretary-General. Beyond the staff working within the different units mentioned above, the EFTA Secretariat also seconds experts to EUROCUSTOMS (Association pour la gestion du Groupement Eurodouane), EUROSTAT (EU Statistical Office) and MEDSTAT (Euro-Mediterranean Programme of Statistical Cooperation).

56. For a presentation of the finances of the EFTA Secretariat, *see infra* Part I, Ch. 5.

Chapter 3. Activities

51. The activities of EFTA can be divided into three main areas: The first area concerns the relationship between the EFTA States themselves, which is governed by the EFTA Convention, the legal basis of the organization. The intra-EFTA activities under the EFTA Convention will be described below in §1. The second set of activities covers the relationship between EFTA and third countries other than the Member States of the EU. EFTA has, in line with the broad objectives of the EFTA Convention, developed relations with a large number of third countries. The activities in relation to third countries will be described below in §2. Finally, EFTA also deals with the relationship between some EFTA States and the EU. Three of the four EFTA States, namely Iceland, Liechtenstein and Norway, and the Member States of the EU are signatories to the EEA Agreement, through which these EFTA States participate in the EU's Internal Market. EFTA's activities in the framework of the EEA Agreement will be described in Part II.[57]

§1. Intra-EFTA Activities

52. The origin of EFTA was the objective of providing a framework for the liberalization of trade in goods among its Member States. The original EFTA Convention thus contained basic rules regarding free trade in goods and related disciplines. The EFTA Convention established a free trade area, not a customs union. Trade policy was outside the scope of the EFTA Convention and remained the competence of its Member States.

53. The growing importance of the service and investment sectors and the conclusion by Switzerland in 1999 of a set of bilateral agreements with the then EC prompted the EFTA States to modernize the EFTA Convention.

54. The revised EFTA Convention renders the economic relations between the four EFTA States more cohesive and gives the Members an improved instrument to manage their internal relations and those with present and potential partner countries.[58] The functions of the EFTA Council were broadened to reflect changes that have taken place in EFTA since the 1980s. The scope of the Convention was expanded to include new areas of trade such as services and investment, mutual recognition of diplomas, land and air transport, public procurement and intellectual property rights.

57. In this respect, it should, however, not be overlooked that the FTAs concluded between the EFTA States and the then EEC in 1972 and 1973 have not been terminated by the entry into force of the EEA Agreement but continue to coexist separately. *See* Case E-2/03 *Ásgeirsson* [2003] EFTA Court Report, 185.
58. Article 49(2) of the EFTA Convention clarifies that the Convention is without prejudice to the rules applicable to Member States governed by the EEA Agreement, the Nordic cooperation and the regional union between Switzerland and Liechtenstein.

55. Another novelty of the revised EFTA Convention is that it is updated on a continuous basis in order to align its content to the lowest common denominator between the content of the Swiss-EU bilateral agreements and the EEA Agreement. The first review of the Convention started three months after its entry into force and has already resulted in numerous amendments to the Convention.

56. Although formally an agreement between all the EFTA States, the EFTA Convention applies mainly to the relationship between Switzerland, on the one hand, and, on the other hand, the other EFTA States, since the EEA Agreement applies to trade relations between Iceland, Liechtenstein and Norway. Indeed, Iceland, Liechtenstein and Norway, in their capacity as EEA Member States, had already removed between themselves (and vis-à-vis the EU) the obstacles that were subsequently removed under the revised EFTA Convention.[59] It is only in the field of trade in fish and fish products that the EFTA Convention goes beyond the EEA Agreement and is of direct relevance for the relationship between all the EFTA States.

57. The revised EFTA Convention is divided into eighteen Chapters, with a total of fifty-nine Articles, twenty-two Annexes (Annexes A–X)[60] and the Protocol regarding the free movement of persons between Switzerland and Liechtenstein.[61] The first chapter deals with the objectives of EFTA. The subsequent chapters set out the substantive trade rules applicable to trade between the EFTA States (*see infra* section I). The institutional provisions are contained in Chapter 16 and have already been outlined *supra* in Chapter 2. However, the main text of the EFTA Convention is silent on the procedures for the updating of the EFTA Convention. These procedures are, to a large extent, dealt with in the different Annexes to the EFTA Convention, which cover fields that are subject to updating (*see infra* section II). Chapter 17 regulates the consultations and dispute settlement procedures, which will be analysed *infra* in Chapter 4. Finally, Chapter 18 of the EFTA Convention contains some general provisions.

I. Substantive Rules Applicable to Intra-EFTA Trade

58. Chapters 2–15 set out the substantive trade rules applicable to trade between the EFTA States. Chapter 2 of the EFTA Convention covers the provisions on free movement of goods. Chapter 3 contains rules on TBT. Chapter 4 lays down the rights and obligations of the Member States relating to State aid. Chapter 5 deals with public undertakings and monopolies. Chapter 6 provides for rules of competition and Chapter 7 deals with the protection of intellectual property. Chapter 8

59. Regarding the EEA Agreement, *see infra* Part II.
60. Annexes C and D were repealed by Council Decision No. 2/2012.
61. Convention establishing the EFTA, last amended on 1 Nov. 2021. The EFTA Convention is available on the EFTA Secretariat's website: https://www.efta.int/sites/default/files/documents/legal-texts/efta-convention/Vaduz%20Convention%20Agreement.pdf.

regulates the free movement of persons and Chapter 9 investments. Chapter 10 covers trade in services. Chapter 11, entitled Dumping, briefly mentions trade protective instruments. Chapter 12 deals with public procurement. Chapter 13 regulates current payments. Chapter 14 provides for rules on exceptions and safeguards. Finally, rules on economic and monetary policy cooperation are mentioned in Chapter 15. Some of these chapters will now be described in more detail.

A. *Free Movement of Goods*

59. To ensure the free movement of goods between the EFTA States, it is prohibited to impose customs duties or quantitative restrictions on imports and exports (Articles 3 and 7 of the EFTA Convention). With regard to customs duties, Article 3 of the EFTA Convention stipulates that customs duties on imports and exports, including customs duties of a fiscal nature, and any charges having equivalent effect, are prohibited between the Member States. Consequently, anti-dumping measures, countervailing duties and measures against illicit commercial practices attributable to third countries are not applicable in relations between the Member States (Article 36 of the EFTA Convention). Such protective trade measures, normally operated by way of special customs duties, would indeed run counter to the idea of a free trade area. Also prohibited between the Member States are quantitative restrictions on imports and exports and all measures having equivalent effect (Article 7 of the EFTA Convention). In order to ensure the free movement of goods, payments connected with the movement of goods are free of all restrictions (Article 28 of the EFTA Convention). In relation to the prohibition to introduce or maintain quantitative restrictions on imports and exports and all measures having equivalent effect (Article 7), Article 13 of the EFTA Convention states that Member States are not precluded from introducing or maintaining prohibitions or restrictions on imports, exports or goods in transit justified on grounds of public morality; public policy or public security; the protection of health and life of humans, animals or plants and of the environment; the protection of national treasures possessing artistic, historic or archaeological value; or the protection of industrial and commercial property. However, such prohibitions or restrictions cannot constitute a means of arbitrary discrimination or a disguised restriction on trade between the Member States.

60. In order to guarantee goods from other EFTA States the same national treatment and not to undermine, by way of indirect measures, the idea of free movement of goods, Article 4(1) of the EFTA Convention states that Member States are prohibited from imposing, directly or indirectly, any internal taxation of any kind in excess of that imposed on similar domestic products on the products of other Member States. Furthermore, no Member State may impose any internal taxation of such a nature as to afford indirect protection to other products or products of other Member States (Article 4(2) of the EFTA Convention). Equally harmful are export subsidies, which would provide exported goods with an artificial price advantage as compared to competing products on the export market. Article 4(3) of the EFTA Convention thus stipulates that where products are exported to the territory of any

Member State, any repayment of internal taxation shall not exceed the internal taxation imposed on them whether directly or indirectly.

61. To identify the products which originate in the Member States and thereby benefit from the above-mentioned provisions on the free movement of goods, Article 5 of the EFTA Convention refers to Annex A, which sets out the provisions on rules of origin and administrative cooperation. Article 1(1) of Annex A states that with respect to the rights and obligations of the Member States concerning rules of origin and administrative cooperation between the customs authorities of the Member States, Appendix I and the relevant provisions of Appendix II to the Regional Convention on pan-Euro-Mediterranean preferential rules of origin (PEM Convention), as it may be subsequently amended, apply and are incorporated into and made part of the EFTA Convention, *mutatis mutandis*, without prejudice to Article 15 of the PEM Convention. In addition, Article 2(1) of Annex A clarifies that notwithstanding Article 1, for the purpose of implementing the EFTA Convention, products which acquire preferential origin in accordance with the provisions set out in Appendix A to this Annex ('alternative rules') are also considered as originating in a Member State.

62. Provisions governing agricultural goods are mentioned in Article 8 of the EFTA Convention and in Annexes V, W and X to the EFTA Convention. Article 8 states that certain provisions and parts of the EFTA Convention, for example, Articles 2, 3, 4 and 7, Chapter IV on State aid, Chapter VI on competition and Chapter XII on public procurement, are not applicable to agricultural goods classified under Chapters 1–24 of the Harmonized Commodity Description and Coding System (HS) or specified in Annex X, except as provided for in Annex V (in relation to basic agricultural products) or Annex W (in relation to processed agricultural products) to the EFTA Convention. The provisions of the EFTA Convention also apply in relation to fish and other marine products (Article 10 of the EFTA Convention).

63. In addition, trade in seeds and organically produced agricultural products is considerably facilitated by the reduction or elimination of a number of technical barriers according to the same rules as under the EEA Agreement and the Swiss-EU Agricultural Agreement (Article 11 in conjunction with Annexes E and F to the EFTA Convention).

64. As regards sanitary and phytosanitary measures, the World Trade Organization (WTO) Agreement on Application of Sanitary and Phytosanitary Measures provides the rules for the EFTA Convention. However, more specific arrangements are included in the EFTA Convention as developments in the EEA Agreement occur (Article 12 in conjunction with Annex G to the EFTA Convention).

65. Article 6 of the EFTA Convention regulates mutual assistance in customs matters in conjunction with Annex B to the EFTA Convention. Annex B to the EFTA Convention on mutual administrative assistance in customs matters applies to all products whether or not covered by the provisions of the EFTA Convention.

B. Technical Barriers to Trade

66. Article 14(1) of the EFTA Convention requires the Member States to notify the EFTA Council at the earliest practicable stage of all draft technical regulations or amendments thereto. The provisions on the notification procedure are set out in Annex H (Article 14(2) of the EFTA Convention). The EFTA Convention incorporates the rules on mutual recognition of conformity assessments established under the bilateral agreement between Switzerland and the EU in this area, as well as the corresponding provisions of the EEA Agreement (Article 15 in conjunction with Annex I to the EFTA Convention). The products covered by the EFTA Convention for the purposes of the mutual recognition of conformity assessments are the following: machinery; personal protective equipment; equipment; toys; medical devices; gas appliances and boilers; pressure vessels; telecommunications terminal equipment; equipment and protective systems intended for the use in potentially explosive atmospheres; electrical equipment and electromagnetic compatibility appliances; construction plant and equipment; measuring instruments and prepackages; motor vehicles; agricultural and forestry tractors; good laboratory practice (GLP); medicinal products good medicinal practice inspection and batch certification; construction products; lifts; biocidal products, cableway installations; and explosives for civil use (excluding ammunition).

C. State Aid, Public Undertakings, Monopolies and Competition Rules

67. The rights and obligations of the Member States relating to State aid are governed by Article 16 of the EFTA Convention with special rules concerning the air transport sector mentioned in Annex Q to the EFTA Convention.[62] Article 16(1) merely refers to the Member States' rights and obligations based on Article XVI of the GATT 1994 and the WTO Agreement on Subsidies and Countervailing Measures.[63] Article 16(2) of the EFTA Convention clarifies that countervailing measures are not applicable between the Member States. Article 16(3) requires Member States to review the scope of application of Chapter IV on State aid with a view to extending the disciplines with respect to State aid to the field of services, taking into account international developments in the sector. The reviews take place at yearly intervals.

68. With regard to public undertakings,[64] Article 17(1) of the EFTA Convention requires Member States to ensure that public undertakings refrain from applying

62. Annex Q on Air Transport was amended by Council Decision Nos 1/2006, 5/2007, 4/2009, 7/2011, 1/2012, 4/2012, 1/2013, 1/2014, 2/2015, 4/2015, 5/2015, 1/2017 and 2/2017.
63. GATT 1994 and the Agreement on Subsidies and Countervailing Measures. Both Agreements are published in *The Results of the Uruguay Round of Multilateral Trade Negotiations* (published by the GATT Secretariat), Geneva 1994.
64. Public undertakings are defined in Art. 17(2) of the EFTA Convention, which states that '[f]or the purpose of this article, "public undertakings" means central, regional, or local government

measures which afford protection to domestic production by means of a duty or a charge with equivalent effect, quantitative restriction or government aid, or trade discrimination on ground of nationality insofar as it frustrates the benefits expected from the removal or absence of duties and quantitative restrictions on trade between Member States. According to Article 17(3) of the EFTA Convention, the competition provisions in Article 18(1) of the EFTA Convention are applicable to the activities of public undertakings, and undertakings for which the Member States grant special or exclusive rights, insofar as the application of these provisions does not obstruct the performance of the particular public tasks assigned to them. Article 17(3) of the EFTA Convention applies equally to the air transport sector in Annex Q to the EFTA Convention (Article 17(4) of the EFTA Convention). Article 17(6) of the EFTA Convention clarifies that where Member States do not have the necessary legal powers to control the activities of regional or local government authorities or enterprises under their control in these matters, they shall nevertheless endeavour to ensure that those authorities or enterprises comply with the provisions of this Article.

69. The competition rules are laid down in Article 18 of the EFTA Convention. That Article states, in its first paragraph, that Member States recognize that the following practices are incompatible with the Convention insofar as they frustrate the benefits arising from the Convention: (a) agreements between enterprises, decisions by associations of enterprises and concerted practices between enterprises which have as their object or result the prevention, restriction or distortion of competition; (b) abuse by one or more undertakings of a dominant position in the territories of the Member States as a whole or in a substantial part thereof. Should a Member State consider that a given practice is incompatible with this article, it may ask for consultations in accordance with the procedures set out in Article 47 of the EFTA Convention[65] and take appropriate measures under the conditions set out in paragraph 2 of Article 40 to deal with the difficulties resulting from the practice in question (Article 18(2) of the EFTA Convention).

D. *Intellectual Property Rights*

70. Under the EFTA Convention, the EFTA States grant each other adequate and effective protection of intellectual property rights and combat infringement, for instance, through counterfeiting and piracy, of such rights (Article 19(1) in conjunction with Annex J to the EFTA Convention). Member States accord each other's nationals treatment no less favourable than they accord to their own nationals or nationals of any other States. Exemptions from this obligation have to be in

---

authorities, public enterprises and any other organisation by means of which a Member State, by law or in practice, controls or appreciably influences imports from, or exports to, the territory of a Member State'.

65. *See infra* Part I, Ch. 4, §1.

accordance with the substantive provisions of the Trade-Related Aspects of Intellectual Property Rights (TRIPS) Agreement[66] (Article 19(2) and (3) of the EFTA Convention). According to Article 19(4) of the EFTA Convention, Member States agreed, upon request of any Member State, to review the provisions on the protection of intellectual property rights contained in Article 19 and in Annex J, with a view to further improve levels of protection and to avoid or remedy trade distortions caused by actual levels of protection of intellectual property rights.

E. *Movement of Persons, Social Security and Mutual Recognition of Diplomas*

71. The EFTA Convention introduced the free movement of persons by opening the labour markets of the EFTA States (Article 20 in conjunction with Annex K to the EFTA Convention and the Protocol to Annex K).[67] The Convention applies to workers, self-employed and persons who otherwise have sufficient financial means, including, under certain conditions, their family members. They have the right of access to work, entry/exit and establishment (residence), the right to provide services for a period of up to ninety days per year and the right to equal treatment. In the case of Switzerland, a few special provisions have been elaborated: Free movement of Swiss citizens to Iceland and Norway took effect upon entry into force of the revised EFTA Convention. The freedom of movement to Switzerland for citizens of the other EFTA States was subject to transitional periods lasting up to five years. Switzerland has introduced special quotas for EFTA citizens, which could later be adjusted by the decision of the EFTA Council. Special rules govern individuals living in border areas and working in Switzerland as well as public service activities and the acquisition of real estate in Switzerland. EFTA citizens living in Switzerland are now granted the same rights as Swiss nationals. Liechtenstein will gradually reduce its limitations to the free movement of Swiss nationals to its territory to the level of liberalization currently in force under the EEA Agreement. Payments connected with the movement of persons are free of all restrictions (Article 38 of the EFTA Convention).

72. The free movement of persons also covers social security issues by establishing a system of coordination between the EFTA States (Article 21 in conjunction with Appendix 2 of Annex K and the Protocol to Annex K to the EFTA Convention). The objective is to apply common principles and rules so that differences in national legislation do not hinder the mobility of persons who move within the EFTA area.

73. In order to make it easier for nationals of the Member States to take up and pursue activities as workers and self-employed persons, the Member States agreed to take measures concerning the mutual recognition of diplomas, certificates and

66. Articles 3 (national treatment), 4 (MFN treatment) and 5 (multilateral agreements on acquisition or maintenance of protection) of the TRIPS Agreement.
67. Annex K on Free Movement of Persons was amended by Council Decision Nos 2/2007, 4/2007 and 5/2015.

other evidence of formal qualifications. The mutual recognition of professional diplomas has therefore been introduced under the EFTA Convention (Article 22 in conjunction with Appendix 3 to Annex K and the Protocol to Annex K to the EFTA Convention). Qualifications obtained in an EFTA State under so-called general systems for the recognition of higher-education diplomas and of professional education or training or in the following specialized areas are recognized in the other EFTA States. This concerns, *inter alia*, legal professions, medical and paramedical activities, architecture, commerce and intermediaries.

F. Investment and Establishment

74. The EFTA Convention includes a comprehensive framework for the general liberalization of investment and trade in services between EFTA States. Chapter 9 on Investment is divided into two sections. The first section deals with establishment, and the second section deals with capital movement.

75. According to Article 23(1) of the EFTA Convention, there shall generally be no restrictions on the right of establishment of undertakings, formed in accordance with the law of a Member State,[68] subject to the exceptions provided for in Article 27 of the EFTA Convention. Article 27 of the EFTA Convention provides for exceptions such as activities connected, even occasionally, with the exercise of official authority or special treatment for foreign undertakings on grounds of public policy, public security, public health or the environment. However, these exceptions should not be used as a means of arbitrary or unjustifiable discrimination between States (Article 27(3) of the EFTA Convention). From entry into effect of the Convention, the EFTA States may not adopt any new discriminatory measures as regards establishment or trade in services (Article 23(4) of the EFTA Convention). However, some reservations remain in effect, which are subject to review with a view to their eventual removal (Article 23(3) of the EFTA Convention). Annexes L–O to the EFTA Convention contain specific provisions and exemptions regarding the right of establishment. In sectors covered by an exemption, each Member State accords companies or firms of another Member State treatment no less favourable than that accorded to companies or firms of third parties other than the EU (Article 23(5), first sentence, of the EFTA Convention). As regards any new agreements concluded between any Member State and the EU, the Member States further undertake to extend to each other, on the basis of reciprocity, the benefits of such agreements (Article 23(5), second sentence, of the EFTA Convention).[69] Subject to these reservations, a company or firm may set up and operate its business in another EFTA State. EFTA States grant to companies of any other EFTA States national treatment (Article 24 of the EFTA Convention) and Most-Favoured-Nation (MFN) treatment (Article 23(5) of the EFTA Convention). The right of establishment in the field of

68. The right of establishment of natural persons is governed by the provisions of Art. 20, Annex K and the Protocol to Annex K on movement of persons between Liechtenstein and Switzerland (Art. 23(7) of the EFTA Convention).
69. Subject to a decision by the EFTA Council.

road, rail and air transport is governed by the provisions of Article 35 and Annexes P and Q, subject to the specific provisions and exemptions set out in Annexes L and M (Article 23(6) of the EFTA Convention). Further, the right of establishment of natural persons is governed by the provisions of Article 20, Annex K and the Protocol to Annex K on movement of persons between Liechtenstein and Switzerland (Article 23(7) of the EFTA Convention).

76. According to Article 24(1) of the EFTA Convention, within the scope of application of Chapter IX, and without prejudice to any special provisions contained therein: (a) Member States have to grant treatment no less favourable than that accorded to their own companies or firms; (b) each Member State may regulate the establishment and operation of companies or firms on its territory, in so far as these regulations do not discriminate against companies or firms of the other Member States in comparison to its own companies or firms.

77. However, according to Article 24(2) of the EFTA Convention, the provisions of Article 24 do not preclude the application by a Member State of particular rules concerning the establishment and operation in its territory of branches and agencies of companies of another Member State not incorporated in the territory of the first Member State, which are justified by legal or technical differences between such branches and agencies as compared to branches and agencies of companies incorporated in its territory. The difference in treatment cannot go beyond what is strictly necessary as a result of such legal or technical differences.

78. In respect of financial services, the chapter on investment does not prejudice the right of Member States to adopt measures necessary for prudential grounds in order to ensure the protection of investors, depositors, policy holders, or persons to whom a fiduciary duty is owed, or to ensure the integrity and stability of the financial system (Article 25(1) of the EFTA Convention).[70]

79. A Member State may enter into an agreement or arrangement with a particular State providing for the recognition of standards, criteria for authorization, licensing or certification of service suppliers, in which case it offers adequate opportunity for any other Member State to negotiate its accession to such an agreement or arrangement or to negotiate comparable ones with it (Article 26(1) of the EFTA Convention). Where a Member State accords such recognition autonomously, it affords adequate opportunity for any other Member State to demonstrate that experience, licences or certifications obtained or requirements met in that other Member State's territory should be recognized (Article 26(2) of the EFTA Convention).

70. Furthermore, Art. 25(2) of the EFTA Convention clarifies that nothing in Ch. 9 shall be construed to require a Member State to disclose information relating to the affairs and accounts of individual customers or any confidential or proprietary information in the possession of public entities.

80. The provisions of Chapter IX do not apply, so far as any given Member State is concerned, to activities which in that Member State are connected, even occasionally, with the exercise of official authority (Article 27(1) of the EFTA Convention). Further, the provisions of Chapter IX and measures taken in pursuance thereof must not prejudice the applicability of provisions laid down by law, regulation or administrative action providing for special treatment for foreign companies or firms on grounds of public policy, public security, public health or the environment (Article 27(2) of the EFTA Convention).

81. The movement of capital is free of any restrictions insofar as it concerns establishment (Article 28(1) of the EFTA Convention). The movement of capital not relating to establishment between the Member States is ensured in accordance with international agreements to which the Member States are parties (Article 28(2) of the EFTA Convention). The rules on capital movements are subject to review within two years after the entry into force of the Convention with a view to their further liberalization (Article 28(3) of the EFTA Convention).

G. *Trade in Services*

82. Regarding cross-border supply of services between EFTA nationals, that is, the use of services by citizens of one EFTA State provided in another EFTA State, and the supply of services by local presence, the EFTA Convention opens up this sector subject to some minor reservations. The Convention establishes the principle in its Article 29(1) that there should be no restrictions on the right to supply services. Payments connected with the supply of services are free of all restrictions (Article 38 of the EFTA Convention). Annexes L–O to the EFTA Convention contain specific provisions and exemptions regarding the right to supply services. The Member States endeavour to gradually eliminate remaining discriminations, which they may maintain in accordance with Annexes L–O to the EFTA Convention (Article 29(3), second sentence, of the EFTA Convention). The reservations are to be reviewed within two years after the entry into force of the revised Convention (Article 29(3), third sentence, of the EFTA Convention). The Member States grant each other national treatment (Article 30 of the EFTA Convention). Any benefits that an EFTA State may grant to the EU in the future in terms of liberalizations of trade in services will have to be extended to the other EFTA States (Article 29(5) of the EFTA Convention). This may be of particular importance if Switzerland were to take further steps in this area vis-à-vis the EU. The reservations maintained by the EFTA States under the Convention in the area of financial services reflect their current commitments under the General Agreement of Trade in Services (GATS). Article 31 of the EFTA Convention concerning financial market regulation basically repeats the text already provided for under the section of establishment in the chapter on Investment (*see supra* in section F).

83. The mutual recognition between the Member States of diplomas, certificates and other evidence of formal qualifications and the coordination of the provisions laid down by law, regulation or administrative action in the Member States concerning the taking up and pursuit of activities by natural person are governed by the relevant provisions of Article 22, Annex K and Appendix 3 thereto and the Protocol to Annex K on movement of persons between Liechtenstein and Switzerland (Article 32(1) of the EFTA Convention). Further, a Member State may enter into an agreement or arrangement with a particular State providing for the recognition of standards, criteria for authorization, licensing or certification of service suppliers, in which case it must offer adequate opportunity for any other Member State to negotiate its accession to such an agreement or arrangement or to negotiate comparable ones with it (Article 32(2) of the EFTA Convention).

84. Article 33 of the EFTA Convention on exceptions basically repeats the wording of Article 27 of the EFTA Convention (*see supra* in section F).

H. Land and Air Transport

85. Special rules apply to transport services. The right to supply services in the field of road, rail and air transport is governed by the provisions of Article 35 and Annexes P and Q,[71] subject to the specific provisions and exemptions set out in Annex M (Article 29(6) of the EFTA Convention). Article 35 of the EFTA Convention, in conjunction with the respective Annexes, basically states that the Member States liberalize the access to each other's transport markets for the carriage of passengers and goods by road, rail and air in accordance with the provisions set out in Annex P and Annex Q respectively. Essential elements of the bilateral Swiss-EU agreements have been transposed into the EFTA Convention, including references to EU rules regarding road, rail and air transport. In the field of land transport, the EFTA Convention now provides for gradual reciprocal opening of the markets for the transport of both persons and goods by road and by rail between all the EFTA States. The rules on civil aviation lay down the terms on which an EFTA State air transport company will have access to the air transport markets of another EFTA State.

I. Public Procurement

86. In the area of public procurement, the EFTA Convention builds on the EFTA States' commitments under the plurilateral WTO Agreement on Government Procurement,[72] to which all EFTA States are Parties (Article 37(1), first sentence, of the EFTA Convention). Moreover, the EFTA Convention goes beyond the WTO rules by extending the sectoral coverage (Article 37(1), second sentence, in conjunction

71. Annex P was amended by Council Decision Nos 1/2007, 3/2010, 6/2011 and 3/2015. Annex Q was amended since 2005 by Council Decision Nos 1/2006, 5/2007, 4/2009, 7/2011, 1/2012, 4/2012, 1/2013, 1/2014, 2/2015, 4/2015, 5/2015, 1/2017 and 2/2017.
72. Agreement on Government Procurement. The Agreement is published in *The Results of the Uruguay Round of Multilateral Trade Negotiations* (published by the GATT Secretariat), Geneva 1994.

with Annex R to the EFTA Convention). This extended coverage includes, for example, purchases of products and services including construction services, by railway operators, entities active in the field of energy other than electricity and private utilities active in the fields of drinking water, electricity, urban transport, ports and airports in the EFTA States. Member States have to secure non-discriminative, transparent and reciprocal access to their respective public procurement markets and must ensure open and effective competition based on equal treatment (Article 37(2) of the EFTA Convention).

J. Economic and Monetary Policy Cooperation

87. The Member States exchange views and information concerning the implementation of the EFTA Convention and the impact of integration on economic activities and on the conduct of economic and monetary policies (Article 42, first sentence, of the EFTA Convention). Furthermore, they may discuss macroeconomic situations, policies and prospects (Article 42, second sentence, of the EFTA Convention). This exchange of views and information takes place on a non-binding basis (Article 42, third sentence, of the EFTA Convention).

II. Procedure for Updating the EFTA Convention

88. In accordance with the Joint Declaration to the EFTA Convention on Development of law, the EFTA States endeavour to regularly update the EFTA Convention, in order to take account of developments of the EEA Agreement and of the bilateral agreements of 21 June 1999 between Switzerland on the one hand and the EU and its Member States on the other hand. In other words, the EFTA Convention is to be aligned to the lowest common denominator between the content of the Swiss-EU bilateral agreements and the EEA Agreement.

89. The procedure for updating the EFTA Convention constitutes a simplified procedure for amending an international agreement. The scope of this simplified procedure is laid down in Article 53(4) of the EFTA Convention.[73]

90. The procedure is, to a large degree, modelled on the EFTA internal procedure preparing for decision-taking under the EEA Agreement.[74] It was the EFTA States' intention that existing structures and resources of the EFTA Secretariat should be used to the greatest extent possible for the updating and operation of the EFTA Convention. As under the EEA Agreement, a similar process takes place at frequent intervals, it was considered useful to entrust the EFTA Secretariat with the

73. It covers in essence amendments to Annexes A, H, S, T, V, W and X as well as the Appendices to Annexes E, F, K, P, Q and R, unless otherwise provided in the Annexes.

74. *See infra* Part II, Ch. 4, §3.

role of updating the EFTA Convention. The whole procedure for updating from its starting point through to the Decision of the EFTA Council should normally take no more than ten weeks.

91. The starting point of the procedure for updating the EFTA Convention is an update of the Swiss-EU bilateral agreements. Once the EFTA Secretariat is informed about such an update, it verifies whether or not the same development has taken place, or will take place, in the EEA Agreement. If the answer is affirmative, the criteria for updating the EFTA Convention, that is, common developments, are fulfilled, and the EFTA Secretariat can formally launch the procedure for updating the EFTA Convention with the EFTA States.

92. It does so by inviting the members of the Vaduz Committee[75] in question to decide on the need to update the EFTA Convention. If all the members of that Committee agree to update the EFTA Convention, the EFTA Secretariat prepares a draft Decision of the EFTA Council amending the EFTA Convention. This draft Decision is submitted to the Vaduz Committee in question for approval.

93. Upon approval of the draft Decision by the Vaduz Committee, the EFTA Secretariat draws up a recommendation inviting the EFTA Council to adopt the decision approved by the Vaduz Committee.[76] Only the Committee on Mutual Recognition in Relation to Conformity Assessment has wider ranging powers and can take a decision amending the EFTA Convention itself.[77] That Committee is entitled to decide on certain amendments of the annex to the EFTA Convention under which it is set up. Nevertheless, it has to notify the EFTA Council of all its decisions without delay.

§2. THIRD-COUNTRY RELATIONS

94. Article 56(2) of the EFTA Convention is the legal basis for the third-country relations of EFTA. It states that the EFTA Council may negotiate agreements with other States, unions of States or international organizations, creating an association embodying such reciprocal rights and obligations, common actions and special procedures as may be appropriate.

I. Joint Declarations on Cooperation

95. Joint Declarations on Cooperation are a first step on the way to free trade between trading partners. The objective is to promote the harmonious development

75. *See supra* Part I, Ch. 2, §2, II, A.
76. A complete list of Council Decisions amending the EFTA Convention is available at: www.efta.int/legal-texts/efta-convention/council-decisions-amending-the-convention.aspx.
77. *See supra* Part I, Ch. 2, §2, II, A.

of economic relations and to create an environment supportive of private entrepreneurship, based on free competition and market forces. Another objective is to examine ways and means of expanding and liberalizing the trade relations between the trading partners. The Joint Declarations on Cooperation are based on mutual benefit, non-discrimination and reciprocity. They cover trade-related issues such as: TBT; developing customs and tariff cooperation; facilitating exchange of information on foreign trade; facilitating exchange of views on conditions for free and undistorted competition; exchanging information on opening-up public procurement markets; and encouraging cooperation in the area of intellectual property rights.

96. Under the Joint Declarations on Cooperation, EFTA States and the relevant third countries are to encourage and stimulate business contacts, notably between enterprises and organizations concerned with foreign trade, with the aim of developing their mutual trade. Furthermore, the Parties to the Joint Declarations on Cooperation shall seek to improve conditions for the implementation of private sector industrial cooperation projects, *inter alia*, by creating favourable conditions conducive to capital flows and investment in all economic sectors of mutual concern, as well as securing the interest of the partners involved. The Joint Declarations on Cooperation also serve as a basis for offering scholarships and extending technical assistance in areas such as customs and origin matters and statistics. Joint Committees, established under the respective Joint Declarations on Cooperation,[78] review the cooperation in areas covered by the Joint Declarations and discuss any other issues of mutual interest. The Joint Committees formulate appropriate recommendations on any cooperation between the EFTA States and the third countries. In 2023, Joint Declarations on Cooperation existed with: Algeria, Kosovo, Malaysia, Mauritius, Mercosur, Mongolia, Myanmar, Nigeria and Pakistan.[79]

II. Free Trade Agreements

97. The EFTA FTAs establish free trade areas between the trading partners, which cover substantially similar areas as those of the EFTA Convention. The terms 'EFTA Free Trade Agreement' or 'EFTA third-country relations' need to be qualified. Indeed, EFTA as such is not a party to the FTAs. The Contracting Parties to an FTA are the EFTA States on the one side and the partner country on the other side. Equally, as the foreign trade policy remains within the competence of the EFTA States and since EFTA is not a customs union, EFTA States are in principle free to

78. The secretariat services for the Joint Committees are preformed jointly by the EFTA Secretariat and the respective Ministries in the third countries.

79. The dates of signature of these Joint Declarations on Cooperation are: 12 Dec. 2002, 23 Nov. 2018, 20 Jul. 2010, 9 Jun. 2009, 19 Jan. 2017, 28 Jun. 2007, 24 Jun. 2013, 12 Dec. 2017 and 12 Nov. 2012, respectively. Furthermore, EFTA concluded Joint Declarations on Cooperation with the following partners prior to starting free trade negotiations on or concluding an FTA: Albania, Colombia, Croatia, Egypt, Georgia, Gulf Cooperation Council (GCC), Jordan, Lebanon, Malaysia, Macedonia, Montenegro, Morocco, Palestinian Authority, Panama, Peru, Philippines, Serbia, Tunisia and Ukraine.

conclude unilaterally FTAs with third countries.[80] For example, on 8 July 2021, Iceland, Liechtenstein and Norway (the EEA-EFTA States) and the United Kingdom (UK) signed a comprehensive FTA.[81] Switzerland earlier concluded a bilateral FTA with the UK.[82]

98. Initially, the purpose of the FTAs was twofold. First, they were designed to assist some of the Central and Eastern European Countries in the transition from a centrally administered economy to a free market economy. Second, the EFTA States wanted to make sure that their economies would not suffer a competitive disadvantage in the transition economies of the Central and Eastern European States after the EU had concluded the so-called Europe Agreements with these newly emerging economies.

99. The first FTAs were so-called first generation agreements. They mainly covered free trade in goods (including processed agricultural products). Regarding the liberalization of services and investment, the EFTA States and their free trade partners merely agreed on a non-binding evolutionary clause that recognized the growing importance of the liberalization of services and investment. These evolutionary clauses contained an agreement on the aim of achieving gradual liberalization and mutual opening of markets, should the parties consider this to be useful in the future.

100. In 1995, the EFTA States, for the first time, decided to extend the geographical scope of their FTAs beyond the immediate confines of Europe. They confirmed the will of the EFTA States to respond in a dynamic and independent manner to the growing need for political, social and economic stability in Europe, as well as in adjacent regions.[83] Four years later, the EFTA States indicated the potential for widening the scope of the agreements so as to include fields such as services and investment, which were of growing importance in an increasingly interdependent world economy.[84]

---

80. For example, Switzerland has bilateral FTAs with China, Japan and the Faroe Islands. The FTA with Japan entered into force on 1 Sep. 2009 and the FTA with China on 1 Jul. 2014.
81. The EEA EFTA-UK agreement covers the full range of trade in goods, services and investment, digital trade, capital movements, government procurement, intellectual property, competition, subsidies, small- and medium-sized enterprises, good regulatory practices and regulatory cooperation, recognition of professional qualifications, trade and sustainable development. It also encompasses legal and horizontal issues including dispute settlement. The full text of the agreement is available on the EFTA Secretariat's website: www.efta.int/sites/default/files/documents/legal-texts/free-trade-relations/UK/e3-uk-main-agreement.pdf.
82. This Swiss-UK trade agreement includes provisions on trade in goods, including provisions on preferential tariffs, tariff rate quotas, non-tariff measures, including sanitary and phytosanitary measures; intellectual property, including geographical indications; and government procurement. The full text of the agreement is available on the Swiss State Secretariat for Economic Affairs' website: www.seco.admin.ch/seco/en/home/Aussenwirtschaftspolitik_Wirtschaftliche_Zusammenarbeit/Wirtschaftsbeziehungen/brexit.html.
83. EFTA Ministerial Declaration adopted in Bergen in 1995.
84. EFTA Ministerial Declaration adopted in Geneva in 1999.

101. These strategic decisions taken by the EFTA States in the 1990s paved the way for a milestone in the history of EFTA's third-country relations. On 27 November 2000, the four EFTA States concluded an FTA with Mexico.[85] It was not only EFTA's first transatlantic agreement, but also its most comprehensive FTA concluded so far: In addition to the matters normally covered by the first generation agreements, the agreement also contains substantive provisions in the field of services, investment and government procurement. The agreement constitutes what is commonly referred to as a second-generation agreement.

102. Most of the more recent FTAs concluded by the EFTA States are now second-generation agreements. Among these agreements, the one concluded with Singapore on 26 June 2002 is particularly noteworthy.[86] It was concluded after less than a year of negotiations and covers all relevant areas ranging from goods, services and investment, to government procurement, competition and intellectual property. It also contains an effective dispute settlement system. Moreover, it is the first FTA concluded between European and East Asian countries.

103. The FTAs are instruments that are regularly adapted and upgraded in consideration of three main objectives: first, to make them as effective as possible; second, to ensure that they take into account developments at WTO level; and third, to make them compatible with the evolution within the wider European economic integration framework. The FTAs concern primarily, in their day-to-day management, customs and origin matters and processed agricultural products. They also contain evolutionary clauses or in-built agendas allowing the partners to develop or deepen their relationship in certain fields, for instance, as regards services and investment. Institutional provisions establish a Joint Committee separately for each FTA, which supervises the agreement. Dispute settlement provisions normally provide for recourse to arbitration.

104. In 2024, the EFTA States had concluded thirty-two FTAs (covering forty-one countries and territories outside the EU).[87] Eight earlier FTAs with the Czech

---

85. FTA between the EFTA States and the United Mexican States.
86. Agreement between the EFTA States and Singapore.
87. Albania (signature 17 Dec. 2009, entry into force 1 Nov. 2010), Bosnia and Herzegovina (signature 24 Jun. 2013, entry into force 1 Jan. 2015), Canada (signature 26 Jan. 2008, entry into force 1 Jul. 2009), Central American States, i.e., Costa Rica, Guatemala and Panama (signatures 24 Jun. 2013 and 22 Jun. 2015, entry into force 19 Aug. 2014, 29 Aug. 2014, 5 Sep. 2014), Chile (signature 26 Jun. 2003, entry into force 1 Dec. 2004), Colombia (signature 25 Nov. 2008, entry into force 1 Jul. 2011 for Liechtenstein and Switzerland, 1 Sep. 2014 for Norway and 1 Oct. 2014 for Iceland), Ecuador (signature 25 Jun. 2018, entry into force 1 Nov. 2020); Egypt (signature 27 Jan. 2007, entry into force 1 Aug. 2007), Georgia (signature 27 Jun. 2016, entry into force pending), GCC (signature 22 Jun. 2009, entry into force 1 Jul. 2014), Hong Kong (signature 21 Jun. 2011, entry into force 1 Oct. 2012 for Iceland, Liechtenstein and Switzerland, 1 Nov. 2012 for Norway), India (signature 10 Mar. 2024, entry into force pending), Indonesia (signature 16 Dec. 2018, entry into force 1 Nov. 2021), Israel (signature 17 Sep. 1992, entry into force 1 Jan. 1993), Jordan (signature 21 Jun. 2001, entry into force 1 Sep. 2002), Korea, Republic of (signature 15 Dec. 2005, entry into force 1 Sep. 2006 for Norway, Liechtenstein and Switzerland, 1 Oct. 2006 for Iceland), Lebanon (signature 24 Jun. 2004, entry into force 1 Jan. 2007), Macedonia (signature 19 Jun. 2000, entry into force 1 May 2002), Mexico (signature 27 Nov. 2000, entry into force 1 Jul. 2001), Moldova (signature 24 Mar.

Republic, Estonia, Hungary, Latvia, Lithuania, Poland, the Slovak Republic and Slovenia ceased to exist on 1 May 2004 due to these partner States' accession to the EU. Equally, the FTAs with Croatia, Bulgaria and Romania ceased to exist after their accession to the EU. Trade relations with these partner States are now covered by the EEA Agreement and the Swiss-EU bilateral agreements. Ongoing FTA negotiations were pending with five other trading partners.[88]

A. The Scope

105. All FTAs cover trade in industrial products as well as in processed agricultural products and fish. They offer a trade regime similar to the one prevailing among the EFTA States themselves. Arrangements on processed agricultural products (e.g., price compensation systems) are contained in separate protocols to the FTAs.[89] Under these protocols each country has its own table listing the products for which it grants concessions to its partner countries. These concessions represent treatment that is not less favourable than that granted to the EU by each country. The industrial (processing) components are duty-free.

106. The rules of origin have a key function in all the FTAs, since they determine the country of origin of products and thus define which goods are profiting from the FTAs. The FTAs are normally rather liberal in nature and allow for the use of up to 50% of non-originating input in the production of certain products. This being said, each FTA contains specific rules of origin.

107. Since the EFTA States do not have a common agricultural policy, basic agricultural products are dealt with in bilateral arrangements concluded between each EFTA State and the partner country in parallel with the main agreement. These arrangements form part of the instruments creating the free trade area and are inextricably linked with the FTAs.

2023, pending entry into force), Montenegro (signature 14 Nov. 2011, entry into force 1 Sep. 2012 for Montenegro, Liechtenstein and Switzerland, 1 Oct. 2012 for Iceland and 1 Nov. 2012 for Norway), Morocco (signature 19 Jun. 1997, entry into force 1 Dec. 1999), North Macedonia (signature 19 Jun. 2000 entry into force 1 May 2002), Palestinian Authority (signature 30 Nov. 1998, entry into force 1 Jul. 1999), Peru (signature 14 Jul. 2010, entry into force 1 Jul. 2011 for Liechtenstein and Switzerland, 1 Oct. 2011 for Iceland, 1 Jul. 2012 for Norway), Philippines (signature 28 Apr. 2016, entry into force pending), Serbia (signature 17 Dec. 2009, entry into force 1 Oct. 2010 for Liechtenstein and Switzerland, 1 Jun. 2011 for Norway and 1 Oct. 2011 for Iceland), Singapore (signature 26 Jun. 2002, entry into force 1 Jan. 2003), Southern African Customs Union (signature 26 Jun. 2006, entry into force 1 May 2008), Tunisia (signature 17 Dec. 2004, entry into force 1 Jun. 2005), Turkey (signature 10 Dec. 1991, entry into force 1 Apr. 1992) and Ukraine (signature 24 Jun. 2010, entry into force 1 Jun. 2012). The text of the agreements as well as some information related to these agreements are available at http://www.efta.int/free-trade/free-trade-agreements.

88. Kosovo, Malaysia, Mercosur, Thailand and Vietnam.

89. The underlying principle is that duties reflect the difference between the domestic market price and the world market price of the basic agricultural component of the product.

108. The FTAs contain three types of provisions on technical regulations. The FTA with Turkey establishes an information procedure on draft technical regulations. Other FTAs, for example, the FTAs with Israel, Morocco and the Palestinian Authority contain no such information procedure, but provide for provisions on consultation and cooperation. A consultation mechanism is established; thereby extending the scope of issues that might be subject to consultation within the framework of the Joint Committee. They also contain a reference to the WTO Agreement on TBT.[90] In case of consultations, the aim would be to work out solutions in conformity with the TBT Agreement. Finally, the FTAs with Mexico and Chile state that the TBT Agreement governs the rights and obligations of the Parties. They specify areas for cooperation in the framework of the FTAs and oblige the Parties to broaden exchange of information.[91]

109. While earlier FTAs only contain evolutionary clauses on services and investment, in which the Parties undertook to cooperate with the aim of achieving gradual liberalization and mutual opening of markets for investments and trade in services, the FTAs with, for example, Mexico, Singapore and Chile cover all modes of service supply and contain separate sections or annexes relating to specific sectors. They also provide for the gradual liberalization and protection of payments and transfers. All of these later FTAs contain provisions regarding the establishment of foreign investors.

110. With regard to public procurement, all FTAs – with some minor exceptions – include a clause that the parties should aim to accede to the WTO Government Procurement Agreement (GPA). It is only the most recent FTAs that secure substantial access for EFTA operators to the relevant government procurement market. For example, the FTA with Chile is quite far-reaching and grants non-discriminatory access to procurement markets for goods, services and public works at the central government level, the subcentral government level and for entities operating in various utility fields (ports and airports, transport and water supply). Similar far-reaching and detailed provisions on public procurement are contained, for example, in the FTAs concluded with Ecuador, Peru and Ukraine.

111. The provisions on intellectual property in the FTAs provide for adequate, effective and non-discriminatory protection of intellectual property rights including measures for the enforcement of such rights against infringement, counterfeiting

90. Agreement on TBT. The Agreement is published in *The Results of the Uruguay Round of Multilateral Trade Negotiations* (published by the GATT Secretariat), Geneva 1994.

91. Similarly, in the area of sanitary and phytosanitary measures, the FTA with Chile states that the rights and obligations of the Parties are governed by the WTO Agreement on the Application of Sanitary and Phytosanitary Measures (the SPS Agreement). Furthermore, according to Art. 16(6) of the FTA with Chile, Chile and any of the EFTA States may, for better implementation of this article, develop bilateral arrangements including agreements between their respective regulatory agencies.

and piracy. They are based on the principles of MFN treatment and national treatment. In some FTAs the level of protection in certain areas goes beyond what is provided for under the TRIPS Agreement,[92] for example, in the FTAs with Singapore and Chile.

112. All second-generation FTAs include chapters on competition and State aid (CSA). The competition provisions foresee cooperation and exchange of information with the aim of ensuring and facilitating the enforcement of the Parties' respective competition laws. The State aid rules are based on notification requirements and annual reporting, which are the tools available for the parties to assess and control whether the other parties have acted in compliance with the provisions on State aid. The provisions on State aid are those referred to in Article XVI of GATT 1994 and the WTO Agreement on Subsidies and Countervailing Measures.

113. EFTA States also apply and actively promote high standards for sustainable development and inclusiveness in their trade policies and their respective foreign policy. With the adoption of model provisions on trade and sustainable development in 2010, EFTA Ministers acknowledged a need for enhanced policy coherence at the national and international levels to harness the potential for a positive contribution of international trade to the promotion of sustainable development.

114. Since 2010, the EFTA States have developed and systematically included model provisions in their FTAs. The provisions reflect a cooperative approach and put an emphasis on policy coherence. They recognize that economic development, social development and environmental protection are interdependent and mutually supportive components of sustainable development and foresee that the Parties reaffirm their commitment to promote the development of international trade in such a way as to contribute to sustainable development. The provisions of the Trade and Sustainable Development chapter specifically address trade- or investment-related aspects of labour and environmental standards. Some of the standards and obligations referred to in the chapter also have a human rights dimension or may relate to the fulfilment of such rights.

115. Chapters on trade and sustainable development have been included in FTAs with Montenegro (2011), Bosnia and Herzegovina (2013), the Central American States (2013), Georgia (2016), the Philippines (2016), Ecuador (2018), Indonesia (2018) and Mercosur (not yet signed). The EFTA-Hong Kong China FTA (2011) includes a chapter on trade and environment, while a side agreement on labour has been concluded in parallel. A chapter has also been added as part of a comprehensive review of the FTA with Turkey (2018) and has been added to the existing FTAs with Albania (2015) and Serbia (2015).

---

92. Agreement on TRIPS. The Agreement is published in *The Results of the Uruguay Round of Multilateral Trade Negotiations* (published by the GATT Secretariat), Geneva 1994.

B. Institutional Set-Up under the FTAs

116. Each FTA establishes a Joint Committee. These Joint Committees are composed of representatives of the EFTA States and the respective partner countries. The Joint Committees supervise the implementation of the respective FTAs and evaluate the results obtained in their application: They oversee the further elaboration of the FTAs and they endeavour to resolve disputes that may arise regarding the interpretation or application of the FTAs.

117. In performing their mandates, the Joint Committees may take decisions in cases provided for by the FTA in question, and make recommendations in all other cases. Decisions by the Joint Committees are foreseen, for instance, for the adoption of its rules of procedure, the establishment of subcommittees,[93] for amendments of the annexes and protocols to the FTA and, subject to subsequent ratification and approval procedures, amendments to the FTA as such.

118. In practice, the Joint Committees usually meet once every year or every two years. They can, however, be convened more often if an urgent issue needs to be addressed, for instance, to provide a forum for consultations between parties to a dispute.

C. Dispute Settlement under the FTAs

119. FTAs also contain provisions on dispute settlement between the parties. Dispute settlement starts with consultations. The consultations take place before the Joint Committee, established under the FTA, unless the party or parties making or receiving the request for consultations disagree.

120. If the matter has not been resolved during the consultations, it may be referred to arbitration by one or more parties involved by means of a written notification addressed to the party complained against. A request for arbitration gives the reasons for the complaint including the identification of the measure at issue and an indication of the legal basis of the complaint. The procedure is carried out before an arbitration panel. Other parties can intervene in the arbitration panel procedure.

121. The arbitration panel presents its ruling to the parties to the dispute within ninety days from the date of its establishment. Unless the parties to the dispute decide otherwise, the ruling is normally published fifteen days after it is presented to them.

122. Rulings of arbitration panels are final and binding on the parties to the dispute. There is no possibility for an appeal. Consequently, each party to the dispute is bound by the ruling and has to take the measures necessary to comply with the

93. Subcommittees have been established, for example, in the field of customs and origin matters.

ruling. The parties to the dispute shall endeavour to agree on the specific measures that are required for complying with the ruling. The party complained against shall notify the other party within thirty days after the ruling has been transmitted to the parties to the dispute: (a) the specific measures required for complying with the ruling; (b) the reasonable period of time to do so; and (c) a concrete proposal for a temporary compensation until the full implementation of the specific measures required for compliance with the ruling.

123. In case of disagreement between the parties to the dispute on the content of such notification, the complaining party may request the original arbitration panel to rule on whether the proposed measures required for complying with the ruling are in compliance with the ruling. It may also request an opinion on the duration of the period of time and on whether the compensation proposal is manifestly disproportionate.

124. In case a party concerned fails to notify the implementing measures, or where the arbitration panel rules that the implementing measures notified by a party are not in compliance with the ruling, such party, if so requested by the complaining party, enters into consultations with a view to agree on a mutually acceptable compensation. If no such agreement has been reached, the complaining party is entitled to suspend the application of benefits granted under the Agreement equivalent to those affected by the measure found to be inconsistent with, or to impair benefits under, the Agreement. The suspension of benefits shall be temporary and shall only be applied by the complaining party until the measure found to be inconsistent with this Agreement has been withdrawn or amended, so as to bring it into conformity with the Agreement, or the parties to the dispute have reached agreement on a resolution of the dispute.

125. Apart from the dispute settlement procedure outlined supra, the FTAs provide for 'good offices', conciliation or mediation. Good offices, conciliation and mediation are procedures that are undertaken voluntarily if the parties involved so agree. These procedures are not bound by any time limits concerning their beginning or end. Moreover, they are confidential and without prejudice to the rights of the parties in any other proceedings.

III. Technical Cooperation

126. EFTA projects on trade policy issues have a dual purpose: first, to assist free trade partners in the implementation of the FTAs; and second, to assist partners within the framework of the Cooperation Declarations, in order to prepare for free trade relations.[94]

94. Upon request, EFTA arranges seminars, workshops and study visits adapted to the particular needs of individual countries, covering areas such as customs and origin matters, TBT, trade facilitation, intellectual property rights, competition rules, State aid and public procurement.

127. In accordance with the principle of cooperation with third countries laid down by the EFTA Council on the basis of the Declaration adopted at the Ministerial meeting in Bergen in 1995, the main focus of EFTA's technical assistance programme should be on activities supporting existing and possible future FTAs in Europe and beyond. EFTA technical assistance covers a series of programmes and projects funded under EFTA's budget.[95] Priority is given to joint EFTA-EU programmes and trade policy projects, as well as to the EFTA scholarship programme.

128. The EFTA States, Iceland, Liechtenstein and Norway, through their membership in the EEA[96] and Switzerland partly and bilaterally, participated, for example, in EU projects and programmes under Horizon Europe (the EU's Research and Innovation Programme), Digital Europe (the EU's funding programme for digital technology), Life (the EU's funding instrument for the environment and climate action), Erasmus+ (the EU's education programme which aims at boosting skills and employability of students), the Single Market Programme (the EU's financing for a well-functioning internal market), the European Space Programme (EU's programme for implementing space activities), Creative Europe (a programme to support Media and Culture), EU4Health (the EU's programme which contributes to the long-term health challenges by building stronger, more resilient and more accessible health systems) and InvestEU (the EU's programme to support sustainable investment, innovation and job creation).[97] In addition, Iceland, Liechtenstein and Norway are providing for 'EEA and Norway Grants'.[98] The EEA and Norway Grants have two goals: first, they contribute to a more equal Europe, both socially and economically; second, they strengthen the relations between Iceland, Liechtenstein and Norway, and the fifteen Beneficiary States in Europe.[99]

95. For example, in 2022 EFTA spent CHF 3,134,000 on EU-EFTA and EFTA cooperation programmes.
96. The legal framework for cooperation is contained in Part VI of the EEA Agreement (Arts 78 to 88).
97. Information about these EU projects and programmes with the respective EEA EFTA Participation can be found on the Website of the EFTA Secretariat: www.efta.int/eea/eu-programmes.
98. *See infra* Part II, Ch. 3, §9.
99. More information on the EEA and Norway Grants is available under the following website: www.eeagrants.org.

Chapter 4. Enforcement Mechanisms

129. Chapter 17 of the EFTA Convention, entitled 'Consultations and Dispute Settlement', provides for a dispute settlement mechanism to deal with any matters of controversy arising from the Convention. This enforcement mechanism follows a classical arbitration approach, distinguishable both from the judicial procedures available under EEA law, which (in some instances) ultimately refer a matter to a supranational Court,[100] and from the more judicial dispute settlement procedure under the WTO rules.

130. Dispute settlement under the EFTA Convention starts with consultations between the parties in dispute. If consultations between the parties fail to produce an amicable solution, the matter can be brought before an arbitration tribunal,[101] which ultimately decides on the matter with a binding verdict. There is no appeal procedure available against the decision of the arbitration tribunal. In the following, the consultation phase and the arbitration procedure will be described in more detail.

§1. The Consultation Phase

131. The consultation provision is contained in Article 47 of the EFTA Convention. According to Article 47(1) of the EFTA Convention, Member States endeavour to agree on the interpretation and application of the EFTA Convention. The Member States have to make every attempt, through cooperation and consultations, to arrive at a mutually satisfactory resolution of any matter that might affect the operation of the EFTA Convention. Article 47(1) of the EFTA Convention puts an obligation on the Member States to accord sympathetic considerations to and afford adequate opportunity for consultation regarding any representations made by another Member State. This article is also an expression of the view that a solution mutually acceptable to the parties to a dispute and consistent with the EFTA Convention is to be preferred.

132. Any matter concerning the interpretation or application of the EFTA Convention can be brought by a Member State before the EFTA Council. All necessary information has to be provided to the Council, which might be of use in making possible an in-depth examination of the situation, with a view to finding an acceptable solution. To this end, the Council examines all possibilities to maintain the good functioning of the Convention (Article 47(2) of the EFTA Convention). A meeting of the Council will be held within thirty days of the receipt of the request for consultations (Article 47(3) of the EFTA Convention).

100. *See infra* Part II, Ch. 5, §2.
101. The establishment and the functioning of the arbitration tribunal and the implementation of arbitral awards are governed by the rules set out in Annex T to the EFTA Convention (Art. 48(4) of the EFTA Convention).

§2. THE ARBITRATION PROCEDURE

133. Where a Member State considers that a measure applied by another Member State violates the EFTA Convention and the matter has not been resolved within forty-five days after consultations have been held, such matter may be referred to arbitration by one or more Member States parties to the dispute by means of a written notification addressed to the Member State complained against (Article 48(1) of the EFTA Convention). A copy of this notification is then communicated to all Member States so that they are in a position to determine whether they have a substantial interest in the matter. Where several Member States request the submission to an arbitration tribunal of a dispute with the same Member State relating to the same question, a single arbitration tribunal should, whenever feasible, be established to consider such disputes (Article 48(1) of the EFTA Convention).

134. The arbitration procedure provides for the possibility of other Member States to intervene in the disputes. To this end, a Member State which is not party to the dispute, on delivery of a written notice to the disputing Member States, is entitled to make written submissions to the arbitration tribunal, receive written submissions of the disputing Member States, attend all hearings and make oral submissions (Article 48(2) of the EFTA Convention and Article 1(8) of Annex T to the EFTA Convention).

135. In general, unless otherwise agreed between the parties to the dispute, and subject to Article 48 of the EFTA Convention and Annex T, the Optional Rules for Arbitrating Disputes between Two States of the Permanent Court of Arbitration (PCA) apply (Article 1(6) of Annex T to the EFTA Convention). The arbitration tribunal takes decisions by majority vote. Minority opinions are not disclosed (Article 1(7) of Annex T to the EFTA Convention). The arbitral award is rendered within six months of the date on which the President of the arbitration tribunal was appointed. This period can be extended by a maximum of three additional months, if the parties to the dispute agree (Article 1(9) of Annex T to the EFTA Convention). The award of the arbitration tribunal is final and binding upon the Member States to the dispute and has to be complied with promptly (Article 48(3) of the EFTA Convention).

I. The Arbitration Tribunal

136. The arbitration tribunal comprises three members. Their nomination is according to the following procedure (Article 1, paragraphs 2–5, of Annex T to the EFTA Convention): In its written notification the Member State(s) referring the dispute to arbitration has (have) to designate one member of the arbitral tribunal. Within fifteen days from the receipt of the notification, the Member State(s) to which it was addressed has (have), in turn, to designate one member. Within thirty days from the receipt of the notification, the Member States concerned, as opposed to the two arbiters appointed by them, have to agree on the designation of a third member. The third member shall not be a national of the parties to the dispute, nor permanently reside in the territory of either Member State. The member thus appointed will be the President of the arbitration tribunal.

137. If all the three members have not been designated or appointed within thirty days from the receipt of the notification, the President of the International Court of Justice, applying the above-mentioned criteria, shall make the necessary designations, at the request of either party to the dispute. If the President is unable to act or is a national of a party to the dispute, the designation will be effected by the next senior member of the Court who is neither unable to act nor a national of a Member State (Article 1(5) of Annex T to the EFTA Convention).

138. The expenses of the arbitration tribunal, including the remuneration of its members, shall be borne by the parties to the dispute in equal shares (Article 1(10) of Annex T to the EFTA Convention). Fees and expenses payable to members of an arbitration tribunal are subject to schedules established by the Council and in force at the time of the establishment of the arbitration tribunal. Thus, expenses are not allocated like in court proceedings, where the defeating party usually covers the costs of the winning party.

II. Implementation of Arbitral Awards

139. On receipt of the arbitral award, the parties to the dispute agree on the implementation of the arbitral award. Unless they decide otherwise by common accord, this conforms to the determinations and recommendations of the arbitration tribunal (Article 2(1) of Annex T to the EFTA Convention). The parties to the dispute have to notify the other Member States of any agreed resolution of the dispute. Wherever possible, the resolution shall be non-implementation or removal of a measure not conforming to the EFTA Convention or, failing such a resolution, compensation (Article 2(2) of Annex T to the EFTA Convention).

140. In case of disagreement as to the existence or consistency of the measure implementing the arbitral award with the recommendations of the arbitration tribunal, the same arbitration tribunal will decide such dispute before compensation can be sought or suspension of benefits can be applied (Article 2(3) of Annex T to the EFTA Convention). The complaining Member State may not initiate arbitration before a period of twelve months has expired following the rendering of the initial award pursuant to Article 48(3) of the EFTA Convention. The award of the tribunal shall normally be rendered within three months of the request for arbitration (Article 2(4) of Annex T of the EFTA Convention).

III. Non-implementation of Arbitral Awards

141. If the arbitration tribunal has determined that a measure is inconsistent with the obligations of the EFTA Convention, and the Member State complained against has not reached agreement with any complaining Member State on a mutually satisfactory resolution within thirty days of receiving the arbitral award, or if no implementing measures have been taken, such complaining Member State or Member States may: (a) seek compensation through an agreement with the Member State complained against; or (b) suspend the application to the Member State complained against of benefits of equivalent effect until such time as the disputing Member States have reached agreement on a resolution of the dispute (Article 3(1) of Annex T to the EFTA Convention).

142. Upon written request of any party to the dispute delivered to the other Member State or Member States, the same arbitration tribunal shall be reconvened to determine whether the level of benefits suspended by a Member State is of equivalent effect (Article 3(2) of Annex T to the EFTA Convention). The proceedings of the arbitration tribunal are conducted in accordance with the general provisions mentioned above. The arbitration tribunal presents its determination within sixty days after the date of the request or such other periods as the parties to the dispute may agree (Article 3(3) of Annex T to the EFTA Convention).

Chapter 5. Finance

143. Pursuant to Article 44(c) of the EFTA Convention, the EFTA Council is to establish the financial arrangements necessary for the administrative expenses of the Association, the procedure for establishing a budget and the apportionment of those expenses between the EFTA States. On the basis of this provision, the Council has adopted the Financial Regulations and Rules, which have been amended since on numerous occasions.

144. The procedure for the adoption of the budget by the EFTA Council starts with the preparation of the budget proposal by the Secretary-General, who submits it to the Council at least six months preceding the beginning of the financial year. The budget proposal is accompanied with a performance plan, which describes the main aims and expected results of the services provided by the Secretariat.

145. As soon as the Council receives the budget proposal, it is to refer that proposal to the Budget Committee. The Budget Committee will examine the proposal and make a recommendation to the Council not later than two months before the beginning of the financial year.

146. The budget for each financial year is adopted by the EFTA Council upon recommendation of the Budget Committee, with reference to the performance plan. It is drawn up in Euros and Swiss Francs and financed by contributions by Member States in accordance to a scale of contribution determined by the Council and by any other income accruing to the Association. The latter source of income is, however, minimal. In 2022, the total EFTA budget was CHF 23,361,000, and it was entirely sourced from contributions of the EFTA States. Of the total budget in 2022, Iceland covered 4.94%, Liechtenstein 1.09%, Norway 48.31% and Switzerland 45.66%. The reason for the lower contribution from Switzerland is to be found in the fact that Switzerland is not a Contracting Party to the EEA Agreement.

147. When adopting the budget, the EFTA Council also adopts a separate decision on the cost sharing of the budget. This decision is based on two cost-sharing keys, which are based on the gross domestic product (GDP) of each of the EFTA States.

148. The first, and most important, key does not take into account that Switzerland is not part of the EEA Agreement. Consequently, although the EFTA Secretariat provides extensive services in connection with the EEA Agreement, the non-EEA Contracting Party Switzerland contributes fully to the financing of these services. However, with regard to the second key, Switzerland's status as a non-EEA Contracting Party is taken into account. This latter key only concerns the costs incurred for the publication of the EEA Supplement to the Official Journal of the EU. The latter contains the Icelandic and Norwegian language versions. Costs other than Secretariat services and publication of the EEA Supplement incurred by reason of the EEA Agreement are not included in the EFTA budget.

149. With regard to the expenses, a new budget method was applied for the first time in 2004. The budget is divided into two parts. Part I covers the daily operations of the EFTA Secretariat and Part II covers cooperation programmes with partners outside the Secretariat. While no funds may be transferred between the two parts without the approval of the Council, the Secretary-General is, in principle, competent to dispose of the funds within the two parts. This means, in particular, that no restriction on the number of personnel applies other than the general financial framework provided by the budget. In 2022, the EFTA budget was divided into the following posts: (1) Trade relations with countries outside the EU (CHF 4,667,000); (2) EEA-related activities (CHF 8,393,000); (3) EFTA/EU statistical cooperation (CHF 683,000); (4) Horizontal and Governance support (CHF 6,484,000); and (5) EU-EFTA and EFTA cooperation programmes (CHF 3,134,000).

Chapter 6. Network with Other Organizations

150. EFTA operates in a network with several international organizations such as the WTO, the OECD and selected United Nation (UN) bodies in areas that are of interest and relevant for its work. Beyond the technical contacts, which it entertains with these organizations it also enjoys an observer status.

151. Since 1960, for instance, EFTA has observer status in the OECD. Even though the OECD has a much broader field of activities than EFTA, EFTA has specific interests in some of the OECD's activities, particularly in relation to its work in connection with FTAs (trade matters, such as trade in services, investment, capital movements, competition policy, etc.). Consequently, EFTA follows the work of the OECD in the respective committees and the Secretariat makes active use of its observer status and is regularly present at meetings of bodies of the Organization, such as the Trade Committee, the Economic Policy Committee, the Economic and Development Review Committee. In addition, the EFTA Secretary-General regularly attends the OECD Council at Ministerial level.

152. The EFTA Secretariat has an observer status in several WTO-bodies of relevance to its work (e.g., Trade Policy Review Body (TPRB), the Committee on Balance of Payments Restrictions (BOPS), the Committee on Regional Trade Agreements (CRTA), the Committee on Trade and Development (CTD), the Committee on Trade and Environment (CTE) and the Committee on Rules of Origin). EFTA is also regularly invited to attend Ministerial conferences as an observer.

153. Finally, the EFTA Secretariat closely follows events of several UN bodies such as the United Nations Economic Commission for Europe (UNECE) and the United Nations Conference on Trade and Development (UNCTAD). Both UNECE and UNCTAD give EFTA a good opportunity to discuss policy issues and exchange experience with other relevant actors in the field. Representatives of the EFTA Secretariat participate in meetings and activities on issues relevant to the work of EFTA, such as the International Forum on Trade Facilitation and the Commission on Enterprise, Business Facilitation and Development. Development policy issues have, in particular, become more and more relevant for EFTA in recent years due to the negotiation of FTAs with less developed countries.

Part II. The EEA

Chapter 1. Genesis and Historical Development of the EEA

§1. The Luxembourg Process

154. On 9 April 1984, the first ever joint meeting at ministerial level was held between the EC and the EFTA States in Luxembourg. At that meeting the historical decision was taken to establish 'a dynamic European Economic Space'. As would later be seen, the inclusion of the word dynamic implied a change in EC-EFTA cooperation, since, for the first time, it foresaw that the two trade blocs should, in some fields, evolve in parallel with the internal market legislation of the EC.

155. In order to follow-up the Luxembourg Ministerial meeting, several working groups, consisting of officials from the European Commission and the EFTA States, were established. The so-called Luxembourg process thereby started. In the beginning the focus was only on the free circulation of goods. The other main areas of free movement – persons, services and capital – were not mentioned. Only in autumn 1986 did the parties agree to discuss liberalization of trade in services and capital movements.

156. For some time, more in-depth integration between the parties was not the objective. None of the then six EFTA States wished to apply for full EC membership. For different reasons, the four non-NATO EFTA States, Austria, Finland, Sweden and Switzerland, each felt that EC Membership was incompatible with their neutrality status. As for Iceland, it doubted that the all-important 'fisheries question' could be resolved to its satisfaction in an accession treaty with the EC. Finally, in Norway the 'scars of the battle for membership in 1972 were still hurting'.[102] The EFTA States were first and foremost concerned that their economies could be disadvantaged and marginalized, if they did not achieve access to the internal market. They wanted, therefore, to participate to the fullest extent possible in the EC's internal market and to do so in a way that went far beyond the pre-existing bilateral EC-EFTA States FTAs for goods.[103] Consequently, at a meeting between the EFTA

102. K. Børde, 'The European Economic Area, Norway and the European Union: Achievements, Possibilities and Limitations', in *The European Economic Area – Norway's Basic Status in the Legal Construction of Europe* 9(10) (P.C. Müller-Graff & E. Selvig eds, Berlin: Berlin Verlag A. Spitz 1997).

103. *See supra* Part I, Ch. 1.

Ministers in Geneva on the 3 December 1986, a statement was issued that argued for parallelism between the EC's efforts to complete the internal market and the evolution of EC-EFTA cooperation.

157. On the EC side, many stakeholders did not feel it was the right moment to have further enlargement, but preferred to focus instead on 'deepening' the Community. Although the EFTA States qualified for the formal criteria for accession, not all EC Member States were enthusiastic about expanding the Community with a large number of small States that were perceived as more interested in enhanced free trade than political integration. This was especially so since the neutrality of some EFTA States constituted a potential impediment to the development of the European Political Cooperation and an eventual common foreign and security policy.

158. The Community's vision of future cooperation with the EFTA States was reflected in a speech by the then European Commissioner for External Relations and Trade Policy, Willy de Clercq, at the so-called Interlaken Ministerial Meeting in 1988. In his view, the EC's relation to EFTA should be guided by the following three principles. First, there should be a priority for internal EC integration. There could, in other words, be no discussion of the possibility of the EC slowing down, in order for the EFTA States to catch up. Second, the EC's internal decision-making autonomy should be preserved. The greater recourse to qualified majority voting, achieved by the Single European Act, should not be undermined by external obligations, which would render internal decision-making more difficult. Third, a fair balance between benefits and obligations should be achieved. By this third principle, the Community pointed to the risk of imbalance if only the EC and its Member States were subject to legal control when implementing and applying agreements with the EFTA States. The European Court of Justice (ECJ) had already held that economic operators from EFTA States could invoke the free trade provisions of the bilateral EC-EFTA States FTAs before the national courts in the Community.[104] In contrast, no similar judicial protection was guaranteed in the EFTA States where most States adhered to dualistic systems making it impossible to attack national legislation on the grounds that it violated an international agreement.

159. After initial optimism with speedy progress in limited fields, the parties had to acknowledge that a long list of areas was still unresolved and that the functional cooperation approach initiated by the Luxembourg process was inadequate for resolving these problems. Seen from the Community perspective the intergovernmental structure of EFTA and its consensus procedures made it a difficult negotiation partner.[105] Although, from an EFTA perspective, the process had the advantage of allowing the EFTA States to decide which areas they wanted to include in the discussion, most EFTA States felt that the Luxembourg process was not only an exhausting exercise but also that its possibilities were becoming exhausted.

---

104. *See* Case C-104/81 *Kupferberg* [1982] ECR-3641.

105. F. Laursen, 'EC-EFTA Relations: A Game-Theory Perspective', in *The Political Economy of European Integration* 179 (193 and 195) (Laursen ed., Maastricht: Kluwer 1995).

§2. THE DELORS INITIATIVE

160. In a speech to the European Parliament on 17 January 1989, the then President of the European Commission, Jacques Delors, asked the EFTA States how far their ambitions actually went. In Delors' view, it was possible to continue on a bilateral road and end up with a free trade area comprising the EC and each of the EFTA States. Another, more far-reaching solution was to look for a new form of association with common bodies for decision-making and administration. Such an approach would have the advantage of resulting in a more efficient structure. Moreover, the approach would underline the political dimension of cooperation in the areas covered by such an agreement. If the EFTA States were ready to accept not only free trade provisions but also common rules, including adherence to the rules on State aid and competition, as well as a strong supervisory system, then a genuine 'European Economic Space' could be established. The basic idea was thus a widening of the EC's internal market. This idea went beyond the existing bilateral FTAs, since it not only purported to regulate trade between the EFTA States and the EC, but to make the EFTA States an integral part of the EC's internal market.

161. Just eight weeks later, at an EFTA summit in Oslo on 14 and 15 March 1989, the EFTA States expressed their consent to such a more comprehensive and in-depth cooperation. Following the positive response of the EFTA States, it was decided to intensify the cooperation for the establishment of the future EEA. A High Level Steering Group and five working groups were established to discuss possible avenues, notably in relation to the four freedoms (i.e., the free circulation of goods, services, persons and capital), flanking policies (e.g., on social policy, environment, State aid, competition and public procurement) and institutional issues. In contrast to the original Luxembourg process, the new process was to be a 'top-down' approach aiming at a package deal. In addition, the EC required the EFTA States to present a common position, that is, to speak with one voice, in the negotiations. The work of the different working and steering groups was concluded on 20 October 1989. At an EC-EFTA Ministerial meeting on 19 December 1989 the decision was taken to initiate formal negotiations on a global agreement. The European Commission then obtained its negotiation mandate from the Council on 18 June 1990 and formal negotiations started on 20 June 1990.

I. The Acquis Communautaire

162. From the beginning of the formal talks, the EFTA States were, by and large, prepared to take over the rules concerning the four freedoms and competition, as well as the secondary law connected thereto. More than 1,800 Community legal acts were taken over into the future EEA Agreement.[106] It became the basis for a homogeneous internal market governing the whole EEA, in which the same rules applied as in the EC's internal market.

---

106. By the end of 2023, more than 10,000 legal acts have been incorporated into the EEA Agreement by decisions of the EEA Joint Committee, and more than 1,000 legal acts have been incorporated by simplified procedure in the veterinary area.

163. Still, the EFTA States insisted on being granted permanent exceptions to these common rules in areas that they deemed to be vital to them. While originally seemingly open to such views, the negotiation position of the EC changed after the opening of the formal negotiations. After that date, the EC no longer displayed the same acceptance of a possible narrowing of the scope of the acquis communautaire[107] for political or security reasons – a change that for a large part was due to the geopolitical changes following the fall of the Berlin Wall. Second, derogations justified by economic difficulties were now to be limited to relatively short transition periods and safeguard clauses, whereas permanent derogations were excluded. The result was that the character of the negotiations changed to an 'all or nothing' discussion. At the end, EFTA States were forced to withdraw their requests for permanent exceptions with, however, two exceptions. The first exception allowed EFTA States to ban advertising for alcohol and spirits on television programmes broadcasted within their borders. The second exception permitted Norway and Iceland to maintain domestic legislation banning foreign direct investment in the fisheries sector.[108] In addition, EFTA States had to agree to one single horizontal safeguard clause.

II. Decision-Making

164. The institutional aspects of the draft EEA Agreement remained the most controversial and difficult issue. Having agreed in principle to adopt future EC legislation, the EFTA States argued that such acceptance had, as its natural counterpart, the establishment of a new decision-making process in the EEA, where all parties took part on equal footing. In other words, the EFTA States argued for a direct participation in the EC's decision-making process.

165. The Community, for its part, did not deviate from the position expressed by Commissioner Willy de Clercq in his speech at the Interlaken Ministerial Meeting in 1988[109] and insisted that any substantial or formal EFTA influence on the decision-making in the EC was excluded. Giving the EFTA States co-decision rights in future legislation would be incompatible with the autonomy of the EC's decision-making power and its institutional set-up. On that basis, the European Commission suggested a distinction between 'decision-shaping' and 'decision-making' that came to form the basis for the institutional set-up in the final Agreement.[110] President Jacques Delors summarized the position on this issue in his annual speech to the European Parliament, made on the 17 January 1990. He stated that there would have

107. The term 'acquis communautaire' designates everything that was decided and agreed upon since the establishment of the Community, whatever the form in which this was done, whether legally binding or not. It refers to the body of rules, which governs the Community. In other words, it encompasses everything that was 'acquired' by the Community.
108. A sector that in combination with agriculture as such falls outside the scope of the EEA Agreement, *see infra* Part II, Ch. 2, §1, I.
109. *See supra* Part II, Ch. 1, §1.
110. *See infra* Part II, Ch. 4.

to be some osmosis between the Community and EFTA to ensure that EFTA's interests were taken into account in major Community decisions, 'but this process must stop short of decision-making, which would imply Community membership and acceptance of marriage contracts'. Thus, the EC gradually moved away from Delors' original idea, outlined in his speech to the European Parliament on 17 January 1989, of 'common administrative and decision-making institutions' for the entire EEA, recognizing that creation of such common institutions would circumscribe the EC's autonomy. Instead, the EC advocated that the future EEA Agreement be based on a 'two-pillar system' where the EFTA States were to establish their own institutional pillar on the EFTA side mirroring the institutional pillar of the EC.

166. At a joint ministerial meeting on 19 December 1990, the two sides finally agreed to adhere to an approach close to that advocated by the Community. Consequently, there would be continuous information and consultation in the so-called decision-shaping phase. The decision-making procedures of the EC would be left untouched. In return, decisions at EEA level should be taken by consensus and have the character of public international law agreements, thus not entailing any transfer of legislative power to the EEA. In practice, this should be done by establishing two new bodies at EEA level: an EEA Council that would be responsible for general political guidelines and impulse and an EEA Joint Committee that would be responsible for the implementation of EC legislation and the functioning of the Agreement.[111]

167. EFTA States were granted the right to raise a matter of concern at any time before the EEA Joint Committee or the EEA Council – the so-called droit d'évocation. Moreover, it was accepted that the EFTA States could participate in the decision-shaping phase of new EC legislation. Finally, they retained the right to oppose taking over new EC legislation into the future EEA Agreement.[112]

III. The Surveillance Mechanism

168. In order to ensure the correct transposition and application of the EEA rules, the Contracting Parties readily agreed on the need for a surveillance mechanism. Otherwise, the risk would be a legal imbalance between, on the one hand, the situation in the EC Member States, and, on the other hand, the situation in the EFTA States, to the detriment of individuals and economic operators. Moreover, in order to avoid confusion in the EC legal system it was imperative that the EEA rules be interpreted in line with the corresponding EC rules. The main discussions during the negotiations, therefore, did not so much focus on the need for a supervisory and judicial mechanism as on its organizational structure.

111. The EEA Council is described *infra* Part II, Ch. 3, §1, while the EEA Joint Committee is analysed *infra* Part II, Ch. 3, §2.
112. *See infra* Part II, Ch. 4.

169. Some EFTA States were, especially at the beginning of the negotiations, unwilling to accept supranational institutions and originally argued for a purely national solution. Obviously, the Community, and indeed some of the EFTA States themselves, considered that approach inadequate.

170. Having accepted the need for a supranational supervisory body, a possible solution would have been to create one joint structure for surveillance, for example, by letting the European Commission supervise the future EEA Agreement, both in relation to the EC Member States and the EFTA States. Another solution would have been to create a new joint surveillance institution. However, constitutional and political considerations prevented the EFTA States from accepting that they should be bound directly by decisions of EC institutions. On the other hand, the Community, in line with its general approach in the final negotiations, could not accept the establishment of one common body supervising both the EC Member States' and the EFTA States' application of the envisaged Agreement.

171. Finally, a 'two-pillar structure' was also chosen for the surveillance mechanism. The surveillance became divided between the European Commission, controlling the implementation and application of the EEA Agreement in relation to the EC Member States, and a separate institution, called the EFTA Surveillance Authority, in relation to the EFTA States. The parties, moreover, agreed that the EFTA Surveillance Authority should have broadly parallel competences and be guided by procedures that, in essence, corresponded to those applicable to the European Commission. Not only did the homogeneity principle[113] favour such an approach, but also the credibility of the EFTA Surveillance Authority and considerations of administrative convenience led to the conclusion that separate and divergent procedures should not be created.

IV. The Judicial Architecture

172. The bilateral FTAs that were concluded between the EC and the EFTA States in 1972 did not contain provisions on judicial dispute settlement.[114] Instead a joint committee resolved disputes between the Contracting Parties. Where the rights of a Contracting Party were violated, and a conciliatory agreement was not reached through negotiations, retaliatory measures could be taken against the infringing party. The EC did not find such a procedure adequate in the draft EEA Agreement and pushed for the establishment of a 'Court of Law'.

173. Having accepted the need for a judicial organ, the EFTA States suggested that an independent EEA court should be established to function in conjunction with the ECJ. This idea was substantially adopted in a Joint EC-EFTA Ministerial meeting in May 1991 where it was decided that the desired homogeneity was to be

113. Homogeneity refers to the principle that the same rules apply in the EEA as in the Community's internal market, *see infra* Part II, Ch. 2, §1, II.

114. *See supra* Part I, Ch. 1.

ensured, *inter alia*, through the establishment of one joint judicial mechanism functionally integrated within the ECJ. The link to EC law was to be substantiated by the plan that most of the participating judges should come from the ECJ where the same judges should sit.[115] The EEA Court was to be competent to give rulings concerning dispute settlement at the request of the EEA Joint Committee or the Contracting Parties, concerning disputes between the EFTA Surveillance Authority and an EFTA State, and concerning cases brought by enterprises or States against decisions of the EFTA States or the EFTA Surveillance Authority in the field of competition.

174. In addition, the idea was to provide the EFTA States with a similar kind of assistance as that which the ECJ gives to the courts in the EC Member States by virtue of the system of preliminary rulings laid down in what is now Article 267 of the Treaty on the Functioning of the European Union (TFEU). The role of the ECJ barred the Community from accepting that this competence be given to the envisaged EEA Court. As the ECJ was not, however, a court of the EFTA States, those States could not accept that the ECJ should give its opinion in form of an opinion binding on them.[116] That was especially so for Iceland and Switzerland where the resistance to let foreign judges decide matters relevant to those countries had historically played a role for the wish of their peoples to achieve independence.[117] The compromise was therefore to use the expression that the ECJ was to 'express itself' on the interpretation of an EEA rule.

175. Both the existence of a common EEA Court and the idea of non-binding preliminary opinions were, however, rejected by the ECJ as being contrary to EC law.[118] The negotiators thereafter had no choice but to reflect on the 'two-pillar structure' also in connection with the judicial control and to proceed with a double set of judicial mechanisms with the ECJ as the supreme interpreter of EEA law in the EC pillar and a new separate EFTA Court having the task of judging the application of EEA law in the EFTA pillar. Simultaneously, the potential set-back for a homogeneous interpretation and application of EEA and EC law was compensated for through a range of new provisions in the future EEA Agreement. Finally, the possibility for an EFTA State to allow its courts and tribunals to refer questions to the ECJ was changed so that the answer of the ECJ would be binding.[119] In relation to the corresponding competence for the EFTA Court – the avenue actually intended to be used in practice – the EFTA States decided to make that court's preliminary opinions only advisory.

---

115. The different suggestions during the negotiating-process are described by L. Sevón, 'The EEA Judicial System and the Supreme Courts of the EFTA States', in *Accord EEE, Commentaires et réflexions* 603 (604) (Jacot-Guillarmod ed., Zürich: Schulthess 1992).
116. S. Norberg, 'The EFTA Court', in *European Courts, Practice and Precedents* 77 (102) (Plender et al. eds, London: Sweet & Maxwell 1997).
117. *Ibid.*
118. ECJ, Opinion No. 1/91 [1991] ECR I-6079.
119. Protocol 34 to the EEA Agreement.

176. The outcome of the negotiations was submitted to the ECJ for a new opinion on 25 February 1992. In its Opinion 1/92, delivered on 10 April 1992,[120] the ECJ found that the new proposed provisions were compatible with EC law as long as the principle that decisions taken by the EEA Joint Committee would not affect the case law of the ECJ would be laid down in a form binding on the Contracting Parties.

V. The Final Agreement

177. On 2 May 1992 in Oporto, Ministers from the EC and EFTA States and the European Commission signed the Agreement on an EEA – an agreement, which, in its thirteen languages, contained approximately 15,000 pages. Whereas the old FTAs of 1972 and 1973 were based on the former Article 113 of the EEC Treaty (now Article 207 TFEU), the EEA Agreement is a mixed agreement based on the former Article 238 of the EEC Treaty (now Article 218 TFEU) in the sense that both the Community (now the EU) and the Member States are parties to it. The mixed agreement structure was deemed necessary since matters such as cultural cooperation and political dialogue did not fall within the exclusive competence of the Community. Only two of the then three Communities became parties to the EEA Agreement, namely the EC and the ECSC, since the cooperation did not comprise the nuclear sector. EFTA as such does not participate in the Agreement.

178. The same day Ministers from the then seven EFTA States signed three agreements: on a Standing Committee of the EFTA States, on the Establishment of a Surveillance Authority and a Court of Justice (the so-called Surveillance and Court Agreement or just Agreement between the EFTA States on the establishment of a Surveillance Authority and a Court of Justice (SCA)) and on a Committee of Members of Parliament of the EFTA States, thereby creating the necessary institutions and structures required by the 'two-pillar structure' of the EEA Agreement.

179. One year of preparatory work and almost two years of formal negotiations had resulted in the successful establishment of, what was then, the world's largest internal market consisting of eighteen countries with a total of 372 million people. Yet, still more troubles lay ahead. The Agreement should have entered into force on 1 January 1993, after ratification by all Contracting Parties. However, after a negative referendum in Switzerland on 6 December 1992, the remaining Contracting Parties concluded an adjusting protocol, which was signed in Brussels on 17 March 1993. In parallel, the EFTA States signed adjusting protocols to the SCA, to the Agreement on the Standing Committee of the EFTA States and to the Agreement on a Committee of Members of Parliament of the EFTA States. The EEA Agreement between the Community, its then twelve Member States and five of the EFTA States, finally entered into force on 1 January 1994. It had taken nearly ten years for the decision of 9 April 1984 at the first joint EC-EFTA Ministerial meeting on establishing a dynamic European Economic Space to be realized.

120. ECJ, Opinion No. 1/92 [1992] ECR I-2821.

180. For the EFTA States, the EEA Agreement had proved how close to EC membership it was possible to get without becoming a member. The change of the geopolitical situation in Europe, however, meant that most of the EFTA States no longer saw the EEA Agreement as a permanent solution, but now perceived it as a transitional arrangement on their way towards full membership of the Community. This was especially so since, during the negotiations, it had become clear that the acceptance of large and important parts of the acquis communautaire and the case law of the ECJ amounted, in practice, to taking over obligations quite similar to those of membership of the EC without having the same say in the political decision-making process.

181. Even before the formal EEA negotiations opened in June 1990, Austria had applied for accession to the EC. Sweden made a similar move in July 1991 just as Finland, Norway and Switzerland also applied for membership shortly after the conclusion of the EEA negotiations. As the membership negotiations were substantially facilitated by these countries' integration of the acquis communautaire into their national law as a consequence of the EEA Agreement, four of the five EFTA States, namely Austria, Finland, Norway and Sweden, signed an accession treaty with the then twelve EU States[121] already on 24 July 1994, with a view to acceding on 1 January 1995.

182. The implication was that the EEA could consist of an EU of sixteen members on the one side and Iceland as the sole EFTA State participating in the EEA on the other side. A situation where Iceland would, on its own, provide a full-fledged EFTA pillar would have necessitated substantial changes in the Agreement and cast doubt on the entire two-pillar approach. This situation, however, did not materialize, as Norway remained in EFTA following a negative vote in a referendum on 28 November 1994. In fact, as Liechtenstein adhered to the Agreement with effect from 1 May 1995, the EFTA pillar soon came to consist of three states. Austria, Finland and Sweden acceded to the EU on 1 January 1995 and were therefore only EFTA Members of the EEA Agreement for a year.[122]

183. The end result is that the EEA Agreement has become more asymmetrical in political and economic terms than originally envisaged. At the time the Agreement was negotiated, EFTA was a large, powerful group consisting of the Community's biggest trading partners. The originally conceived group of EFTA Members of the EEA accounted for approximately 10% of the population in the EC and a little less than 25% of the Community's external trade. In comparison, even before the accession of the eastern European countries to the EU, the three EFTA States which were parties to the Agreement accounted for less than 5% of the EU's trade with third countries. Moreover, the total population of the three EFTA States is only around 1% of the number of EU citizens.

121. The Lisbon Treaty transferred the legal personality of the EC to the EU.

122. Austria, Finland and Sweden are still parties to the EEA Agreement but now as a part of the EU pillar.

184. It has been argued that the EEA fast became an anachronism, since it was designed as a medium-speed alternative to membership for seven countries on the outskirts of Western Europe that for various reasons either could not, or would not, contemplate full membership of the EU but, which after the fall of the iron curtain, mostly found themselves ready and able to enter mainstream European politics.[123] Such an evaluation highlights the difference between the original expectations of an EEA as it looked in the 1980s and the present EEA. It is certainly true that the idea of an EEA was conceived and developed under one set of assumptions, completed under another and now functions under a third set of circumstances, circumstances that have changed even more after the accession to the EU of a significant number of Central and Eastern European Countries. However, this analysis overlooks the importance the Agreement has had for the EFTA States. It would hardly have been possible for Iceland, Liechtenstein and Norway to negotiate so comprehensive an agreement had they been alone on the EFTA side. Moreover, even though most of EFTA States did become members of the EU shortly after the entering into force of the EEA Agreement, the Agreement should also be considered as having great importance for those States, since it provided an important stepping-stone for them on their way to full membership of the EU.

185. As a consequence of the global financial crisis in 2008 and its impact on the Icelandic economy, Iceland applied in 2009 for membership in the EU. Accession negotiations between Iceland and the EU started in 2010. After a new government took over in May 2013, Iceland put the accession negotiations on hold. In March 2015, Iceland's Government informed the EU that Iceland no longer wished to maintain its status as a candidate country for EU membership.

186. On 31 January 2020, the UK withdrew from the EU, the EEA Agreement and other agreements applicable between the UK and Iceland, Liechtenstein and Norway by virtue of the UK's membership of the EU. Article 126 of the 'Agreement on the withdrawal of the United Kingdom of Great Britain and Northern Ireland from the European Union and the European Atomic Energy Community' ('the Withdrawal Agreement') provided for a transition period from 1 February 2020 to 31 December 2020.[124] Article 129(1) of the Withdrawal Agreement clarified that during the transition period the UK was bound by the obligations stemming from the international agreements concluded by the EU, by Member States acting on its behalf, or by the EU and its Member States acting jointly, which includes the EEA Agreement. The EFTA States agreed to treat the UK as an EU Member State during

123. F. Sejersted, 'Between Sovereignty and Supranationalism in the EEA Context – On the Legal Dynamics of the EEA Agreement', in *The European Economic Area – Norway's Basic Status in the Legal Construction of Europe* 43 (44) (P.C. Müller-Graff & E. Selvig eds, Berlin: Berlin Verlag A. Spitz 1997). Sejersted, however, also states, on 45, that 'even anachronisms do not have to be fixed before they are broken. And the Agreement is working well – in its own pragmatic way.'

124. Agreement on the withdrawal of the United Kingdom of Great Britain and Northern Ireland from the EU and the European Atomic Energy Community (OJ C 384, 12.11.2019, 1).

this transition period. Accordingly, the rights and obligations contained in the EEA Agreement continued to apply between the UK and the EEA-EFTA States until 31 December 2020.[125]

187. On 28 January 2020, an 'Agreement on arrangements between Iceland, Liechtenstein, Norway and the UK following the withdrawal of the UK from the EU, the EEA Agreement and other agreements applicable between the United Kingdom and the EEA EFTA States by virtue of the UK's membership of the EU' ('the Separation Agreement') was signed.[126] The Separation Agreement largely mirrors the Withdrawal Agreement in areas relevant under the EEA Agreement.[127] The Separation Agreement is primarily concerned with the rights of EFTA and UK citizens who have made a home in each other's countries as a result of the right of free movement under the EEA Agreement.

125. *See also* on the EFTA Secretariat's website: 'What is the transition period and what does it mean for the UK's relations with the EEA EFTA States?': https://www.efta.int/About-EFTA/Frequently-asked-questions-EFTA-EEA-EFTA-membership-and-Brexit-328676.

126. The Separation Agreement can be found on the EFTA Secretariat's website: https://www.efta.int/sites/default/files/2020_01_28_UK-EEA-EFTA_separation_agreement_.pdf.

127. The Separation Agreement conferred new powers on the EFTA Surveillance Authority, *see infra* Part II, Ch. 3, §6, I.

Chapter 2. Characteristics of the EEA

188. The EEA Agreement aims at reconciling divergent aims. On the one hand, it aims at creating a homogeneous EEA, in which equal conditions of competition prevail between all the Contracting Parties and in which the same rules apply throughout. On the other hand, it aims at maintaining the institutional autonomy and sovereignty of the Contracting Parties. This has resulted in the EEA Agreement having a hybrid character. The Agreement contains both elements of a classic public international law instrument (which have determined the Agreement's form and decision-making process) and EU law (that has been the source of both the substantive rules of the Agreement and the procedural rules that govern the rules concerning enforcement of the Agreement). Through the EEA Agreement a substantial part of EU law is in effect duplicated and transformed into public international law, albeit of a somewhat special nature, in order to be incorporated into the national legal orders of the EFTA States.

189. The hybrid character is reflected in some of the core institutional provisions of the EEA Agreement. For example, the dispute settlement mechanism is in the first instance a diplomatic one, and matters under dispute are brought before the EEA Joint Committee under a procedure outlined in Article 111 of the EEA Agreement. This procedure is also applicable to resolve any divergence in the case law of the Court of Justice of the European Union (CJEU) and the EFTA Court. While a judicial resolution of disputes is possible, by the Contracting Parties agreeing to request the CJEU to give a ruling, the CJEU has no automatic compulsory jurisdiction.

§1. A Special Relation with the EU Treaties

190. The special relationship with the EU is evident from the history of the conclusion of the EEA Agreement and the way that that Agreement is infused with rules and concepts of EU law. As both the EU (the 'European Community', as it then was) and all the EU Member States are Contracting Parties to the EEA Agreement, the notion of 'Contracting Party' required a specific definition to be inserted, which can be found at Article 2(c) of the EEA Agreement. According to the definition, the notion can, depending on context, refer to the Union and the Member States taken together, or either of them separately.

191. Any European State acceding to the EU is bound, by virtue of Article 128 of the EEA Agreement, to apply to become a Contracting Party to the EEA Agreement. At the same time, members of EFTA merely have the option, but not the obligation, to apply to accede to the EEA Agreement – a nuance that became necessary to accommodate Switzerland. Article 127 of the EEA Agreement makes specific provision for withdrawal from the EEA Agreement and requires a withdrawing Contracting Party to give at least twelve months' notice, triggering a diplomatic conference being convened by the other Contracting Parties to envisage any modifications to the Agreement. Closely connected to this is the territoriality clause contained in Article 126 of the EEA Agreement, whereby the EEA Agreement applies to the territories to which the EU Treaties apply, as well as the territories of Iceland, Liechtenstein and Norway.[128] By way of consequence, EU Member States cannot withdraw from the EEA Agreement without at the same time withdrawing from the EU. By the same token, withdrawal of a Member State from the EU ipso facto results in the EEA Agreement ceasing to apply in its territory, whereas withdrawal of an EFTA State requires modifications to the EEA Agreement – at the very least to Article 126 of the EEA Agreement – and thus necessitates the diplomatic conference contemplated by Article 127 of the EEA Agreement.[129]

I. The Extension of the Internal Market

192. The primary aim of the EEA Agreement is to create an internal market, including not only the current twenty-seven EU Member States, but also the three EFTA States that are Contracting Parties to the EEA Agreement. Therefore, as the TFEU, it guarantees the free movement of goods, persons, services and capital, as well as equal conditions of competition and non-discrimination against individuals in all the Contracting Parties. In order to secure homogeneity between EU law and EEA law, these provisions are drafted in terms as close as possible to the corresponding provisions of the TFEU. The EEA Agreement also contains provisions on a number of EU policies relevant to the four freedoms (so-called horizontal areas) such as labour law, health and safety at work, environment, consumer protection and company law. The EEA Agreement further provides for close cooperation between Contracting Parties to the Agreement in certain fields not related to the four freedoms, such as research and technical development, information services, education and social policy.

193. The EEA Agreement is based on the provisions of the EC Treaty as it stood before the entry into force of the Maastricht Treaty – the treaty formally known as the Treaty on European Union (TEU). Although many of its provisions can now be found in the TFEU, the parallelism is not unlimited. The gap between EU and EEA law has widened over the years.[130] The EU Treaties have been amended four times since 1992, while the main EEA Agreement has remained substantially unchanged. With regard to substance, the most noticeable differences between EU law and the EEA Agreement can be conveniently summarized under the following five headings.

128. Protocol 40 to the EEA Agreement allowed Norway to exempt the territory of Svalbard from the application of the EEA Agreement. Norway has made use of this exemption (*see* s. 6 of the Norwegian EEA Act, Act No. 109 of 27 Nov. 1992).

129. Article 127 of the EEA Agreement was not triggered when the United Kingdom withdrew from the EU, the EEA Agreement and other agreements applicable between the United Kingdom and Iceland, Liechtenstein or Norway by virtue of the United Kingdom's membership of the Union.

130. *See* Case E-28/15 *Yankuba Jabbi* [2016] EFTA Court Report, 577, para. 62.

A. No Customs Union

194. First, the EEA Agreement does not entail a common commercial policy towards third countries. The EFTA States have not transferred their respective treaty-making powers to any kind of supranational organs but remain free to conclude treaties and agreements with third countries in relation to foreign trade.[131] The EEA Agreement is a free trade area without a customs union. In the EU, a product is, in principle, in free circulation once it has been lawfully placed on the market in a Member State. In contrast, according to Article 8 of the EEA Agreement, the principle of free movement of goods as laid down in Articles 11–13 of the EEA Agreement applies only to goods originating in the EEA. In other words, goods from third countries are not covered by the EEA Agreement even if they have been put in free circulation in an EU or EFTA State. For that reason, Protocol 4 to the EEA Agreement contains extensive rules on the origin of a given product. Similarly, the EEA Agreement does not abolish border controls, although it does contain provisions that simplify these controls.[132] Those rules prevent the distortion of trade that would otherwise take place, if products from third countries could benefit from preferential treatment and free circulation in the entire EEA by virtue of being imported into the EEA State that had the lowest custom tariff towards a given third country.

B. Limited Product Scope

195. Second, the product scope of the EEA Agreement, i.e., the types of goods it applies to, is limited and in essence excludes most agricultural products. Unless otherwise specified, the Agreement only covers (a) products falling within Chapters 25–97 of the Harmonized Commodity Description and Coding System, with the exception of those listed in Protocol 2 to the EEA Agreement, and (b) products specified in Protocol 3, subject to the specific arrangements set out in that Protocol (Article 8(3) of the EEA Agreement). This provision also has the effect of excluding the application of the CSA rules to the products not covered by the EEA Agreement.[133] By the same token, the EEA Agreement contains neither a Common Agricultural Policy nor a Common Fisheries Policy and does not impinge on national rules on farming activities of the EFTA States or on the setting of fishing quotas, etc. Instead, the Agreement – notably Article 19 of the EEA Agreement and Protocol 3 thereto – contains aims of progressive liberalization of agricultural trade. Those provisions are different in content from the free trade rights and obligations

---

131. *See* Art. 5 EEA Agreement, Protocol 28 to the EEA Agreement and Case E-2/97 *Mag Instrument* [1997] EFTA Court Report, 127.
132. *See* Protocols 10 and 11 to the EEA Agreement. The above-described differences have lead L. Gormley, 'The European Economic Area and the Europe Agreements', in *The European Economic Area EC-EFTA* 1 (3–4) (Stuyck & Looijestijn-Clearie eds, Dordrecht: Kluwer 2000), to argue that the Agreement neither establishes a common market nor an internal market as these notions are understood in the EC (and now the EU). Compare for a more nuanced view, T. Bruha, 'Is the EEA an Internal Market?', in *EEA-EU Relations* 97 (P.C. Müller-Graff & E. Selvig eds, Berlin: Berlin Verlag 1999).
133. *See infra* Part II, Ch. 5, §1, II, B and II, C, 4.

that regulate other products, since the speed, scope and methods of the liberalization process is for the Contracting Parties to decide. The EFTA Surveillance Authority has no role to play here. Instead, the EFTA States have concluded bilateral agreements with the EU in the field of agriculture.

196. When it comes to trade in fish and other marine products, Protocol 9 to the EEA Agreement contains specific provisions and arrangements. This protocol contains a two-track system on trade, customs duties and market access for specific fish and marine products listed in the appendices to the Protocol. The rules in the Protocol provide a self-standing frame of reference and are not supplemented by the general rules in the Agreement as these are inapplicable by virtue of Article 8 of the EEA Agreement.[134] As Protocol 9 is an integral part of the EEA Agreement, both the EFTA Surveillance Authority and the EFTA Court are in principle competent to deal with matters covered by the Protocol.[135] The EFTA Surveillance Authority, for example, has competence to start proceedings against an EFTA State that introduces charges or measures with equivalent effect contrary to the provisions on customs duties just as it is competent to consider issues of product origin.[136] It is only where a particular provision prescribes an alternative supervisory or dispute settlement procedure that the EFTA Surveillance Authority ('the Authority') and the EFTA Court have no role to play. The Authority does not, for example, have competence to assess State aid in the fisheries sector under Article 4 of the Protocol, since the Contracting Parties, in a joint declaration in the Final Act of the agreement, have stated that distortion of competition is to be assessed by the Contracting Parties themselves.[137] Consequently, the Authority's and the EFTA Court's competence under Protocol 9 must be assessed separately regarding each provision.

197. Notwithstanding the exclusion of agricultural and fisheries products from its product scope, the sectors concerned are to some extent affected by the EEA Agreement. The fundamental freedoms apply to economic activities in general and, with few exceptions, no specific economic sector is in principle excluded from the scope of those provisions. Acquisition of an agricultural farm is, for instance, considered as a capital movement under EEA law and such rules therefore have to respect the EEA Agreement's rules on the prohibition of unnecessary restrictions of capital movements.[138] Moreover, most of the secondary EU legislation concerning veterinary and phytosanitary matters is taken into the EEA Agreement,[139] comprising production requirements covering every aspect of the production, 'from farm to

---

134. Compare S.M. Stefánsson, 'The EEA Agreement and Fish and Other Marine Products', in *Fiskeripolitikken i EØS* 7 (11) (Eisenreich ed., Copenhagen: Norfeir 1996) and T. Foss, 'Fiskeri', in *EØS-håndboken, EØS-Avtalen – innhold og praktisering* 167 (A.D. Gjønnes & S. Knudtzon eds, Oslo: Universitetsforlaget 1998), who both seem to take the opposite view.

135. *See* Case E-2/03 *Ásgeirsson* [2003] EFTA Court Report, 185.

136. *See* Case C-286/02 *Bellio* [2004] ECR I-3465, in which the Court of Justice interpreted Art. 2(5) of the protocol. That provision states that the Community (now the EU) shall apply no quantitative restrictions on imports or measures having equivalent effect on fish and marine products and thus corresponds to Art. 34 TFEU.

137. *See infra* Part II, Ch. 5, §1, II, C, 4.

138. *See* Case C-452/01 *Ospelt* [2003] ECR I-9743.

139. *See* Annex I to the EEA Agreement.

fork', in order to ensure food safety. A number of the acts also concern fish, fishery products and bivalve molluscs, for instance, requirements for production facilities, the use of veterinary medicinal products, packing and transport requirements, requirements for official controls, etc.

C. No Citizenship

198. Third, justice and home affairs and citizenship all fall outside the scope of the EEA Agreement, as there is no equivalent to the relevant provisions of the TFEU, such as Article 20 TFEU which established the concept of Union Citizenship. There is notably broad consensus that immigration policy is not covered by the EEA Agreement.[140] While residence rights for third-country nationals therefore fall outside the scope of the Agreement, the Contracting Parties at the same time recognized that in the case of family members of an EEA national exercising his or her right to free movement under the EEA Agreement, these rights are corollary to the right of free movement of the EEA nationals and should receive some protection. By way of consequence, the Citizenship Directive was incorporated into the EEA Agreement, albeit with certain adaptations renaming it the 'Residence Directive'.[141] The EFTA Court has repeatedly provided a purposive interpretation of the Directive in order to minimize the discrepancy arising between the protection of third-country family members in EU and EFTA States.[142]

D. No Economic or Monetary Union

199. Fourth, the policy areas of economic and monetary union, having come into the EU framework with the Maastricht Treaty only, have no equivalent in the EEA Agreement. Likewise, the EU policies on both direct and indirect taxation and monetary policy fall outside the EEA Agreement. Thus, for example, the EU's directives on VAT have not been taken into the Agreement.[143]

---

140. Joint Declaration by the Contracting Parties annexed to EEA Joint Committee Decision No. 158/2007 of 7 Dec. 2007 (OJ 2008 L 124, 20, and EEA Supplement 2008 No. 26, 17).
141. Directive 2004/38/EC of the European Parliament and of the Council of 29 Apr. 2004 on the right of citizens of the Union and their family members to move and reside freely within the territory of the Member States amending Regulation (EEC) No. 1612/68 and repealing Directives 64/221/EEC, 68/360/EEC, 72/194/EEC, 73/148/EEC, 75/34/EEC, 75/35/EEC, 90/364/EEC, 90/365/EEC and 93/36/EEC (OJ 2004 L 158, 77, as corrected by OJ 2004 L 229, 35, OJ 2005 L 30, 27, and OJ 2005 L 197, 34, and Norwegian EEA Supplement 2012 No. 5, 243) was incorporated into the EEA Agreement at point 1 of Annex V and point 3 of Annex VIII to the Agreement by the EEA Joint Committee Decision No. 158/2007 of 7 Dec. 2007 (OJ 2008 L 124, 20, and EEA Supplement 2008 No. 26, 17), which entered into force on 1 Mar. 2009.
142. *See*, for example, Case E-28/15 *Yankuba Jabbi* [2016] EFTA Court Report, 577, paras 49–82 and Case E-4/19 *Campbell*, paras 57–58. *See also* generally concerning the absence of citizenship notions in the EEA Agreement, Case C-897/19 *PPU Ruska Federacija* EU:C:2020:262.
143. This does not mean that the consequences for national tax provisions that follow from the four freedoms are fundamentally different in the EEA legal order, as these basic freedoms have been taken into the Agreement, *see* Case E-1/03 *EFTA Surveillance Authority v. Iceland* [2003] EFTA Court

E. Limited Horizontal and Flanking Policies

200. Finally, in fields such as research and development, social policy, education and civil protection, only so-called horizontal and flanking policies exist. Whereas in the fields of horizontal policies (*see* Part VI of the EEA Agreement), the EU strives for common rules, these rules are only included in the EEA Agreement to the extent they are considered to be relevant to the four freedoms. The flanking policies, as such, are not directly linked to the internal market. However, the EFTA States and the EU agreed to cooperate in these fields if this is of mutual interest. Likewise, there is no common regional policy.[144] These differences reflect the fact that while in the EU the aim of a common market is merely one, albeit very important, means of achieving political and social integration, that wish is in itself the ultimate, and more limited, aim of the EEA Agreement.

II. Homogeneity with EU Law

201. For an extended internal market to function, it was necessary to ensure that, in the areas covered by the EEA Agreement, the same rules apply in the EEA as in the EU. In other words, homogeneity between the two legal orders had to be ensured, and it may even be said that the homogeneity principle is the single most important principle in the entire EEA Agreement.[145] Indeed, the EEA Agreement contains a vast range of statements and instruments ensuring its homogeneity with EU law. First, the Agreement itself closely follows the wording and the structure of the former EC Treaty. Moreover, in order to fulfil the aim of a homogeneous EEA, the Contracting Parties secure a joint and parallel development of the legal orders of the EU and the EFTA States in areas covered by the Agreement.

202. At the legislative level, homogeneity is addressed by involving experts from the EFTA States in the preparatory work of new EU rules and by permitting the legislative process within the EEA organs to coincide as much as possible in time with the legislative process within the EU Institutions.[146] In fact, virtually all

Report, 143, Case E-1/04 *Fokus Bank* [2004] EFTA Court Report, 11, Case E-7/07 *Seabrokers* [2008] EFTA Court Report, 172, Case E-15/16 *Yara International* [2017] EFTA Court Report, 434 and Case E-3/21 *PRA Group*.

144. However, on the basis of Arts 115 to 117 of Part VIII of the EEA Agreement, the EFTA States have agreed to contribute to the reduction of social and economic disparities between the regions of the EEA. Although these provisions, in connection with Protocol 38 to the EEA Agreement, indicated that this contribution was of a temporary nature only, the EFTA States have agreed to additional commitments for the periods 1999–2003, 2004–2009 (Protocol 38a to the EEA Agreement), 2010–2014 (Protocol 38b to the EEA Agreement) and 2014–2021 (Protocol 38c to the EEA Agreement). On 1 Dec. 2023, the EEA EFTA States and the EU reached an agreement on the contribution for the period 2021–2028.

145. M. Johansson & S. Norberg, 'EFTA-Domstolen – Garant för det homogena EES – Reflektioner i ljuset av 17 års tillämpning av EES-avtalet', *Europarättslig Tidskrift* (2011): 379 (380 and 382). The two authors go as far as arguing that even if, formally speaking, there exists two separate legal orders, EU law and EEA law, in practice they constitute one common European legal system.

146. *See infra* Part II, Ch. 4, §3, II, B, 1.

internal market legislation adopted by the EU ends up being incorporated into the EEA Agreement, with or without adaptations. The fact that the EFTA States introduce rules identical to those of the EU does not, however, suffice to ensure that the same rules are interpreted in a similar manner and respected throughout the entire EEA. For that reason, the fifteenth recital of the Preamble states that:

> in full deference of the courts, the objective of the Contracting Parties is to arrive at, and maintain, a uniform interpretation and application of this Agreement and those provisions of Community legislation which are substantially reproduced in this Agreement and to arrive at an equal treatment of individuals and economic operators as regards the four freedoms and the conditions of competition.

203. This overall goal is substantiated in several provisions in the main Agreement. According to Article 6, without prejudice to future developments of case law, the provisions of the EEA Agreement shall, insofar as they are identical in substance to corresponding rules of EU law, be interpreted in conformity with the relevant rulings of the CJEU given prior to the date of signature of the EEA Agreement, namely 2 May 1992.[147] In consequence, the rules on interpretation applied by the EU courts form the basis for the interpretation of the EEA Agreement.[148]

A. *The Cut-Off Date*

204. The obligation under Article 6 of the EEA Agreement – to interpret EEA law in conformity with EU law – only concerns case law that is older than the date on which the EEA Agreement was signed. Since the EFTA States did not wish to submit themselves to a legislative process in which they did not participate, it was only logical that they did not accept to be bound by future case law of the CJEU which they would not be able to co-determine either.

205. Homogeneity would, however, be difficult to achieve if the interpretation and application of the EEA Agreement were to be 'frozen' and not able to follow the dynamics of the case law of the CJEU after the 2 May 1992. For that reason, Article 3(2) SCA states that the EFTA Court and the Authority shall pay due account to the principles laid down by the relevant rulings of the CJEU given after the date of signature of the EEA Agreement and which concern the interpretation of the EEA

147. The same obligation arise in relation to judgments from the General Court, *see* Case E-2/94 *Scottish Salmon Growers* [1994/1995] EFTA Court Report, 59, and Case E-8/00 *LO* [2002] EFTA Court Report, 114.

148. *See, inter alia*, with regard to the interpretative rule of the CJEU that exceptions to fundamental freedoms are, as a rule, to be interpreted narrowly Case E-2/00 *Allied Colloids* [2000–2001] EFTA Court Report, 35. In Case E-1/02 *EFTA Surveillance Authority v. Norway* [2003] EFTA Court Report, 1, the Court referred to the 'homogeneity objective' and refused to redefine the concept of discrimination on grounds of gender compared to that developed by the ECJ.

Agreement or of such rules of the EC Treaty (now the TEU and the TFEU) insofar as they are identical in substance to the provisions of the EEA Agreement.

206. In practice, the EFTA Court refers to the most recent case law and has hitherto not found reason to distinguish between case law before and after the signature of the EEA Agreement.[149] An example of the Court's approach is found in Ullensaker Kommune,[150] in which the EFTA Court applied the reasoning of the famous Keck judgment of the CJEU to Article 11 of the EEA Agreement, although that judgment was delivered after the cut-off date of 2 May 1992. As the Authority argued in its submissions before the Court, a mechanical focus on the cut-off date (thereby disregarding the Keck doctrine) would open the door to divergent policies in a field of vital importance for the achievement of the objectives of the EEA Agreement. Likewise, where the CJEU has changed its case law after a decision of the EFTA Court following the case law of the CJEU before that change, the homogeneity objective would be better served if the EFTA Court followed the new rather than the older case law.[151] Conversely, if the EFTA Court were faced with a legal problem where there existed only very old precedents of the CJEU, the EFTA Court would probably not regard itself as being bound to follow such precedent, if it considered it likely that the CJEU itself would depart from it. That being said, it might be argued that since the EEA Agreement is not supranational in the same manner as the EU Treaties, the EFTA Court might be induced to show some caution in taking over completely new doctrines that the CJEU might develop. This is especially so if such doctrines would concern vital national interests so that a renegotiation might seem more appropriate than a judicial 'copying'.[152]

B. Rules 'Identical in Substance'

207. According to Article 6 of the EEA Agreement and Article 3 SCA, the obligation to interpret EEA law in conformity with EU law only concerns rules in the Agreement 'in as far as they are identical in substance' with the corresponding provisions in EU law. As pointed out by several authors, the requirement that the two provisions should be identical in substance is, strictly speaking, circular.[153] Only after an interpretation can it be assessed whether the rules are identical in substance. And if this is indeed the case, then there is little need for a rule prescribing that the interpretation should be the same. The very purpose of the homogeneity clause in Article 6 of the EEA Agreement is to obtain an interpretation whereby the

149. *See also* P. Wennerås in Arnesen et al. (ed.), *Agreement on the European Economic Area, A Commentary*, 2018, 213.

150. Case E-5/96 *Ullensaker Kommune* [1997] EFTA Court Report, 30.

151. Case E-10/07 *L'Oréal Norge* [2008] EFTA Court Report, 259.

152. *See* O. Rognstad, 'EF-domstolens og EFTA-domstolens praksis som rettskilder ved tolkning av EØS-aftalen', *Tidsskrift for Rettsvitenskap* (2001): 435 (448–449).

153. *See*, for example, H. Bull, 'EØS-avtalen – litt om avtalens struktur og om prinsippene for gjennemføring I norsk rett', *Lov og Rett* (1992): 583 (595) and F. Arnesen et al., *Oversikt over EØS-retten* 41 (Oslo: Universitetsforlaget, 2022).

substance of the two sets of rules becomes the same. Still, as the provision is formulated, the duty to construe EEA Agreement provisions in line with their EU counterparts only arises if, on proper construction, the first rules in any event correspond to the latter. The meaning of the phrase is, however, fairly clear. Where a provision in the EEA Agreement has been copied from the EU Treaties, the former provision must be understood in the same manner as the CJEU has interpreted the latter. The idea behind the words 'in substance' is thus to indicate that an identical wording of the two provisions is not required in order for Article 6 of the EEA Agreement to apply.

208. The EFTA Court has had occasions to rule on nearly all of the most important substantive provisions in the main part of the EEA Agreement corresponding to the EU rules on nationality discrimination, free movement and CSA. In all situations the Court has interpreted the EEA Agreement rule in line with the corresponding EC Treaty provision and, after the Lisbon Treaty, the corresponding provision in the TFEU.[154] Moreover, the EFTA Court has also drawn on the case law of the CJEU in relation to those rules on the burden of proof that the CJEU has developed in relation to provisions corresponding to the ones in the EEA Agreement.[155]

209. Homogeneity, however, becomes difficult to achieve when the relevant provision in EU law has been changed after the conclusion of the EEA Agreement without leading to a similar change in the applicable EEA rule. This problem has become increasingly relevant, as the EC Treaty was changed several times since the 1992 and has subsequently been replaced by the TEU and the TFEU.[156] These changes can raise questions on the understanding of the corresponding EEA rule in, at least, two situations.

---

154. *See*, for example, Case E-/98 *Fagtún* [1999] EFTA Court Report, 51 (Art. 4 of the EEA Agreement); Case E-1/01 *Einarsson* [2002] EFTA Court Report, 1, and Case E-6/07 *HOB vín ehf* [2002] EFTA Court Report, 128; Case E-5/96 *Ullensaker Kommune* [1997] EFTA Court Report, 30; Case E-6/06 *Wilhelmsen* [1997] EFTA Court Report, 53, and Case E-3/00 *EFTA Surveillance Authority v. Norway* [2000–2001] EFTA Court Report, 73 (Arts 11 and 13 of the EEA Agreement); Case E-1/94 *Restamark* [1994–1995] EFTA Court Report, 15; Case E-5/96 *Ullensaker Kommune* [1997] EFTA Court Report, 30; Case E-4/01 *Karlsson* [2002] EFTA Court Report, 240, and Case E-4/05 *HOB-vín* [2006] EFTA Court Report, 4 (Art. 16 of the EEA Agreement); Case E-26/13 *Gunnarsson* [2014] EFTA Court Report, 254; Judgment of 7 Jul. 2023 of the EFTA Court in Case E-11/22 *RS* (Art. 28 of the EEA Agreement), Case E-4/00 *Brändle* [2000–2001] EFTA Court Report, 123; Case E-5/00 *Mangold* [2000–2001] EFTA Court Report, 163; Case E-6/00 *Tschannet* [2000–2001] EFTA Court Report, 203, and E-8/04 *EFTA Surveillance Authority v. Liechtenstein* [2005] EFTA Court Report, 46 (Art. 31 of the EEA Agreement); Case E-1/03 *EFTA Surveillance Authority v. Iceland* [2003] EFTA Court Report, 143 (Art. 36 of the EEA Agreement); Case E-1/00 *Islandsbanki-FBA* [2000–2001] EFTA Court Report, 2 (Art. 40 of the EEA Agreement); Case E-3/97 *Jæger* [1998] EFTA Court Report, 1, and Case E-8/00 *LO* [2002] EFTA Court Report, 114 (Art. 53 of the EEA Agreement); Case E-6/98 *Norway v. EFTA Surveillance Authority* [1999] EFTA Court Report, 74 (Art. 61 of the EEA Agreement), and Case E-2/06 EFTA *Surveillance Authority v. Norway* [2007] EFTA Court Report, 164 (Art. 125 of the EEA Agreement). As for the corresponding case law of the ECJ *see infra* section E.
155. *See*, for example, Case E-1/94 *Restamark* [1994–1995] EFTA Court Report, 15.
156. Case E-28/15 *Yankuba Jabbi* [2016] EFTA Court Report, 577, para. 62. For a more detailed examination of this issue, *see* N. Fenger, 'Limits to a Dynamic Homogeneity between EC Law and EEA Law', in *Liber Amicorum Claus Gulmann*, ed. Fenger & Hagel-Sørensen og Vesterdorf, 131 and H.

210. The most obvious situation is where the relevant treaty provision itself has been changed. In Case E-1/02 *EFTA Surveillance Authority v. Norway*,[157] the Norwegian Government argued that the EFTA Court should take into account a directive on gender discrimination that had not been taken into the EEA Agreement just as it suggested that the Court should apply the rule on positive discrimination in Article 141(4) EC Treaty (now Article 157 TFEU) by analogy, although the EEA Agreement only mirrors the original Article 119 of the EC Treaty that did not contain a provision on positive discrimination. The Court refused to do so since, as these provisions had not been made part of EEA law, they could not provide a legal basis to decide a case under EEA law, be that directly or by analogy. The Court, however, added that substantial changes have occurred in the legal framework on the EU side and that inevitably, the interpretation of the directive in EEA law would reflect both the evolving legal and societal context in which it operates.

211. The issue has also arisen in the field of capital movements where the difference between the two legal systems is due to the fact that the applicable EEA rules correspond to those found in EU law before the Maastricht Treaty, that is, Directive 88/361 on liberalization of capital movements. Taking a more flexible view than that expressed in the above-mentioned *EFTA Surveillance Authority v. Norway*, both the CJEU and the EFTA Court have played down the differences between the two legal orders. According to the two courts, the rules governing the free movement of capital in the EEA Agreement are essentially identical in substance to those in the EU law. This more flexible approach entails that case law concerning Article 63 TFEU becomes guiding also for the interpretation of Article 40 of the EEA Agreement.[158]

212. A similar problem arises if the provision in the EC Treaty which served as a blueprint for the relevant EEA rule (and which can now be found in either the TEU or the TFEU) has not itself been textually modified after the signature of the Agreement but where other articles in the governing treaties of the EU have been inserted which may affect the contextual interpretation of that EU provision. This concerns, for example, cases where the CJEU's case law concerning free movement of persons has been influenced by the later concept of citizenship – a concept that had not been taken over in the EEA Agreement.[159] Similarly, it could be argued that the interpretation of the EU's rules on CSA might be influenced by the insertion by the Amsterdam Treaty of what is now Article 14 TFEU concerning services of general interest.

Haukeland Fredriksen, 'Er EFTA-domstolen mer katolsk enn paven? Noen betraktninger om EFTA-domstolens dynamiske utvikling av EØS-retten og streben etter dialog med EF-domstolen', *Tidsskrift for Rettsvitenskap* (2009): 507 (563–570).

157. Case E-1/02 *EFTA Surveillance Authority v. The Kingdom of Norway* [2003] EFTA Court Report, 1.

158. Case C-452/01 *Ospelt* [2003] ECR I-9743; Case C-10/10 *Commission v. Austria* EU:C:2011:399 and Case E-10/04 *Piazza* [2005] EFTA Court Report, 76.

159. *See*, for example, Case E-28/15 *Yankuba Jabbi* [2016] EFTA Court Report, 577 and EFTA Court judgment of 13 May 2020 in Case E-4/19 *Campbell*.

213. In *Einarsson*,[160] the EFTA Court held that it would not be proper exercise of its judicial function to extend the scope of the EEA Agreement by reference to a provision in the Treaty of Amsterdam. In light of the content of the national legislation at stake, it seems unlikely that the result would, in fact, have been different had it been assessed under the EC Treaty as it then was. Nevertheless, the judgment shows that there are limits in the Court's attempt to construe the EEA Agreement in light of present day EU law.[161] The judgment can thereby be seen as a 'warning signal' that the failure to amend the text of the EEA Agreement may pose problems to the maintenance of the homogeneity sought by that agreement.[162] It can indeed be difficult to expand the application of an EEA act, which has been adopted on now changed provisions in the EU, so that the act also covers considerations addressed in the new EU provision. Sometimes it might be possible to solve the problem by way of an extensive interpretation of the EEA Agreement. However, as argued by the EFTA Court's former president Thór Vilhjálmsson, such an interpretation will, occasionally, imply too great deviations from the wording and scope of the EEA Agreement.[163]

214. A related problem of homogeneity arises when secondary EU rules are not taken into the EEA Agreement in a way that assures simultaneous application in the two legal systems. In *Jæger*,[164] one of the parties to the main proceedings argued that even if an EC block exemption regulation in the field of competition was not formally in force in the EFTA State concerned, it should none the less be considered applicable for reasons of homogeneity with Community law. The EFTA Court rejected that argument and underlined that it was for the EEA Joint Committee to bring new legislation into the EEA by adopting amendments to the Annexes and Protocols to the EEA Agreement. Although homogeneity is indeed one of the fundamental principles of the EEA Agreement, it follows from the structure of the Agreement and the legislative procedure provided for therein that this might not be fully achieved in terms of simultaneous application of legislative measures. Thus, Article 102 of the EEA Agreement provides that decisions of the EEA Joint Committee shall be made 'as closely as possible' to the adoption by the EU of the corresponding new EU legislation with a view to permitting a simultaneous application

---

160. Case E-1/01 *Einarsson* [2002] EFTA Court Report, 1.

161. *See also* Case E-3/00 *EFTA Surveillance Authority v. Norway* [2000–2001] EFTA Court Report, 73, where the EFTA Court, however, managed to evade the homogeneity problem since clear traces of the legal concept at stake – the so-called precautionary principle – could be found in case law dating from before this principle was explicitly introduced in Community law by the Maastricht Treaty.

162. *See* C. Baudenbacher, 'The EFTA Court – An example of the judicialisation of international economic law', *European Law Review* (2003): 880 (891). There are no signs that the EU is getting more open to renegotiation. As bluntly stated by M. Everson et al., *Navigating by the Stars*, 4: 'From Brussels' standpoint … the EEA relationship is looking more and more like a systemic anachronism, yet a revision of the EEA Treaty would be a complex task that would be extremely time-consuming for all its institutions. It would therefore not merit priority alongside the EU's huge agenda of other competing demands.'

163. *See* T. Vilhjálmsson, 'EFTA-domstolen', in *Rettsteori og Rettsliv – Festskrift til Carsten Smith* 897 (902 and 908–909) (Lødrup et al. eds, Oslo: Universitetsforlaget, 2002).

164. Case E-3/97 *Jan and Kristian Jæger AS* [1998] EFTA Court Report, 1.

within the EU and EFTA pillars. Where the decision of the Joint Committee implies that, during a transitional period, there will not be full homogeneity, such a decision cannot be challenged on grounds of homogeneity. The Court, moreover, refused to interpret Article 53 of the EEA Agreement in a manner that brought it within the terms of the block exemption regulation concerned since the block exemption could not be seen as a tool for interpreting Article 53 of the EEA Agreement but rather as an instrument which derogated from that provision.

C. Homogeneity and the SCA

215. The obligation in Article 6 of the EEA Agreement and Article 3 SCA to interpret EEA law in conformity with rulings of the CJEU concerning provisions that are identical in substance to provisions in EU Law does not cover all parts of EEA law. For instance, those provisions do not encompass the rules of the SCA itself.[165] The reason for this might be that the dangers to homogeneity are smaller when a divergence in the case law concerns procedural questions. The EFTA Court has nevertheless sought to apply the case law of the CJEU to such procedural questions. This is so, both in relation to the infringement procedure in Article 31 SCA, the rules on advisory opinions in Article 34 SCA, the annulment procedure in Article 36 SCA and the provision on applications for failure to act in Article 37 SCA.[166]

D. CJEU Rulings Relevant in an EEA Context

216. According to Article 6 of the EEA Agreement and Article 3 SCA, the obligation to interpret EEA law in conformity with rulings of the CJEU depends on whether these rulings are relevant in an EEA context. The conditions of relevance are notably raised in relation to the general principles of EU law; a question, which will be dealt with separately.[167] Moreover, the question can be raised whether seemingly similar provisions in the EEA Agreement must be interpreted differently because the EC's aim of an ever-closer Union as a self-standing goal does not appear in the EEA Agreement. According to Article 1 of the EEA Agreement, the

165. However, Protocols 1–4 and Annexes I and II to the SCA are subject to Art. 3 SCA.
166. *See infra* Part II, Ch. 5, §2. In Case E-4/97 *Norwegian Bankers' Association* [1999] EFTA Court Report, 1, the EFTA Court applied Art. 1 of Protocol 3 to the Surveillance and Court Agreement in a way that corresponds to the similar provision in Art. 108 TFEU. *See* similarly with regard to the requirement to provide statements of reasons in Art. 16 SCA Joined Cases E-4/10, E-6/10 and E-7/10 *Liechtenstein, Reassur Aktiengesellschaft and Swisscom RE Aktiengesellschaft v. EFTA Surveillance Authority* [2011] EFTA Court Report, 22. In two orders regarding costs for lawyers' fees in Case E-9/04 *Bankers' and Securities Dealers' Association of Iceland* [2007] EFTA Court Report, 74, and 220, the EFTA Court noted that whilst, in interpreting its Rules of Procedure, the EFTA Court is not required to follow the ECJ or the General Court's interpretations of their corresponding Rules of Procedure, the Court nevertheless attaches importance to these provisions 'in the interest of equal treatment and foreseeability for parties appearing before the [ECJ], the CFI and the EFTA Court'.
167. *See infra* Part II, Ch. 2, §1, III.

aim of the Agreement is limited to promoting continuous and balanced strengthening of trade and economic relations between the Contracting Parties with equal competition, and the respect for the same rules, with a view to creating a homogenous EEA.

217. It has sometimes been suggested that this difference in the objectives of the two Agreements should imply that the interpretation of the two legal systems must differ.[168] Any departure from the principle of homogeneity will however be likely to remain an exception.

218. As a starting point, EEA provisions that are substantially identical to corresponding EU provisions should be interpreted in conformity with the CJEU's case law without regard for the considerations and underlying objectives that may have inspired or initiated such case law.[169] Already as a matter of practicality, it makes sense to start from the presumption that substantially identical provisions should be interpreted in the same manner and the EFTA Court has understandably on occasion focused on the fact that it has 'not been presented with any specific circumstance which would compel it to disregard the case law' of the CJEU in relation to the corresponding provision in the EU treaties.[170] Accordingly, where parallel provisions are to be interpreted, homogeneity should prevail unless specific circumstances indicate that the differences in the scope and purpose of the EEA Agreement as compared to the EU treaties should lead to another interpretation than the one given to the those latter treaties.[171]

219. The EFTA Court has been particularly insistent on ensuring the homogeneity objective when interpreting the fundamental freedoms and principles contained in the EEA Agreement and has, for example, stringently followed the case law of the CJEU concerning the relationship between, on the one hand the rules on free movement and, on the other hand, national rules on taxes although taxation is to a much lesser extent covered by the EEA Agreement than by EU law.

220. The EFTA Court has, however, at the same time, recognized that there are differences in scope and purpose of the EEA Agreement as compared to the TEU

168. *See*, for example, Opinion 1/91 [1991] ECR I-6079, and N. Wahl, 'Relevanta avgöranden av EG-domstolen', in *EES-avtalet i svensk rätt* 181 (190) (Bernitz et al. eds, Stockholm: Juristförlaget 1993).
169. *See* W. van Gerven, 'The Genesis of EEA Law and the Principles of Primacy and Direct Effect', *Fordham International Law Journal* 3 (1992): 955 (977). *See* for a broadly similar line of reasoning, S. Norberg, 'The EFTA Court, One of the Two Main Components of the EEA Judicial Mechanism', in *The European Economic Area EC-EFTA* 9 (30) (Stuyck & Looijestijn-Clearie eds, Dordrecht: Kluwer 2000). According to Norberg, a limitation to judgments delivered in the fields actually covered by the Agreement would not be compatible with spirit of the Agreement.
170. *See* Case E-4/00 *Brändle* [2000–2001] EFTA Court Report, 123; Case E-5/00 *Mangold* [2000–2001] EFTA Court Report, 163, and Case E-6/00 *Tschannet* [2000–2001] EFTA Court Report, 203.
171. *See* Case E-3/98 *Rainford-Towning* [1998] EFTA Court Report, 205.

and the TFEU and has stated that these differences might, under specific circumstances, lead to differences in interpretation.[172] That being said, in the only case which actually turned on a divergence between the EFTA Court's own and the CJEU's case law – *L'Oréal Norge* – the EFTA Court, although recognizing that there was scope for different interpretations of the same substantive provisions, held that it was subject to an obligation to not deviate from the CJEU's case law, unless there are compelling grounds to do so.[173]

221. The presumption in favour of an interpretation in conformity with EU law should also guide the solution in cases where the question is whether differences in the structure of, one the one hand, the EEA Agreement and, on the other hand, the TEU and the TFEU should lead to divergent interpretations. According to Article 119 of the EEA Agreement, the legal acts included in the annexes to the Agreement constitute an integral part of the Agreement and the incorporation of new acts into the Agreement is done through separate international agreements. Still, the principle of the CJEU, according to which secondary EU law must be interpreted in conformity with the EU Treaties because of the higher rank of those treaties, should also be applied in an EEA context regardless of the fact that acts integrated in the annexes to the Agreement formally have the same legal status as the main part of the Agreement.[174]

E. The Duty of Homogeneous Interpretation in the EU Courts

222. As the EEA Agreement is also, through EU law, a part of the legal order of all the EU Member States, the EU Courts should, likewise, interpret provisions in the EEA Agreement in same manner as corresponding provisions in EU law, and vice versa. Otherwise, one could be faced with a situation in which different rules apply for the EFTA States. And indeed, the CJEU has in a long range of cases held that various provisions in the EEA Agreement should be interpreted in the same manner as the corresponding provisions in the TEU and the TFEU.[175]

---

172. Case E-2/97 *Mag Instruments* [1997] EFTA Court Report, 127.

173. *See* Case E-10/07 *L'Oréal Norge* [2008] EFTA Court Report, 259. *See also* T. van Stiphout, 'The l'Oreal Cases – Some Thoughts on the Role of the EFTA Court in the EEA Legal Framework: Because It's Worth It!', *Jus & News* 1 (2009): 7.

174. *See* Case E-3/02 *Paranova* [2003] EFTA Court Report, 101.

175. *See* Case C-286/02 *Bellio* [2004] ECR I-3465; Case C-143/06 *Ludwigs-Apotheke* [2007] ECR I-9623; Case C-265/06 *Commission v. Portugal* [2008] ECR I-2245 (Arts 11 and 13 of the EEA Agreement and Arts 34 and 36 TFEU); Case C-104/06 *Commission v. Sweden* [2007] ECR I-671; Case C-345/05 *Commission v. Portugal* [2006] ECR I-10633, and Case C-155/09 *Commission v. Greece*, judgment of 20 Jan. 2011 (Arts 4, 28 and 31 of the EEA Agreement and Arts 18, 45 and 49 TFEU); Case C-471/04 *Keller Holding* [2006] ECR I-2107, Case C-157/07, *Krankenheim Ruhesitz* [2008] ECR I-8061 and C-48/11, *Veronsaajien oikeudenvalvontayksikkö* EU:C:2012:485 (Art. 31 of the EEA Agreement and Art. 49 TFEU); Case C-522/04 *Commission v. Belgium* [2007] ECR I-5701, Case C-153/08 *Commission v. Spain* [2009] ECR I-9735 and Case C-897/19 *PPU Ruska Federacija* EU:C:2020:262 (Art. 36 of the EEA and Art. 56 TFEU); Case C-521/07 *Commission v. Netherlands* [2009] ECR I-4873, Case C-562/07 *Commission v. Spain* [2009] ECR I-9553, Case C-540/07 *Commission v. Italy* [2009] ECR I-10983, Case C-72/09 *Établissements*

223. The question to what extent the CJEU is bound to have regard to the case law of the EFTA Court when interpreting EEA law is not without practical significance as the two-pillar structure[176] implies that in EEA law there is no single Court that has the final competence to decide, with effect for the entire EEA system, on the correct interpretation of the EEA Agreement. In the absence of an EEA Court, this task is now divided between the EFTA Court, having the competence to clarify the obligations of the EFTA States, and the CJEU with the competence to give the final interpretation of EEA law in the EU Member States.[177]

224. While Article 3 SCA only relates to the EFTA Court and the EFTA Surveillance Authority, the rules in the EEA Agreement are in principle binding on the EU as a Contracting Party, and thus on its institutions, including its courts. The CJEU pays regard to the case law of the EFTA Court. As the former President of the CJEU Vassilios Skouris has pointed out extrajudicially, ignoring the precedents of the EFTA Court would be incompatible with the overriding objective of homogeneity in the EEA Agreement.[178] The CJEU moreover has not only the task, within the Union legal order, of ensuring that uniformity is safeguarded as regards the interpretation of the EEA Agreement itself, but also that an interpretation is given which is uniform as regards the interpretation of identical or comparable provisions of the TFEU.[179]

225. While the rules in Article 6 of the EEA Agreement and Article 3 SCA only relate to the EFTA Court and the EFTA Surveillance Authority, the rules in the EEA Agreement are in principle binding on the EU as a Contracting Party, and thus on its institutions, including its courts. In this regard, Article 105(1) of the EEA Agreement, entitled 'Homogeneity', records the (common) objective of the Contracting Parties to arrive at as uniform an interpretation as possible of EU legislation substantially reproduced in the EEA Agreement. At the same time, no provision expressly obliges the CJEU to take EFTA Court precedents into account. A provision to that effect was contained in the first version of the EEA Agreement with regard to the suggested EEA Court, but was taken out in the final agreement, due to

---

Rimbaud, judgment of 28 Oct. 2010, Case C-267/09 *Commission v. Portugal*, judgment of 5 May 2011, Case C-20/09 *Commission v. Portugal*, judgment of 7 Apr. 2011, and Case C-10/10 *Commission v. Austria*, judgment of 16 Jun. 2011 (Art. 40 of the EEA Agreement and Art. 63 TFEU), and Joined Cases T-117/07 and T-121/07 *Areva v. Commission*, judgment of 3 Feb. 2011 (Art. 51(1) of the EEA Agreement and Art. 101(1) TFEU).

176. *See supra* Part II, Ch. 1, §2, II–IV and *infra* Part II, Ch. 2, §2, II, A.

177. *See* Andenas & Baudenbacher, 'What is the significance of EFTA Court rulings for the ECJ? – AG Emiliou's opinion in Case C-128/22 *BV NORDIC INFO v. Belgian State*', in *Op-Ed of 12 Oct. 2023, EU Law Live*.

178. Vassilios Skouris, 'The ECJ and the EFTA Court under the EEA Agreement: A Paradigm for International Cooperation between Judicial Institutions', in *The EFTA Court Ten Years On* 123, 125 (Carl Baudenbacher, Per Tresselt & Thorgeir Örlysson eds, Oxford and Portland, Oregon: 2005).

179. Opinion of Advocate General Geelhoed in Case C-452/01 *Margarethe Ospelt and Schlössle Weissenberg Familienstiftung*, EU:C:2003:232, para. 67.

the CJEU's findings in Opinion 1/91.[180] It has been argued that such an obligation nevertheless follows from the spirit of the EEA Agreement.[181]

226. Potential problems might arise if the CJEU is called upon to interpret an EEA Agreement provision where the EFTA Court has already given an interpretation of the relevant EEA rule, which differs from that which the CJEU would like to give of the equivalent EU rule.[182] An example is the EFTA Court's judgment in *Fred. Olsen*, establishing that the fundamental freedoms are applicable in respect of trusts even though they lack legal personality.[183] The same question was subsequently raised in the CJEU in Case C-646/15 *Panayi*, where the EFTA Surveillance Authority submitted that the judgment of the EFTA Court should be accorded strong persuasive authority by the CJEU, while the Norwegian Government intervened to submit that the CJEU should diverge from *Fred. Olsen*. In the event, the CJEU decided the matter in the same way as the EFTA Court, but without making any reference to the *Fred. Olsen* judgment.[184] Where the EFTA Court was the first EEA court to have ruled on a particular question of interpretation of EEA law, the CJEU should, in a similar way as when it is confronted with one of its own previous decisions, exercise caution and pay due regard to the needs for legal certainty and homogeneity in the legal order of the EEA as a whole before departing from such a judgment of the EFTA Court.

F. When Homogeneity Fails

227. Article 105 of the EEA Agreement concerns the situation that there is a difference in the case law of the CJEU and the EFTA Court. The Contracting Parties have entrusted the EEA Joint Committee[185] with the responsibility of keeping under

180. Opinion 1/91 [1991] ECR I-6079.
181. *See* for an advocate of this point of view C. Baudenbacher, 'The Legal Nature of EEA Law in the Course of Time', in *Afmælisrit Tor Vilhjálmsson* 39 (48) (Björgvinsson ed. Reykjavik: Bókaútgáfá Orators 2000), but contrast G. Mathisen, 'Om EFTA Domstolen', *Europarättslig Tidskrift* (2010): 13 (22–23). *See also* V. Skouris, 'The ECJ and the EFTA Court under the EEA Agreement: A Paradigm for International Cooperation between Judicial Institutions', in *The EFTA Court Ten Years On* 123 (125) (Baudenbacher, Tresselt & Orlygsson eds).
182. In Case C-189/95 *Franzen* [1997] ECR I-5909, the CJEU ignored an earlier ruling of the EFTA Court concerning a factual situation very similar to the one before the CJEU. In Case C-355/96 *Silhouette* [1998] ECR I-4799, the CJEU came to a different result in the interpretation of Directive 89/104/EEC on Trade Marks than had the EFTA Court done in Case E-2/97 *Mag Instruments* [1997] EFTA Court Report, 127. In Joined Cases E-9/07 and Case E-10/07 *L'Oréal Norge* [2008] EFTA Court Report, 259, the EFTA Court concluded that the two judgments could not be distinguished by reason of the fact that the EEA Agreement does not entail a customs union but only an enhanced free trade area. Accordingly, the EFTA Court reversed its case law as laid down in *Mag Instruments* and instead adopted the approach taken by the CJEU in *Silhoutte*.
183. Joined Cases E-3-13 and E-20/13 *Fred. Olsen and Others v. the Norwegian State* [2014] EFTA Court Report 400.
184. Case C-646/15 *Trustees of the P Panayi Accumulation & Maintenance Settlements* EU:C:2017:682.
185. *See infra* Part II, Ch. 3, §2, I.

constant review the development of the case law of the two courts and of taking necessary action to preserve the homogeneity of the Agreement.[186] Article 105 of the EEA Agreement does not provide for the possibility that the EEA Joint Committee change any judgments. On the other hand, the EEA Joint Committee is not bound by the existing rules when making its decision that will have effect ex nunc. The task attributed to the Committee should therefore be seen as more political than legal and is not part of the judicial structure of the EEA Agreement. The role is more akin to that of any other lawmakers who wish to change the law as a consequence of a decision of the judiciary.[187] If a difference in the case law of the two Courts has been brought before the EEA Joint Committee and that committee has not been successful within two months in preserving homogeneous interpretation, the dispute settlement procedures of Article 111 of the EEA Agreement may, according to Article 105(3) of the EEA Agreement, be applied.[188] According to Protocol 48 to the EEA Agreement, decisions taken by the EEA Joint Committee under Articles 105 and 111 of the EEA Agreement may not affect the case law of the CJEU.[189]

III. General Principles Inspired by the EU Treaties

228. In the light of the importance of the principle of homogeneity, it is not surprising that some of the general principles of the EU law have found their way into the EEA Agreement. For instance, the case law of the CJEU concerning general principles as regards, for example, legitimate expectation and legal certainty has been received into the EEA Agreement by the EFTA Court.[190] Thereby, the Court has confirmed the – for EEA lawyers – famous phrases of Walter van Gerven: 'Stripping Community law of its general principles amounts to taking its heart. An EEA legal system that would not encompass such general principles would therefore be a legal system that is not at all homogeneous with Community law.'[191] Still,

186. *See also* H. Fredriksen in Arnesen et al. (eds), *Agreement on the European Economic Area, A Commentary*, 2018, 826.
187. As Protocol 48 to the EEA Agreement provides that the decisions taken by the EEA Joint Committee under Arts 105 and 111 of the EEA Agreement may not affect the case law of the ECJ, Sevón has suggested that measures adopted by the EEA Joint Committee would most likely either have to contain a solution of recognizing the differences or, in one way or another, imply that the interpretation of the ECJ will prevail, *see* L. Sevón, 'The ECJ, the EFTA Court and the national courts of the EFTA Countries', in *Rettsteori og Rettsliv – Festskrift til Carsten Smith* 721 (729) (Lødrup et al. eds, Oslo: Universitetsforlaget 2002). S. Norberg, 'The EFTA Court', in *European Courts, Practice and Precedents* 77 (94) (Plender ed., London: Sweet & Maxwell, 1997), does not exclude an action in the form of expressing support for a certain interpretation.
188. *See infra* Part II, Ch. 6, §1. The procedure set out in Art. 105(3) of the EEA Agreement has never been used. *See* H. Fredriksen in Arnesen et al. (eds), *Agreement on the European Economic Area, A Commentary*, 2018, 835.
189. Páll Hreinsson, 'General Principles', in *The Handbook of EEA Law* 350–351 (Carl Baudenbacher ed., Switzerland: Springer International Publishing 2015).
190. Joined Cases E-5/04, E-6/04, and E-7/04 *Fesil and others* [2005] EFTA Court Report, 117.
191. W. van Gerven, 'The Genesis of EEA Law and the Principles of Primacy and Direct Effect', *Fordham Int. Law Journal* 3 (1992): 955 (972–973).

as will be explored in more detail below, the more limited aim of the EEA Agreement – and especially the lack of transfer of legislative powers – has as a consequence that not all general principles of EU law can be applied in the EEA legal order.

A. *Direct Effect and Supremacy*

229. In the EU pillar the question of the effect of the EEA Agreement in the legal order of the EU Member States is assessed according to the general principles of EU law itself. In consequence, as the approach of EU law is monistic, provisions of EEA law can have direct effect in the EU Member States. Being part of EU law, they must, moreover, be given primacy over conflicting national rules and over secondary EU legislation.[192]

230. In the EFTA pillar, the question of the effect of EEA law in the EFTA States cannot be solved by recourse to general principles of EU law, but must be decided on the basis of EEA law and the internal law of each EFTA State. In this respect, Protocol 35 to the EEA Agreement on the implementation of EEA rules is of particular interest. The Preamble to Protocol 35 to the EEA Agreement underlines that the aim of the Agreement is to achieve a homogeneous EEA, based on common rules, without requiring any Contracting Party to transfer any legislative powers to any institution of the EEA, and that, therefore, this homogeneity will have to be achieved through national procedures. The sole Article of Protocol 35 to the EEA Agreement hereinafter states the following:

> For cases of possible conflicts between implemented EEA rules and other statutory provisions, the EFTA States undertake to introduce, if necessary, a statutory provision to the effect that EEA rules prevail in these cases.

231. Protocol 35 to the EEA Agreement implies that individuals and economic operators in cases of conflict between implemented EEA rules and national statutory provisions must be entitled to invoke at the national level any rights that can be derived from provisions of the EEA Agreement, as being or having been made part of the respective national legal order, if they are unconditional and sufficiently precise.[193] The scope of Protocol 35 to the EEA Agreement is, however, fairly limited. The undertaking of the EFTA States assumed under that Protocol relates only to the EEA rules that have already been implemented into national law. Moreover, it does not extend to every provision in the main part of the EEA Agreement, but only to those provisions that are framed in a manner capable of creating rights that individuals and economic operators may invoke before national courts and thus only to provisions that are unconditional and sufficiently precise.[194]

192. *See* Case T-115/94 *Opel Austria* [1997] ECR II-39.
193. *See* Case E-1/94 *Restamark* [1994–1995] EFTA Court Report, 15 and EFTA Court judgment of 4 Jul. 2023 in Case E-11/22 *RS*.
194. *See* Case E-1/01 *Einarsson* [2002] EFTA Court Report, 1.

232. For a long time, it was discussed in legal literature whether non-implemented EEA rules could have direct effect in the same manner as in EU law. Some authors argued that the principle of direct effect had not been taken into the EEA Agreement.[195] A similar view seems to have been taken by the CJEU in Opinion 1/91 on the EEA Agreement, where the CJEU stated that it appeared from Protocol 35 to the EEA Agreement that the Contracting Parties did not recognize the principles of direct effect and primacy. On the other hand, two former EFTA Court judges argued that if the balance of rights and obligations under the EEA Agreement were to be maintained, and the homogeneity objective not jeopardized, the principle of direct effect and primacy would have to apply also in the EEA, although possibly in a slightly modified form to fit the EEA.[196]

233. In *Karlsson*,[197] the EFTA Court followed the traditionalist view by stating that it followed from Article 7 of the EEA Agreement and Protocol 35 to the EEA Agreement that EEA law did not entail a transfer of legislative powers. Therefore, EEA law does not require that individuals and economic operators can rely directly on non-implemented EEA rules before national courts. In consequence, it is for the domestic legal order of the EFTA States to decide what effect they give to non-implemented EEA rules in their internal legal system. The net effect is that the EEA Agreement de facto has a larger status in the monistic Liechtenstein[198] legal system than in the dualistic ones of Norway and Iceland.

234. In conclusion, the answer to the question of the legal effect of EEA rules in the EFTA States depends on whether the issue is raised in relation to provisions that have been made part of national law, but where national law contains conflicting provisions, or in relation to provisions that have not been incorporated into national law. The main part of the Agreement will – by virtue of Protocol 35 to the EEA Agreement combined with the fact that it has been incorporated into national law – in practice obtain the same status as EU law has in EU Member States. Thus, as far

195. *See*, for example, H. Bull, 'EØS-avtalen – litt om avtalens struktur og om prinsippene for gjennemføring i norsk rett', *Lov og Rett* (1992): 583 (595), F. Arnesen, *Statslig Styring og EØS-retlige skranker* 24 (Oslo: Universitetsforlaget 1996), P.C. Müller-Graff, 'EEA-Agreement and EC Law: A Comparison in Scope and Content', in *The European Economic Area – Norway's Basic Status in the Legal Construction of Europe* 17 (35) (Müller-Graff & Selvig eds, Berlin: Berlin Verlag 1997) and R. Barents, 'The Court of Justice and the EEA Agreement: Between Constitutional Values and Political Realities', in *The European Economic Area EC-EFTA* 57 (64) (Stuyck & Looijestijn-Clearie eds, Dordrecht: Kluwer 2000).

196. *See* L. Sevón & M. Johansson, 'The Protection of the Rights of Individuals under the EEA Agreement', *European Law Review* (1999): 373 (385) and S. Norberg, 'Perspectives on the Future Development of the EEA', in *Afmælisrit Thor Vilhjálmsson* 367 (374) (Björgvinsson eds, Reykjavik: Bókaútgáfá Orators). *See also* U. Bernitz, 'Om EES-avtalet. Bakgrund, utformning och tolkning', in *EES-avtalet i svensk rätt* 7 (26) (J. Rósen ed., Stockholm: Juristförlaget 1993), W. van Gerven, 'The Genesis of EEA Law and the Principles of Primacy and Direct Effect', *Fordham Int. Law Journal* 3 (1992): 955 and Bekkedal, Tarjei, 'Understanding the nature of the EEA Agreement: On the direct applicability of regulations.' *Common market law review (2020),* 773.

197. Case E-4/01 *Karl K. Karlsson hf. v. The Icelandic State* [2002] EFTA Court Report, 240.

198. *See* M. Sánchez Rydelski, 'Private Enforcement of EEA Law in Liechtenstein', *Liechtensteinische Juristen-Zeitung*, LJZ 3/23 (2023).

as the EEA Agreement provisions reflecting the rules in the TFEU on free movement, CSA are concerned no substantial difference is felt in the daily application of the two legal systems. In contrast, in cases of non-implementation of directives or regulations the rights for individuals will – in the dualistic legal systems of Norway and Iceland – have to be secured via the principles of State liability and interpretation of national provisions in conformity with EEA law.[199]

B. State Liability

235. As with the EU Treaties, the EEA Agreement contains no explicit provision establishing a basis for State liability arising from national legislation or administrative acts that violate EEA law. The question is, therefore, whether such a State obligation may nevertheless be derived from the purpose and structure of the EEA Agreement. In the EU pillar, this question is without practical significance, as a breach of an EEA Agreement provision must be able to create State liability under the conditions provided for in *Francovich*,[200] and *Brasserie du Pecheur*.[201] In contrast, the question has huge practical importance in the EFTA pillar.

236. In *Sveinbjörnsdóttir*,[202] the EFTA Court concluded that an EFTA State is obliged to provide for compensation for loss and damage caused to individuals as a result of breaches of the obligations under the EEA Agreement for which that State can be held responsible. This was so, notwithstanding that the EEA Agreement does not entail a transfer of legislative powers, since the principle of State liability must be seen as an integral part of the EEA Agreement as such, and since it was therefore 'natural to interpret national legislation implementing the main part of the Agreement as also comprising the principle of State liability'. The Court further noted that the conditions under which State liability gives rise to compensation must depend on the nature of the breach. In the event of incorrect implementation of a directive in national law contrary to Article 7 of the EEA Agreement, the effectiveness of that rule requires that there should be a right to reparation provided that three conditions are fulfilled. First, the directive in question must be intended to confer rights on individuals the content of which can be identified on the basis of the provisions of the directive. Second, the breach must be sufficiently serious. Third, and finally, there must be a causal link between the breach and the loss and damage suffered by the injured parties. As to the second condition, the EFTA Court held that condition to be fulfilled where the State concerned had 'manifestly and gravely disregarded the limits on its discretion'. The Court, moreover, established the same guiding criteria as the CJEU had earlier done in, *inter alia*, the *Brasserie de Pecheur* case.

199. Case E-1/07 *Criminal proceedings against A* [2007] EFTA Court Report, 246. As explained *infra* in Part II, Ch. 2, §2, I, the EEA legal order distinguishes itself from EU law thereby that not only directives but also regulations should be made part of national law by way of national implementing measures, *see* Art. 7 of the EEA Agreement.
200. Joined Cases C-6 and C-9/90 [1991] ECR I-5357.
201. Joined Cases C-46/93 and C-48/93 [1996] ECR I-1029.
202. Case E-9/97 [1998] EFTA Court Report, 95.

237. The EFTA Court's reasoning was further elaborated in Karlsson,[203] where the Court held that the principle of State liability was not limited to incorrect implementation of directives. Thus, the three general conditions for State liability to be incurred could be satisfied both where the loss for which compensation was sought is the result of a failure to act on the part of the EEA State, and where it is the result of the adoption of a legislative or administrative act in breach of EEA law. Furthermore, an EEA State can be held liable for its breaches of its obligations under both secondary acts of EEA legislation and the main part of the EEA Agreement. In conclusion, notwithstanding a different theoretical basis, the EFTA Court has constructed a principle of the State liability in EEA law that de facto broadly corresponds to that found in EU law. Moreover, according to both systems the said conditions are minimal conditions in the sense that they are supplemented by national law within the general limitations set by the principle of equivalence and effectiveness.[204]

C. Fundamental Rights

238. The EEA Agreement does not include provisions that state whether fundamental rights are part of the Agreement nor does it contain a document akin to the Charter of Fundamental Rights of the European Union. The closest allusion is a consideration in the Preamble to the Agreement, according to which the Contracting Parties are convinced that an EEA will contribute to the construction of a Europe based on peace, democracy and human rights.

239. Fundamental rights, nevertheless, form part of EEA law and influence the way in which the Agreement should be interpreted. This has been confirmed in several judgments by the EFTA Court. This is most clearly so in relation to situations where the question of fundamental rights arises in relation to the interpretation of a regulation or directive incorporated into the Agreement. The CJEU has constantly held that secondary EU law is to be interpreted in a way that brings it in conformity with fundamental rights including, in addition to the Charter, common constitutional values of the EU Member States, and international human rights instruments such as the European Convention on Human Rights (ECHR),[205] the International Covenant on Civil and Political rights of 19 December 1966,[206] the European Social Pact, and International Labour Organization (ILO) Convention 111[207] on

203. Case E-4/01 [2002] EFTA Court Report, 240. *See also* Case E-8/07 *Nguyen* [2008] EFTA Court Report, 224, and Case E-2/10 *Kolbeinsson* [2009–2010] EFTA Court Report, 234.
204. *See* Case E-4/01 *Karlsson* [2002] EFTA Court Report, 240, and compare with Case C-424/97 *Haim* [2000] ECR I-5213.
205. Convention for the Protection of Human Rights and Fundamental Freedoms, Rome, 4 Nov. 1950.
206. United Nations, *Treaty Series*, vol. 999, 171.
207. ILO Convention C111 Discrimination (Employment and Occupation) of 1958.

discrimination in employment.[208] Moreover, as provisions in EEA law should be interpreted in line with their EU counterparts, the general quest for homogeneity enshrined in Article 6 of the EEA Agreement and Article 3 SCA in such situations itself speaks in favour of an interpretation of the EEA acts in a manner which is in line with fundamental rights.

240. The EFTA Court has gone further and integrated fundamental rights into the EEA legal order. In *TBW and Bellona v. EFTA Surveillance Authority*,[209] the Court briefly discussed the application of the criteria of direct and individual concern in Article 36 SCA in the light of human rights and access to justice. Moreover, in *Ásgeirsson*,[210] the Court held that both the EEA Agreement and the SCA should be interpreted in the light of fundamental rights.[211] It further stated that the ECHR and the judgments of the European Court of Human Rights are important sources for determining the scope of these rights. In *Holship*,[212] the Court stated that fundamental rights form part of the unwritten principles of EEA law and that the fundamental rights guaranteed in the EEA legal order are applicable in all situations governed by EEA law. And furthermore, that where overriding reasons in the public interest are invoked in order to justify measures which are liable to obstruct the exercise of the right of establishment, such justification, provided for by EEA law, must be interpreted in the light of the general principles of EEA law, in particular fundamental rights. In *Clauder*,[213] the Court noted that in the EU the same right as that at issue in the proceedings was protected by Article 7 of the Charter of Fundamental Rights without however saying more about what consequences it drew from that observation.

It follows implicitly from the case law of the EFTA Court that the Authority must take into account fundamental rights, including the case law of the European Court of Human Rights in its dealings with the EFTA States, individuals and economic operators, just as the EFTA States must respect the same rights when implementing EEA acts. In *Kerim*,[214] the Court noted that the States, in particular their courts, not only must interpret their national law in a manner consistent with EEA law but also are under an obligation to ensure that the interpretation and application of acts incorporated into the EEA Agreement do not result in a conflict with fundamental rights protected by EEA law. Moreover, both *Ásgeirsson* and *Clauder* indicate that the ECHR is not the only source of fundamental rights that the Court will take into consideration when interpreting the EEA Agreement.

208. *See*, for example, Case 230/78 *Eridania* [1979] ECR-2749, and Case 63/83 *Kirk* [1984] ECR-2689, and *see also*, with regard to the importance of opinions of the Human Rights Committee established under Art. 28 of the International Covenant on Civil and Political rights of 19 Dec. 1966, Case C-249/86 *Grant* [1998] ECR I-621.
209. Case E-2/02 [2003] EFTA Court Report, 52.
210. Case E-2/03 [2003] EFTA Court Report, 185, para. 23. *See also* Case E-15/10 *Posten Norge* [2012] EFTA Court Report, 246, paras 85–86.
211. *See also* EFTA Court Judgment of 21 Mar. 2024 in case E-5/23 *LDL*, para 94.
212. Case E-14/15 [2016] EFTA Court Report, 240, para. 123.
213. Case E-4/11 [2011] EFTA Court Report, 216.
214. EFTA Court judgment of 9 Feb. 2021 in Case E-1/20 *Kerim*, para. 43.

§2. An Agreement of Public International Law Nature

I. The Structure of the EEA Agreement

241. The EEA Agreement consists of the main Agreement, fifty-two Protocols, twenty-two Annexes as well as a final act. The main Agreement comprises a preamble and 129 Articles setting out in Part I the objects and principles; in Part II, the free movement of goods; in Part III, the free movement of persons, services and capital;[215] in Part IV, the competition and State rules; in Part V, the horizontal provisions relevant to the four freedoms;[216] in Part VI, rules on cooperation outside the four freedoms; in Part VII, the institutional provisions; in Part VIII, rules of the financial mechanism; and in Part IX, the general and final provisions.

242. As already indicated, one of the basic concepts underlying the EEA Agreement is the principle of homogeneity. With a view to achieving homogeneity, the EEA Agreement not only mirrors large parts of the EU primary law in the main Agreement but also includes EU secondary law referred to in its Annexes. Each of the twenty-two Annexes is established by an article in the main Agreement. For example, Article 17 sets out that Annex I contains specific provisions and arrangements concerning veterinary and phytosanitary matters, and Article 23 refers to Annex II on technical regulations, standards, testing and certification. Hence, the twenty-two Annexes, as established in the main Agreement, set out the material scope of the EEA Agreement.

243. The basic set-up for each of the Annexes follows a specific template: first, for transparency and as a reminder, there is a reference to Protocol 1 on horizontal adaptations; second, most of the Annexes contain sectoral adaptations applying to all the acts referred to in that Annex;[217] third, the Annexes list the acts referred to. This is normally referred to as the acts incorporated into the EEA Agreement.

244. Pursuant to Article 119 of the EEA Agreement, the Annexes to the EEA Agreement and the acts referred to therein, as well as the Protocols, constitute integral part of the EEA Agreement. Hence, from a formal viewpoint, there is no hierarchy between the main Agreement and the Annexes and the Protocols.

245. As Article 119 of the EEA Agreement indicates, the incorporation of EU secondary legislation into the EEA Agreement is done through a technique of reference to the relevant EU acts. Each act referred to in an Annex is inserted with an

215. The freedoms mentioned in Parts II and III are also jointly referred to as 'the four freedoms'.
216. Such as social policy, consumer protection, environment, statistics and company law.
217. There are sectoral adaptations to Annexes I, II, V, VI, VII, VIII, IX, XII, XIII, XIV, XV, XVI, XCII, XIX, XX, XXI and XXII.

individual number followed by a reference to the Celex number,[218] the name and the publication reference of the acts in question. Amending acts are listed as indents under the acts that are amended. This technique thus identifies unequivocally all the acts that apply in the EEA. It also means that it has not been necessary to reproduce the complete text of the directives and regulations taken into the Agreement itself. In some cases, however, acts are incorporated with adaptations for the purposes of the EEA Agreement, and such specific adaptations are reflected in the Annexes. A specific adaptation to an EU act incorporated into the EEA Agreement implies that the act, or a specific provision of that act, should be read in a certain way or that the text of certain provision should be replaced or disapplied for the purposes of the EEA Agreement.[219]

246. It could be argued that not all the EU secondary legislation that is referred to in the EEA Agreement constitutes an integral part of the EEA Agreement. Some acts are included under the heading 'acts of which the EFTA States and the EFTA Surveillance Authority shall take due account' or 'acts of which the Contracting Parties shall take note'. The acts referred to under these headings are typically non-binding acts such as recommendations and opinions.

247. The Agreement, moreover, includes a wide range of Protocols. Those protocols contain rules on various specific issues, such as the product scope, rules of origin, mutual assistance in customs matters and trade in fish. The Protocols are in general more static than the annexes, but a few are updated on a regular basis.

248. If an act is referred to in an Annex of the EEA Agreement, it has to be read in the light of all relevant adaptations for the purposes of the EEA Agreement. These adaptations constitute the key to how to read secondary EU legislation in an EEA context. Those adaptations can be horizontal, sectoral or specific adaptations. The horizontal adaptations are set out in Protocol 1 to the EEA Agreement on Horizontal adaptations. They adapt a series of more or less standard provisions contained in EU acts that are referred to in the twenty-two Annexes to the EEA Agreement. The provisions in question concern, *inter alia*, the setting-up of procedures for adapting and amending EU acts, the exchange of information, the rights and obligations imposed upon Member States or their public entities, undertakings and individuals, the language requirements and the publication requirements. These horizontal adaptations apply, unless either the sectoral or the specific adaptations provide for the contrary.

---

218. The Celex number is the document identification number used in Celex, which is the official legal database of the EC. Celex is no longer updated after 31 Dec. 2004. Reference is made to EUR-Lex http://eur-lex.europa.eu – *see* http://eur-lex.europa.eu/homepage.html?locale=en.

219. *See* Adaptation texts to EU Acts upon incorporation into the EEA Agreement, in *EFTA Bulletin June 2019, Legal Notes by the EFTA Secretariat on the EEA Agreement* (available at www.efta.int) and C. Frommelt, 'Ausnahmeregelungen un Anpassungen im EWR-Recht', in Müller & –Schroeder (eds), *25 Jahre Europäischer Wirtschaftsraum* (2020): 101–123.

249. The sectoral adaptations are set out at the beginning of each Annex and adapt all the acts contained in that Annex. They thus concern only the rules in a certain field of law. The specific adaptations are applicable in the context of the EU act in question only. In particular the specific adaptations can sometimes be of a substantive nature in that they grant one or more of the EFTA States a temporary or even permanent derogation from the EU act in question.

250. In addition, and as reflected in Article 7 of the EEA Agreement, EEA law operates with the same distinction between regulations and directives as in EU law. Thus, acts corresponding to an EU regulation shall 'as such' be made part of the internal legal order of the Contracting Parties while acts corresponding to an EU Directive shall leave the choice of form and method of implementation to the authorities of the Contracting Parties. However, Article 7 of the EEA Agreement also illustrates the non-supranational character of the EEA Agreement. In fact, unlike EU law it prescribes that not only directives, but also regulations, should be made part of the national legal orders.[220] That difference to EU law was necessary, first, in order to reflect the basic premise behind the Agreement that it should not entail any transfer of legislative powers, and second, in order to avoid that due to the public international law character of the EEA Agreement, acts corresponding to directives would be more binding under EEA law in monistic legal systems (such as the one in Liechtenstein)[221] than under EU law.

251. Accordingly, with a view to obtaining the full picture of how an EU act referred to in the EEA Agreement applies in the EEA, it is not enough to examine the EU act in question. It is necessary to read the EU act in conjunction with all the adaptations that may be applicable. In addition, the general characteristics of the EEA Agreement have to be always kept in mind.

II. The Dynamic Development of the EEA

252. The EEA Agreement foresees two different procedures for ensuring a development of the EEA Agreement. The first procedure is set out in Articles 98 and 102 of the EEA Agreement and is designed to allow for the dynamic development within the fields already covered by the EEA Agreement. The second procedure is based on Article 118 of the EEA Agreement, the so-called evolutionary clause, and allows for the development of the EEA Agreement into fields currently not covered by the EEA Agreement.

220. *See* Art. 7(a) of the EEA Agreement. *See* in this context also, for example, Case E-3/08 *EFTA Surveillance Authority v. Iceland* [2008] EFTA Court Report, 308, Case E-2/09 *EFTA Surveillance Authority v. Iceland* [2009–2010] EFTA Court Report, 12 and EFTA Court judgment of 12 Jul. 2023 in Case E-15/22 *EFTA Surveillance Authority v. Norway*.

221. *See* M. Sánchez Rydelski, 'Private Enforcement of EEA Law in Liechtenstein', *Liechtensteinische Juristen-Zeitung*, LJZ 3/23 (2023).

A. *Dynamic Development Within the Fields Already Covered by the EEA Agreement*[222]

253. As a starting point, only EU acts falling within the scope of the EEA Agreement are incorporated into the Annexes to the EEA Agreement. This is generally referred to as a question of 'EEA relevance'. At the outset, EU acts are considered EEA relevant if they contribute to fulfilling the aim of Article 1 of the EEA Agreement, meaning that they are relevant for the fulfilment of the internal market and ensure equal conditions of competition. This means that certain areas of law falling within the competence of the EU fall outside the scope of the EEA Agreement, and EU acts in these areas would not be incorporated.

254. In most cases, the assessment of EEA relevance is unproblematic and rather straightforward, especially where new EU acts are replacing or amending acts already incorporated into the EEA Agreement. However, there have been several examples of challenging discussions between the EFTA States and the EU related to EEA relevance, for example, concerning the relevance of rules on criminal sanctions and on rules concerning the EU's trade relations with third countries.[223]

255. At the time of the signature of the EEA Agreement, the then existing internal market legislation was to a large extent reflected in the EEA Agreement. However, as it was clear that the rules of the Community (and now the Union) would further develop after the signing of the EEA Agreement, the homogeneity achieved in the negotiations for the EEA Agreement would disappear over time if no mechanism were found for a parallel development of the two legal orders. For the EEA Agreement to function, an institutional mechanism had to be set up for this parallel development to take place. In other words, the principle of homogeneity had to contain a dynamic element.

256. When designing this institutional mechanism, the negotiators faced several, to a certain degree conflicting, demands from either side. On the one hand, the Community, as it then was, required that its decision-making autonomy with regard to its internal rules would be safeguarded. On the other hand, the EFTA States required participating in the decision-making process of the decisions to which they would subsequently be subjected. Finally, the EFTA States could not accept a transfer of decision-making power to a supranational body.

---

222. For other descriptions of the same topic, *see* G. Baur, 'Decision-Making Procedure and Implementation of New Law', in Baudenbacher (ed.), *The Handbook of EEA law* (2016): 45; D. Tynes in Arnesen et al. (eds), *Agreement on the European Economic Area, A Commentary* (2018): 782–788; M. Dystland, F. Finstad & I. Sørebø, in Arnesen et al. (eds), *Agreement on the European Economic Area, A Commentary* (2018): 795–824; K. Isaksen, 'The Process of Incorporating EU Acts into the EEA Agreement', in Müller & Schroeder (eds), *25 Jahre Europäischer Wirtschaftsraum* (2020): 53–68 and F. Arnesen et al., *Oversikt over EØS-retten* 68 (Oslo: Universitetsforlaget, 2022).

223. *See* H. Fredriksen & G. Mathisen, *EØS-rett 4. utgave* 223 (Fagbokforlaget 2022) and M. Dystland, F. Finstad & I. Sørebø, in Arnesen et al. (eds), *Agreement on the European Economic Area, A Commentary* (2018): 807.

With a view to reaching a compromise between all these demands, the negotiators envisaged an institutional mechanism, which ensures that neither group of Contracting Parties to the EEA Agreement can interfere with the internal matters of the other group of Contracting Parties. This system is commonly referred to as the two-pillar system. For the two pillars to communicate appropriately with each other, it was necessary to create the necessary forums to this effect. The different organs of this institutional system as well as the decision-making procedure in the EEA Agreement will be described in more detail *infra* in Chapters 3 and 4 respectively.

257. The main expression of the two-pillar system is the fact that the EFTA States have not transferred any decision-making power to a supranational body. Therefore, the adoption of an EU act by the EU does not ipso facto lead to a modification of the EEA rules. The incorporation of new EU acts into the EEA Agreement takes the form of amendments of the EEA Agreement. This is so because the acts referred to in the Annexes and Protocols to the EEA Agreement form an integral part thereof. These amendments of the EEA Agreement, by which new EU acts are incorporated into the EEA Agreement, are themselves agreements of a public international law nature.[224]

258. This being said, it would have been inconceivable to reconvene all Contracting Parties for agreeing on the incorporation of an EU act into the EEA Agreement, using general treaty amending procedures under public international law, each time the EU bodies have adopted an act of EEA relevance. Using such general procedures would be cumbersome bearing in mind the high number of EU acts that are incorporated into the EEA Agreement, and it would render the achievement of the objective homogeneity difficult. Therefore, the Contracting Parties agreed on a 'simplified' procedure for modifying Annexes and certain Protocols to the EEA Agreement. That procedure is laid down in Articles 98 and 102 of the EEA Agreement,[225] whereby EEA-relevant EU legislation is incorporated into the EEA Agreement by way of EEA Joint Committee decisions. This competence for the EEA Joint Committee is essential to the functioning of the EEA Agreement, and its importance can be illustrated by the amendments to the main Agreement of the EEA Agreement in connection with the EU enlargements in 2004, 2007 and 2014. For the first two amendments, the time needed from signature to ratification was twenty months and more than four years, respectively. The third EEA Enlargement Agreement from 2014 regarding Croatia is [as of December 2023] still pending ratification and is currently provisionally applicable.[226]

259. Even if the decisions of the EEA Joint Committee constitute agreements of a public international law nature, this does not mean that EFTA States' Parliaments do not play any role. Article 103 of the EEA Agreement provides that if a decision of the EEA Joint Committee can be binding on a Contracting Party only after the

224. *See* Case E-6/01 *CIBA* [2002] EFTA Court Report, 32, para. 33.
225. *See infra* Part II, Ch. 4, §3.
226. *See* K. Isaksen, 'The Process of Incorporating EU Acts into the EEA Agreement', in Müller & Schroeder (eds), *25 Jahre Europäischer Wirtschaftsraum* (2020): 65.

fulfilment of constitutional requirements, the decision shall enter into force only after the Contracting Party concerned has notified the other Contracting Parties that the constitutional requirements have been fulfilled. As a matter of consistent practice of the Contracting Parties, a delay in the entry into force of a Joint Committee decision relates only to its binding effect, but does not prevent the act in question from being incorporated into the EEA Agreement immediately. This distinction can be of importance as an act which has been made part of the EEA Agreement will, for example, already have to be taken into account by national courts, e.g., when interpreting national law, irrespective of whether the act in question already has binding effects in the national legal order.[227]

260. What has to be understood under the term 'constitutional requirements' depends on the national legal systems, but the wording indicates that the Governments of the EFTA States, due to the national constitutions, need the approval of the Parliament. The term can refer to a need of approval of the EEA Joint Committee decision or to a need of amendments to existing legislation by the national Parliament. It is for each of the EFTA States to decide if there is a need for constitutional requirements in respect of an EU acts. However, if Article 103 of the EEA Agreement is used in a situation where no new legislation or amendments to national legislation are necessary or where no parliamentary approval otherwise is needed, this would be contrary to the wording of that provision.[228]

261. As set out in the first sentence of Article 103(2) of the EEA Agreement, a Joint Committee Decision does not enter into force until all Parties have notified that the constitutional requirements have been fulfilled. If such notifications have not taken place upon the expiry of a period of six months after the adoption of the Joint Committee Decision, the Decision shall be applied provisionally pending the fulfilment, unless an EFTA State has indicated that such provisional application cannot take place.[229] However, in cases where an EFTA State is not in a position to fulfil the constitutional requirements within the six-month deadline, the States systematically notify the EU of the delay and that provisional application pending fulfilment is not possible for constitutional reasons.[230] It should be noted that a notification arriving after the expiry of the six-month period cannot reverse the provisional application of the Joint Committee Decision. Were an EFTA State to be

227. Case E-3/15 *Liechtensteinische Gesellschaft für Umweltschutz v. Gemeinde Vaduz* [2015] EFTA Court Report, 74.
228. *See also Procedures in the EEA EFTA States, the EFTA Secretariat and the EU for the incorporation of legislation into the EEA Agreement*, Note by the Secretariat 8 Sep. 2022, Ref. 17-1402, para. 98, published on www.efta.int.
229. *See* G. Baur, 'Decision-Making Procedure and Implementation of New Law', in *The Handbook of EEA Law* 63 (Baudenbacher ed., Springer 2016); M. Dystland, F. Finstad & I. Sørebø, in Arnesen et al. (eds), *Agreement on the European Economic Area, A Commentary* (2018): 820–821.
230. A list of constitutional requirements indicated since 2004, available on the website of the EFTA Secretariat, shows that in a majority of the cases, one or more EFTA States notified a delay and that provisional application pending fulfilment is not possible.

permitted at any point after the expiry of the six-month period to revoke unilaterally the provisional applicability, this would be contrary to the express wording of Article 103 of the EEA Agreement and, thus, incompatible with the general principle of legal certainty.[231]

262. Article 103(2), second sentence, of the EEA Agreement sets out what happens if a Contracting Party notifies the non-ratification of a Joint Committee Decision. Non-ratification in this situation refers to a situation where the constitutional requirement cannot be lifted because it is not possible to obtain approval from the national parliament. This has never occurred, but such a situation would be treated as if an agreement on incorporation cannot be reached, and pursuant to Article 103(2), second sentence, the suspension provided for in Article 102(5) of the EEA Agreement takes effect one month after a notification of non-ratification. Based on the wording of Article 103(2), second sentence, the same shall also apply where an EFTA State has notified that provisional application cannot take place, which happens on a regular basis. As described below,[232] in situations falling under Article 102(4) and (5), a Contracting Party needs to expressly mention that it considers the suspension of the affected part of an Annex to be triggered, and the same should apply to situations falling under Article 103(2), second sentence. This interpretation is supported by more than twenty-five years of practice, as there has never been any use of the suspension provided for in Article 103(2), even though there has been a number of notifications of delays of fulfilling constitutional requirements and that provisional application pending fulfilment is not possible. Effectively, in most cases, a suspension of the affected part of an Annex would be a disproportionate reaction, as most such cases concern a delay of the incorporation of one or a limited number of acts for a few months and the non-provisional application for these acts during the period of this delay, which in fact is a very different situation from not reaching an agreement pursuant to Article 102(4) and (5).

263. In conclusion, and notwithstanding the fact that the same substantive rules should apply in the EEA and in the EU, the EEA and the EU constitute two quite distinct legal systems. The EEA Agreement applies to the relations between both the EFTA States and EU and its Member States and between the EFTA States themselves. The TEU and the TFEU govern the relations between the EU Member States.

B. Dynamic Development Beyond the Fields Already Covered by the EEA Agreement

264. According to Article 118 of the EEA Agreement, where a Contracting Party considers that it would be useful in the interests of all Contracting Parties to develop the relations established by the EEA Agreement by extending them to fields not covered by the Agreement, it shall submit a reasoned request to the other Contracting

231. Case E-17/11 *Aresbank* [2012] EFTA Court Report, 916, para. 77.
232. *See infra* Part II, Ch. 4.

Parties within the EEA Council. This so-called evolutionary clause was not strictly necessary in the context of the EEA Agreement. First, the droit d'évocation[233] would already suffice to allow a Contracting Party to raise the issue regarding a possible amendment of the main body of the EEA Agreement and, second, the 1969 Vienna Convention on the law of treaties foresees that an agreement can be modified by the common accord of the parties thereto (Article 39 Vienna Convention).[234] The evolutionary clause has been introduced into the EEA Agreement, because it was of great political importance for the Contracting Parties.[235] They wanted to signal that the integration between the Contracting Parties could be further developed and that the conclusion of the EEA Agreement was not the end of the integration process.[236]

265. According to Article 118 of the EEA Agreement, the procedure of amending the EEA Agreement by extending it to fields not covered thereby is initiated by a Contracting Party who considers such extension appropriate. It does so by submitting a reasoned request to the other Contracting Parties in the EEA Council.[237] After having received the reasoned request, the EEA Council has three options. The EEA Council may instruct the EEA Joint Committee to examine all the aspects of this request and to issue a report (Article 118(1)(1) of the EEA Agreement), or it may take a political decision with a view to opening negotiations between the Contracting Parties (Article 118(1)(2) of the EEA Agreement). The third option is only implicit in Article 118 of the EEA Agreement. The EEA Council could immediately come to the conclusion that it would not be appropriate to engage in a process of extending the scope of the EEA Agreement.[238]

266. Once the EEA Council has taken the political decision with a view to opening the negotiations between the Contracting Parties, the Contracting Parties will negotiate an amendment of the EEA Agreement. The EEA Council is not involved at this stage of the process. The agreements resulting from the negotiations will be subject to the ratification or approval by the Contracting Parties in accordance with their own procedures (Article 118(2) EEA of the Agreement).

267. With regard to the expression 'extending the relations to fields not covered by the EEA Agreement' found in Article 118 of the EEA Agreement, it has to be

233. *See* for an explanation of this concept *infra* Part II, Ch. 3, §1, I and Part II, Ch. 6, §2.
234. *See* Haas & V. Zellweger, 'Allgemeine und Schlussbestimmungen', in *Accord EEE – Commentaires et réflexions* 672 (O. Jacot-Guillarmod ed., Zürich: Schulthess 1992). The Vienna Convention on the Law of Treaties can be found at: United Nations, *Treaty Series*, vol. 1155, 331.
235. S. Norberg et al., *The European Economic Area, EEA Law, A Commentary on the EEA Agreement* 293 (Stockholm: Fritzes 1993).
236. *See* for the particular case of Switzerland: G. Haas & V. Zellweger, 'Allgemeine und Schlussbestimmungen', in *Accord EEE – Commentaires et réflexions* 670 (O. Jacot-Guillarmod ed., Zürich: Schulthess 1992).
237. *See infra* Part II, Ch. 3, §1, I.
238. G. Haas & V. Zellweger, 'Allgemeine und Schlussbestimmungen', in *Accord EEE – Commentaires et réflexions* 671 (O. Jacot-Guillarmod ed., Zürich: Schulthess 1992).

recalled that the EEA Agreement covers, in principle, the four freedoms, the competition rules and the horizontal and flanking policies. Accordingly, possible extensions of the scope to the EEA Agreement to other fields of cooperation, such as asylum or agriculture would follow the procedure foreseen in Article 118 of the EEA Agreement.

Article 118 of the EEA Agreement has never been triggered. However, it could be argued that, to some extent, the EEA Agreement has nevertheless been extended to new fields without the use of Article 118 of the EEA Agreement. First, at least ad hoc, through the ordinary incorporation procedure set out in Articles 98 and 102 of the EEA Agreement, due to the somewhat elastic notion of EEA relevance. Second, the scope of the EEA Agreement has evolved as a result of the case law of the EFTA Court.[239] As regards the dynamic development through the procedure set out in Articles 98 and 102 of the EEA Agreement, a number of EU acts supposedly falling outside the scope of the EEA Agreement have been incorporated. For most of these acts, however, it could be argued that these are incorporations ad hoc of specific acts falling entirely or partly outside the scope rather than extensions to fields not already covered by the EEA Agreement. At least, this is the impression when analysing the declarations concerning the incorporation of certain acts attached to decisions of the EEA Joint Committee, where it is stated that the acts fall outside the scope of the EEA Agreement and that the incorporation is without prejudice to the scope. Such declarations can be joint by the Contracting Parties or by the EFTA States only. Examples of acts where such declarations can be found are within the areas of judicial cooperation in criminal matters, trade relations with third countries, climate change and common foreign and security policy.[240] Hence, the Contracting Parties occasionally agree to ad hoc extend the scope of the EEA Agreement by incorporating EU acts that fall entirely or partly outside the scope, but an extension, as such, of a field not covered, should be based on Article 118 of the EEA Agreement.

C. Technical Updates of the EEA Agreement Through the EEA Enlargement Agreements

268. The procedure applicable to amendments of the main text of the EEA Agreement as well as those protocols that cannot be amended by decision of the EEA Joint Committee[241] are cumbersome. Therefore, and notwithstanding the development of EU terminology, the Contracting Parties to the EEA Agreement have decided not to systematically update these parts of the EEA Agreement.

---

239. *See also* C. Hillion, in Arnesen et al. (eds), *Agreement on the European Economic Area, A Commentary* (2018): 905–906.

240. *See*, for example, Joint Committee Decision Nos 87/2006, 158/2007, 80/2008, 20/2009. 39/2009, 141/2009, 127/2010, 6/2011, 32/2012, 53/2012, 83/2013, 164/2013, 188/2015, 191/2015, 63/2020, 228/2021 and 337/2022. Some of these declarations specifically mention that they are without prejudice to Art. 118 of the EEA Agreement.

241. *See supra* Part. II, Ch. 2, §2, II, B.

269. Rather, the Contracting Parties have hitherto seized the opportunity offered by the EU's 2004 enlargement, which eventually also resulted in enlargements of the EEA, and therefore required a full national ratification procedure anyway, with a view to proceeding to the certain updates.[242]

270. On that occasion, the Contracting Parties even agreed to amend an uncontentious issue, such as the modification of Protocol 36 to the EEA Agreement on the Statute of the EEA Joint Parliamentary Committee. The amendment consisted in the reduction of the number of members of the EEA Joint Parliamentary Committee to twenty-four members.[243]

---

242. *See* Agreement on the participation of the Czech Republic, the Republic of Estonia, the Republic of Cyprus, the Republic of Latvia, the Republic of Lithuania, the Republic of Hungary, the Republic of Malta, the Republic of Poland, the Republic of Slovenia and the Slovak Republic in the European Economic Area of 14 Oct. 2003 (OJ L 130, 29.4.2004, 11; EEA Supplement No. 23, 29.4.2004, 1).
243. *See* Art. 2 para. 2 a) of the Agreement on the participation of the Czech Republic, the Republic of Estonia, the Republic of Cyprus, the Republic of Latvia, the Republic of Lithuania, the Republic of Hungary, the Republic of Malta, the Republic of Poland, the Republic of Slovenia and the Slovak Republic in the European Economic Area of 14 Oct. 2003 (OJ L 130, 29.4.2004, 11; EEA Supplement No. 23, 29.4.2004, 1).

Chapter 3. Institutional Set-Up

271. The institutional set-up of the EEA Agreement is a result of the Contracting Parties' requirement that their respective decision-making autonomy is fully respected. To this end, the Contracting Parties decided to adopt the so-called two-pillar structure[244] which means that the EU and the EFTA side each take care of their own internal matters. Decisions taken by one pillar cannot bind the Contracting Parties of the other pillar. Each pillar has its own institutions for decision-making, surveillance and judicial review.

272. For this two-pillar system to function well, a full-fledged EFTA pillar had to be established. EFTA, which previously operated like a traditional international organization without any element of supranationality, had to adapt its institutional set-up to that prevailing in the EU pillar. The EFTA States not only established a Standing Committee of the EFTA States entrusted with the coordination of the EFTA States' position in the EEA Joint Committee (*see* Agreement on the establishment of a Standing Committee of the EFTA States)[245] but also had to establish the EFTA Surveillance Authority and the EFTA Court. This has been done by way of the Surveillance and Court Agreement between the EFTA States. The tasks of the latter two institutions reflect respectively the tasks of the European Commission and the CJEU in the EU pillar.

273. However, the establishment of some common institutions could not be avoided, in particular with a view to maintaining homogeneity in the EEA through joint decision-making and dispute settlement. These common institutions are the EEA Council, the EEA Joint Committee, the EEA Joint Parliamentary Committee and the EEA Consultative Committee. Their legal framework is laid down in Chapter 1 (The structure of the Association) of Part VII (Institutional provisions) of the EEA Agreement. A common feature of all these joint institutions is that both the EU side and the EFTA side have the same weight therein.

§1. The EEA Council

274. Article 89 of the EEA Agreement establishes an EEA Council, which is the highest political body in the EEA. It is responsible for giving the political impetus in the implementation of the EEA Agreement and lays down the general guidelines for the EEA Joint Committee. Accordingly, the EEA Council serves as a forum for exchanges of views between EFTA and the EU regarding the EEA Agreement and related matters.

244. *See supra* Part II, Ch. 1, §2, II–IV and Part II, Ch. 2, §2, II, A. *See also* 'The Two-Pillar System of the EEA Agreement: Legal framework and overview of cases raising two-pillar challenges', in *EFTA Bulletin June 2019, Legal Notes by the EFTA Secretariat on the EEA Agreement* (available at www.efta.int).

245. Agreement on a Standing Committee of the EFTA States, signed in Porto on 2 May 1992. The Agreement is available on the EFTA Secretariat's website: www.efta.int/legal-texts/committees.

I. Functions of the EEA Council

275. Article 89(1) of the EEA Agreement specifies that the EEA Council shall assess the overall functioning of the EEA Agreement and take the political decisions leading to amendments of the EEA Agreement. While the overall functioning of the EEA Agreement is assessed at every meeting and summarized in the conclusions of the EEA Council meeting, the EEA Council has hitherto never been requested to take a political decision leading to amendments of the EEA Agreement.

276. However, the functions of the EEA Council, as mentioned in Article 89(1) of the EEA Agreement, are not the only ones that the EEA Council exercises. Among the other functions are the EEA Council's role in connection with the droit d'évocation of Article 5 of the EEA Agreement (concerning the right of the Contracting Parties to the EEA Agreement to raise any matter of concern at the level of the EEA Joint Committee or the EEA Council),[246] the so-called evolutionary clause in Article 118 of the EEA Agreement (setting out the procedure for amending the EEA Agreement),[247] as well as the participation of third countries in the EEA as provided for in Article 128 of the EEA Agreement.[248]

277. The droit d'évocation set out in Article 5 of the EEA Agreement as well as the evolutionary clause in Article 118 of the EEA Agreement are an expression of the EEA Council's task to give the political impetus in the implementation of the EEA Agreement. In contrast, this is less obvious with regard to Article 128 of the EEA Agreement. In connection with the latter article, the EEA Council merely acts as a mailbox for the applications of candidate Contracting Parties. It does not take any – not even political – stance on the incoming applications.

278. In addition to the functions expressly foreseen in the EEA Agreement, the EU and its Member States and the EFTA States are to hold informal exchanges of views at ministerial level at meetings of the EEA Council. This political dialogue initially foreseen has been strengthened by the fact that following a Joint Declaration of 30 May 1995, the EFTA States may subscribe to declarations adopted by the EU Member States in the framework of the political dialogue. This political dialogue goes beyond the stricter confines of the EEA Agreement, typically on topical foreign policy issues.[249] The EEA Council also takes into consideration resolutions adopted by the EEA Joint Parliamentary Committee and the EEA Consultative Committee.

246. *See infra* Part II, Ch. 6, §2 for a more thorough description of the *droit d'évocation.*
247. *See supra* Part II, Ch. 2, §2, II, B.
248. Article 128 of the EEA Agreement provides that 'any European State becoming a member of the Community shall, and the Swiss Confederation or any European State becoming a member of EFTA may, apply to become a Party to this Agreement. It shall address its application to the EEA Council'.
249. J. Forman, 'The EEA Agreement Five Years on: Dynamic Homogeneity in Practice and Its Implementation by the Two EEA Courts', *Common Market Law Review* (1999): 36/751 (761).

II. Organization and Composition

279. Pursuant to Article 90(2) of the EEA Agreement, decisions by the EEA Council are to be taken by agreement between the EU, on the one hand, and the EFTA States, on the other hand. This provision has two implications. First, it means that as long as no decision is to be taken, the Contracting Parties may express their views individually within the Council. Second, it means that each Contracting Party as defined in Article 2 of the EEA Agreement has the right to veto a decision.

280. Pursuant to Article 91(2) of the EEA Agreement, the EEA Council is to be convened twice a year by its President, who is to preside at the meetings. The office of President of the EEA Council alternates between the EU and the EFTA States every six months. It is to be held either by a member of the EU Council or a member of a Government of an EFTA State. The meetings are normally held in Brussels. The EEA Council does not have a permanent secretariat supporting it, as preparations are done independently in each of the two pillars. In the EFTA pillar, the EFTA Secretariat in Brussels is supporting the EFTA States.

281. The EEA Council consists of the members of the EU Council and of the European Commission on the one hand and of one member of the Government of each of the EFTA States on the other (Article 90(1) of the EEA Agreement). The EEA Council was meant to be meeting at Ministerial level. Like the EU Council, the EEA Council is not a fixed body. It could be formed by different Ministers (and officials of the European Commission) each time it meets according to the subject matters to be discussed.[250]

§2. The EEA Joint Committee

282. Article 92 of the EEA Agreement establishes an EEA Joint Committee, which is to ensure the effective implementation and operation of the EEA Agreement and is designed to function as an institution working in the pursuit of the common interest of the EU side and the EFTA side. The EEA Joint Committee is responsible for the day-to-day management of the EEA Agreement and is the EEA Agreement's main decision-making body. The continuous contacts between the Contracting Parties will take place within the framework of the meetings of the EEA Joint Committee. However, it has to be kept in mind that the EEA Joint Committee does not have any supranational competences.

I. Functions

283. The EEA Joint Committee is responsible for a number of different tasks. The wide array of tasks to be carried out by the EEA Joint Committee implies that

250. C. Bright & K. Williams, 'Understanding the European Economic Area: Context, Institutions, and Legal Systems', in *Business Law in the European Economic Area* 6 (Oxford: Oxford Press 1994).

the EEA Joint Committee cannot be compared to the secretariat of an intergovernmental organization. Indeed, the EEA Joint Committee can be distinguished from a secretariat insofar as it not only prepares and implements decisions but can also take decisions that are binding upon the Contracting Parties.

284. The tasks that the EEA Joint Committee assumes can be divided into three main areas. First, the EEA Joint Committee is the body that decides which acts of secondary EU legislation should be incorporated into the EEA Agreement. Second, according to Article 105 of the EEA Agreement, it is required to 'act so as to preserve the homogeneous interpretation of the EEA Agreement' when it comes to judgments of both the CJEU and the EFTA Court (a measure the EEA Joint Committee has not yet had the occasion to exercise). Third, the EEA Joint Committee has a central role in the cross-pillar dispute settlement procedure.

285. The ensuing presentation will be based on the classification contained in the wording of Article 92(1) of the EEA Agreement, according to which the EEA Joint Committee carries out exchanges of views and information and take decisions in the cases provided for by the EEA Agreement.

A. Exchanges of Views and Information

286. Like the EEA Council, the EEA Joint Committee plays a role in connection with the politically important droit d'évocation provided for by Article 5 of the EEA Agreement, which basically means that a Contracting Party may at any time raise a matter of concern at the level of the EEA Joint Committee or the EEA Council.[251]

287. In addition, there are numerous other occasions when the EEA Joint Committee is to carry out exchanges of views and information: first, to keep under constant review the development of the case law of the CJEU and the EFTA Court and to act so as to preserve the homogeneous interpretation of the EEA Agreement (Article 105(2) of the EEA Agreement);[252] second, to set up a system of exchange of information concerning judgments by the EFTA Court, the CJEU and the courts of last instance in the EEA-EFTA States (Article 106 of the EEA Agreement); third, to settle disputes between the two surveillance authorities (Article 109(5) of the EEA Agreement) as well as cross-pillar disputes between Contracting Parties (Article 111 of the EEA Agreement);[253] and fourth, to consult on possible safeguard measures considered by one of the Contracting Parties with a view to finding a commonly acceptable solution (Articles 112 of the EEA Agreement et seq.).[254] All these tasks are, however, only very seldom or never carried out.

251. For a presentation of the *droit d'évocation*, *see supra* Part II, Ch. 3, §1, I and *infra* Part II, Ch. 6, §2.
252. *See supra* Part II, Ch. 2, §1, II, F.
253. *See infra* Part II, Ch. 6, §1.
254. *See infra* Part II, Ch. 6, §1, II.

288. Finally, the EEA Joint Committee prepares and issues annual reports on the functioning and the development of the EEA Agreement (Article 94(4) of the EEA Agreement). These reports are addressed to the EEA Council as well as to the EEA Joint Parliamentary Committee. These reports are published on the website of EFTA, based on Article 21(3) of the Rules of Procedure of the EEA Joint Committee.[255]

B. Decisions in the Cases Provided for by the EEA Agreement

289. The EEA Agreement does not foresee that the EEA Joint Committee is to take decisions in a wide number of cases. The main category of decisions to be taken by the EEA Joint Committee is that under Article 98 of the EEA Agreement, pursuant to which the EEA Joint Committee may take decisions leading to amendments of the Annexes or Protocols to the EEA Agreement.[256] In most cases, these Decisions incorporate EU acts into the EEA Agreement.

290. The mandate of the EEA Joint Committee should not be interpreted in an overly restrictive manner. Indeed, pursuant to Article 102(3) of the EEA Agreement, the EEA Joint Committee is to make all efforts to arrive at an agreement on 'matters relevant to this Agreement'. The operative goal of this provision is to 'arrive at an agreement'. For this to carry any practical meaning in relation to the effective implementation and operation of the EEA Agreement, such an agreement cannot be restricted to a mere incorporation of secondary EU legislation.[257] The EEA Joint Committee must also have the competence to agree on adaptations to EU acts to be incorporated into the EEA Agreement or to provide for exemptions from certain provisions of these EU acts. This means that the Joint Committee can make substantive changes as compared to the original EU act when incorporating that act into the EEA Agreement and, for example, decide that the act shall not, or only partially, be applicable in a given EFTA State.

II. Organization and Composition

A. Composition

291. Article 93(1) of the EEA Agreement provides that the EEA Joint Committee consists of representatives of the Contracting Parties. It is made up of high-ranking officials from both pillars of the EEA Agreement. The EFTA States are normally represented in the EEA Joint Committee by their respective ambassadors to the EU. The EU, in turn, sends representatives of the Secretariat-General of the

---

255. Decision of the EEA Joint Committee No. 1/94 adopting the rules of procedure of the EEA Joint Committee (OJ L 85, 30.3.1994, 60, EEA Supplement No. 1, 30.3.1994, 1).
256. For a presentation of the procedure of the decision-making by the EEA Joint Committee *see infra* Part II, Ch. 4, §3, II, B.
257. *See* Case E-6/01 *CIBA* [2002] EFTA Court Report, 32.

European Commission, normally the Head of Unit responsible for the EEA Agreement. It is only rarely that delegates of the different EU Member States participate in the meetings.

292. In addition to the representatives of the Contracting Parties, representatives of the EFTA Surveillance Authority, in practice the College, as well as, under certain conditions, a representative of the European Investment Bank, are admitted to sit on the EEA Joint Committee as observers. Also, the EU Council's Secretariat can participate as an observer on the basis of Article 1(3)(3) of the rules of procedure. In addition, the EEA Joint Committee can decide to admit other persons to its meetings.[258] The meetings are not public.

293. As with the EEA Council, the office of President of the EEA Joint Committee alternates between the EU and the EFTA side every six months. During the period in which the EU holds the Presidency, a representative of the European Commission occupies the office of President. This distinguishes the office of President of the EEA Joint Committee from the one of the EEA Council, where a member of the EU Council holds the office. Accordingly, while all the Contracting Parties on the EU side have a seat in the EEA Joint Committee, it is only the representative of one of the Contracting Parties – namely the EU itself – that is eligible for holding the office of President on the EU side.

294. On the EFTA side, the office of the President is held by a representative of one of the EFTA States. Where it is up to the EFTA side to hold the office of President, it is the representative of the EFTA State that holds the Presidency in the Standing Committee of the EFTA States that holds the office of President in the EEA Joint Committee.

B. Voting Arrangements

295. The decisions in the EEA Joint Committee are taken by agreement between the EU, on the one hand, and the EFTA States, speaking with one voice, on the other hand (Article 93(1) of the EEA Agreement). The rule that the EFTA States have to speak with one voice has been presented as being liable to amount, de facto if not de jure, to majority voting within the EFTA itself (i.e., within the Standing Committee of the EFTA States). This argument was based on the idea that the political pressure would be exerted on potential reluctant countries.[259] Practice has shown, however, that this not the case. The Standing Committee still operates with the rule of unanimity.[260]

258. Article 1(3) of Decision of the EEA Joint Committee No. 1/94 adopting the rules of procedure of the EEA Joint Committee (OJ L 85, 30.3.1994, 60, EEA Supplement No. 1, 30.3.1994, 1).

259. *See* C. Reymond, 'Institutions, Decision-Making Procedure and Settlement of Disputes in the European Economic Area', *Common Market Law Review* (1993): 30/449, 458.

260. With regard to the few exceptions to this rule, *see infra* Part II, Ch. 3, §5, II, B.

296. Although not explicitly stated in Article 93(3) of the EEA Agreement, also the EU must speak with one voice. This can be deduced from the fact that unlike Article 92(2) of the EEA Agreement, Article 93(2) of the EEA Agreement does not state that the EU and its Member States shall act in their respective fields of competence. Accordingly, the EU Member States can sit on the meeting as observers.[261] Council Regulation (EC) No. 2894/94 of 28 November 1994 concerning arrangements for implementing the Agreement on the EEA[262] lays down the rules pursuant to which the EU adopts its position internally.[263]

C. Procedural Aspects of the Joint Committee's Work

297. In theory, the EEA Joint Committee is to meet at least once per month. In practice it meets only about once every six weeks with a break during summer. Over the last years, the EEA Joint Committee held about eight ordinary meetings each year. Extraordinary meetings are possible by virtue of Article 94(2) of the EEA Agreement. They are convened either on the initiative of the President of the EEA Joint Committee or at the request of one of the Contracting Parties in accordance with Article 2 of the rules of procedure.

298. The meetings of the EEA Joint Committee are held in English and all documents, except the decisions that amend the EEA Agreement, are drawn up in English only. However, if one member of the EEA Joint Committee so wishes, simultaneous translation can be provided for in the meeting.

299. The EEA Joint Committee does not have its own secretariat. Instead, pursuant to Article 15 of the rules of procedure of the EEA Joint Committee, it shall be assisted in its work by five subcommittees, dealing with free movement of goods, free movement of capital and services, free movement of persons, horizontal and flanking policies and finally legal and institutional matters (respectively called subcommittees I, II, III, IV[264] and V).[265] These subcommittees are made up of a small group of officials from the Commission who follow EEA matters as well as their EFTA States' counterparts. In some instances, these officials are joined by officials who are experts in the subject matter of a piece of legislation to be discussed in the subcommittees. As it is the case under the EEA Joint Committee, representatives of the EFTA Surveillance Authority are allowed to sit in on the meetings as observers.

---

261. *See* D. Felder, 'Structure institutionnelle et procédure décisionnelle de l'EEE', in *Accord EEE – Commentaires et réflexions* 574 (O. Jacot-Guillarmod ed., Zürich: Schulthess 1992).
262. OJ L 305, 30.11.1994, 6.
263. *See infra* Part II, Ch. 4, §3, II, A, 2.
264. Although subcommittees I, II, III and IV continue to be formally independent, they have been merged for practical purposes: the same people sit in all four committees and the committees meet back to back.
265. Although subcommittee V on legal and institutional matters has a formal existence (*see* Art. 15(1)I of the rules of procedure of the EEA Joint Committee), it normally only meets informally.

300. If the subcommittees deem it useful, they are free to hold joint meetings between the working groups of the substructure of the Standing Committee of the EFTA States and the European Commission. In addition, the subcommittees can decide to establish ad hoc working groups in connection with subject matters that cannot be attributed to one of the working groups. However, in practice, the meetings between the European Commission and the EFTA working groups are held at an informal level.

§3. The EEA Joint Parliamentary Committee

301. The EEA Agreement refers to the concept of 'democracy', in the first recital of its preamble. Furthermore, Article 95 of the EEA Agreement establishes an EEA Joint Parliamentary Committee, and Protocol 36 to the EEA Agreement contains the Statute of that Committee.

I. Functions

302. The EEA Joint Parliamentary Committee is to contribute, through dialogue and debate, to a better understanding between the EU and the EFTA States in the fields covered by the EEA Agreement (Article 95(3) of the EEA Agreement). Thus, the Committee merely has a consultative function. The legal instruments it can adopt correspond to the consultative functions it has. Pursuant to Article 95(4) of the EEA Agreement, the EEA Joint Parliamentary Committee may express its views in the form of reports or resolutions.

303. The consultative function of the EEA Joint Parliamentary Committee does not extend to a role in connection with the EU legislative process corresponding to that of the European Parliament, nor to a similar role in relation to the adoption of the decisions of the EEA Joint Committee. Even de facto it is excluded from the decision-making procedure, because it meets only twice a year. Nor does it exercise any genuine political control with the other EEA organs. Only on very few occasions has the Committee adopted resolutions that can be directly linked to (a set of) legislative proposals.

304. Concerning the contacts between the EEA Joint Parliamentary Committee and other common institutions between the EFTA and the EU sides, Article 95(5) of the EEA Agreement states that the President of the EEA Council may appear before the EEA Joint Parliamentary Committee in order to be heard by it. It is not the EEA Joint Parliamentary Committee that may call the President of the EEA Council, but it is the President of the EEA Council who may appear before the Committee.

305. The EEA Joint Parliamentary Committee also examines the annual report of the EEA Joint Committee on the functioning and the development of the EEA

Agreement.[266] The examination results in the adoption by the EEA Joint Parliamentary Committee of a resolution on the annual report of the EEA Joint Committee. However, the EEA Agreement does not foresee any direct contacts between the EEA Joint Parliamentary Committee and the EEA Joint Committee.

306. Both the possibility of hearing the President of the EEA Council and the obligation to examine the annual report of the EEA Joint Committee, give the EEA Joint Parliamentary Committee a grain of power of control over the other institutions. In practice, the EEA Joint Parliamentary Committee has the right to put oral and written questions to the representatives of the EEA Council and of the EEA Joint Committee. Moreover, at each meeting, the EEA Joint Parliamentary Committee has discussions with representatives of the EEA Council, the EEA Joint Committee and the EFTA Surveillance Authority.

II. Organization and Composition

307. The EEA Joint Parliamentary Committee was intended to have sixty-six members.[267] When Austria, Finland and Sweden left the EFTA pillar to join the EU, it was decided to limit the number of the members of the Committee to twenty-four members. The practice received formal confirmation with the entry into force of the EEA Enlargement Agreement of 14 October 2003.[268]

308. Article 95(1) of the EEA Agreement provides that an equal number of members shall be appointed by the European Parliament and by the Parliaments of the EFTA States respectively from among their respective members. On the EU side, membership in the EEA Joint Parliamentary Committee is primarily based on considerations of political colour of the respective members. On the EFTA side, membership in the EEA Joint Parliamentary Committee flows from the Agreement on a Committee of Members of Parliament of the EFTA States.[269] This Committee of Members of Parliament of the EFTA States has to be distinguished from the Committee of Members of Parliament of the EFTA Countries, which serves as a consultative body to the EFTA Council under the EFTA Convention.[270]

309. Article 1 of the Agreement on a Committee of Members of Parliament of the EFTA States clarifies that the members of Parliament appointed to the Committee of Members of Parliament of the EFTA States are, at the same time, members of the EEA Joint Parliamentary Committee. This results in a personal union between

266. *See supra* Part II, Ch. 3, §2, I, A.
267. Article 2(1) of Protocol 36 on the Statute of the EEA Joint Parliamentary Committee.
268. Article 2(2)(a) of the EEA Enlargement Agreement.
269. Based on Art. 47 of the Surveillance and Court Agreement the Committee of Members of Parliament of the EFTA States has the power to give its opinion on the budget of the EFTA Surveillance Authority before the Governments of the EFTA States adopt that budget (*see infra* Part II, Ch. 7, §2).
270. *See supra* Part I, Ch. 2, §2, II, C.

the memberships in the two Committees. Switzerland enjoys observer status both in the Committee of Members of Parliament of the EFTA States and the EEA Joint Parliamentary Committee.[271]

310. Some commentators expected at the beginning of the EEA Agreement, that horizontal political structures, such as political groups, would be created in the EEA Joint Parliamentary Committee.[272] However, perhaps due to the fact that the EEA lost its weight with three EFTA States joining the EU, this never happened.[273]

311. Unlike in the EEA Council and the EEA Joint Committee, the office of the President of the Committee is held alternately, for a period of one year (instead of six months) by a member from the EFTA side and by a member from the EU side. The Committee itself elects the person who is going to hold the office (Article 3 of Protocol 36 to the EEA Agreement). The Committee holds two ordinary meetings per year, which take place alternately in the EU and in an EFTA State (Article 4 of Protocol 36 to the EEA Agreement).

§4. EEA Consultative Committee

I. Functions

312. Pursuant to Article 96(1) of the EEA Agreement:

> Members of the Economic and Social Committee and other bodies representing the social partners in the Community and the corresponding bodies in the EFTA States shall work to strengthen contacts between them and cooperate in an organized and regular manner in order to enhance the awareness of the economic and social aspects of the growing interdependence of the economies of the Contracting Parties and of their interests within the context of the EEA.

313. Such cooperation between the social partners of the initial Contracting Parties preceded the conclusion of the EEA Agreement. The EFTA Consultative Committee, which existed since 1961, cooperated with its EC counterpart since 1980. The EEA Agreement has formalized that informal cooperation. Article 96(2) of the EEA Agreement thus establishes the EEA Consultative Committee.

314. Compared to the European Economic and Social Committee (EESC), the EEA Consultative Committee only plays a minor role, as it is not involved in the decision-making process under the EEA Agreement. For example, the EEA Consultative Committee does not have a right to receive draft decisions of the EEA Joint

271. *See* EFTA Factsheet, *EFTA & EEA Parliamentary Committees*, 1.

272. *See* R. Bieber, 'EWR-Abkommen und parlamentarische Zusammenarbeit', in *Accord EEE – Commentaires et réflexions* 786 (O. Jacot-Guillarmod ed., Zürich: Schulthess 1992).

273. Lately this weight seems to have diminished so much that sometimes the necessary quorum to adopt declarations cannot be attained due to lacking participation from the EU-members of the EEA Joint Parliamentary Committee.

Committee, in order to provide its opinion.[274] The difference between the two bodies reflects the very structure of the EEA Agreement: the decisions of the EEA Joint Committee are, in most cases, nothing more than an ex-post facto incorporation into the EEA Agreement of acquis communautaire in the fields covered by the EEA Agreement.[275] The substantive decisions are mostly taken within the EU pillar, on which the EFTA social partners may try to exercise influence indirectly via the EEA Consultative Committee.

315. The EEA Consultative Committee can express its views on any question that concerns the EEA Agreement. It can do so in the form of reports or resolutions (Article 96(2) of the EEA Agreement in fine), which are normally sent to the EEA Joint Committee or the EEA Council. The latter body would normally take note of them in the meetings.

II. Organization and Composition

316. The EEA Consultative Committee is composed of an equal number of members of the EESC and members of the EFTA Consultative Committee.[276] Contrary to what is the case in relation to the EEA Joint Parliamentary Committee, the EEA Agreement does not specify the number of members of the EEA Consultative Committee. Accordingly, the rules of procedure of the EEA Consultative Committee determine the number of members themselves. While originally the EEA Consultative Committee was composed of thirty members of each of the two Committees, the EEA Consultative Committee decided in January 1996 to reduce the number of members of each Committee to nine. Beyond its eighteen members, the rules of procedure of the EEA Consultative Committee allow both UNICE and ETUC to participate in its meetings as observers. As is the case in the parliamentary cooperation, Switzerland has observer status both in the EFTA and EEA Consultative Committees.

317. Initially, the EEA Consultative Committee intended to meet twice each year. However, after Austria, Finland and Sweden left the EFTA pillar to join the EU, it was decided to only hold one meeting per year, which is held alternately in an EU Member State or an EFTA State.

318. Although the meetings of the EEA Consultative Committee are the most visible result of Article 96(1) of the EEA Agreement, it is not the only means of cooperation between the social partners in the EEA. Article 96(1) of the EEA Agreement, which invites the members of the EESC and other bodies representing the social partners in the EU and the corresponding bodies in the EFTA States to

274. *See* C. Reymond, 'Institutions, Decision-making Procedure and Settlement of Disputes in the European Economic Area', *Common Market Law Review* (1993): 462.
275. *See* F. Weiss, 'The Oporto Agreement on the European Economic Area – A Legal Still Life', *Yearbook of European Law* 12 (1992): 421.
276. For a presentation of the EFTA Consultative Committee, *see supra* Part I, Ch. 2, §2, II.

strengthen contacts between them and cooperate in an organized and regular manner, allows for cooperation that goes beyond meetings in the framework of the EEA Consultative Committee.

319. Accordingly, the EEA Consultative Committee has established the so-called OSMOSIS procedure. It allows representatives of the EFTA Consultative Committee to participate in the work of EESC and vice versa. Through the OSMOSIS procedure, a regular dialogue has been established between the EFTA Consultative Committee and EESC. All this is proof of the fact that the cooperation between the social partners plays an important role in context of the EEA Agreement. Indeed, due to the OSMOSIS procedure the awareness of the EEA among the members of EESC has increased and is often reflected in opinions from EESC.

§5. The Standing Committee of the EFTA States

320. The Standing Committee of the EFTA States has been set up by a separate agreement between the EFTA States beyond their obligations under the EEA Agreement.[277] The main purpose of the Standing Committee of the EFTA States is to facilitate the elaboration of decisions to be taken by the EEA Council and the EEA Joint Committee.[278] The establishment of a Standing Committee of the EFTA States was considered necessary because the EFTA States are to speak with one voice in the EEA Joint Committee, as set out in Article 93(2) of the EEA Agreement.[279] The main function of the Standing Committee is thus to provide for a platform for political and legal discussions in the EFTA pillar, in order to have a coordinated approach, when a certain matter is taken up with the EU in either the EEA Council or, more frequently, in the EEA Joint Committee. Thus, the Standing Committee of the EFTA States ensures that political discussions between the EFTA States can be concluded before the relevant matter is discussed in those two institutions.

321. Initially, the EFTA States considered making use of the institutional structures foreseen by the EFTA Convention (i.e., the EFTA Council)[280] for the tasks allocated to the Standing Committee. However, for political and practical reasons, as well as because it was realized that it could not be excluded that one or more of the EFTA States could remain outside the EEA Agreement (as Switzerland indeed did), it was considered necessary to be able to differentiate between the cooperation of EFTA States on EEA matters and cooperation in other fields.[281] Eventually, the EFTA States agreed to set up a separate institution in the form of the Standing Committee.

---

277. Agreement on a Standing Committee of the EFTA States, signed in Porto on 2 May 1992. The Agreement is available on the EFTA Secretariat's website: www.efta.int/legal-texts/committees.
278. *See* recital 3 to the Standing Committee Agreement.
279. *See* S. Norberg et al., *The European Economic Area, EEA Law, A Commentary on the EEA Agreement* 685 (Stockholm: Fritzes 1993).
280. *See supra* Part I, Ch. 2, §2, I.
281. *See* S. Norberg et al., *The European Economic Area, EEA Law, A Commentary on the EEA Agreement* 685 (Stockholm: Fritzes 1993).

I. Functions

322. The Standing Committee carries out functions in respect of decision-making, administration and management, as well as consultations among EFTA States (Article 1(1) of the Standing Committee Agreement). The Standing Committee only carries out functions in connection with the EEA Agreement and does not have a mandate to discuss issues that are not of relevance for the EEA Agreement. It cannot be used to discuss matters that concern, for example, the EFTA Convention. For these matters the EFTA Council remains exclusively competent.

Because of the different tasks of which the Standing Committee is in charge, it is possible to distinguish its role as a forum for the preparations of the meetings of the EEA institutions and its role in the administration and management of the rules of the EEA Agreement.

A. Preparations of the Meetings of the EEA Institutions

323. Articles 90(2) and 93(2) of the EEA Agreement require the EFTA States to speak with one voice when it comes to adopting decisions in the EEA Council and the EEA Joint Committee. It is therefore necessary for the EFTA States to discuss their position in either of these meetings beforehand. The Standing Committee serves as a forum for discussion in this connection. Article 2 of the Standing Committee Agreement states that the EFTA States 'shall, when appropriate, consult within the Standing Committee for the purpose of taking decisions in the EEA Council and the EEA Joint Committee'.

324. The words 'when appropriate' indicate that the EFTA States have not accepted an obligation to hold consultations in the Standing Committee, from which they would be exempted in exceptional circumstances. They remain free to hold consultations outside the Standing Committee, as they occasionally do. This is in line with the fact that it is not EFTA as such, but the individual EFTA States that are Contracting Parties to the EEA Agreement.[282] It also corresponds to the very purpose of the Standing Committee, which is to facilitate the elaboration of decisions to be taken by the EEA institutions.

325. The practice with regard to Article 2 of the Standing Committee Agreement has been different depending on whether the EFTA States had to coordinate their views regarding decisions to be taken by the EEA Joint Committee or by the EEA Council. While the EFTA States' views on matters on the agenda of the EEA Joint Committee are mostly discussed in the Standing Committee, this is not the case regarding matters on the agenda of the EEA Council. Accordingly, the Standing Committee meets, almost systematically, on the eve of any meeting of the EEA Joint Committee. In contrast, it does normally not meet prior to a meeting of the EEA Council.

---

282. *See* S. Norberg et al., *The European Economic Area, EEA Law, A Commentary on the EEA Agreement* 687 (Stockholm: Fritzes 1993).

B. Administration and Management of the Rules of the EEA Agreement

326. Article 3 of the Standing Committee Agreement provides a long list of different tasks, which the Standing Committee is to carry out. Rather than listing these tasks in detail, the following is designed to categorize those tasks in a more systematic manner.

327. The first set of tasks follows from the application of Protocol 1 to the EEA Agreement on Horizontal adaptations to the EEA Agreement. Article 3(1)(a) of the Standing Committee Agreement explicitly refers to Protocol 1 to the EEA Agreement. The tasks concerned are review and reporting tasks and tasks in the context of procedures for verification or approval, information, notification or consultation and similar matters, which the European Commission is to carry out pursuant to acts referred to in the EEA Agreement.[283]

328. Protocol 1 to the EEA Agreement does not take a position on whether those tasks have to be carried out by the Standing Committee or the EFTA Surveillance Authority, but merely specifies that they shall be carried out according to procedures established among the EFTA States. The latter therefore had to define a division of the tasks. It can be found in Protocol 1 SCA and in Article 1 of Protocol 1 to the Standing Committee Agreement.

329. Protocol 1 SCA and Protocol 1 to the Standing Committee Agreement only contain a general description of the Standing Committee's and the Authority's respective tasks. It does not provide a clear picture of the competences of the Standing Committee and the Authority under Article 3(1)(a) of the Standing Committee Agreement. Therefore, and with a view to specifying the tasks of the Standing Committee and of the EFTA Surveillance Authority, the EFTA Secretariat draws up a non-binding list of the division of tasks identified in the acts that are incorporated into the EEA Agreement.

330. In general, it can be said that functions which are more related to surveillance or monitoring have been entrusted to the EFTA Surveillance Authority, while functions which include elements of a legislative or political nature, as well as certain administrative functions, remain within the remit of the Standing Committee.[284] It can nevertheless sometimes be difficult to ascertain whether a particular provision in an incorporated act entails a task of surveillance character, which is to be allocated to the EFTA Surveillance Authority.[285]

331. The remaining tasks which follow from the application of Protocol 1 to the EEA Agreement, are those mentioned in Article 3(1)(c) and (d) of the Standing

283. *See* paras 4(d) and 5 of Protocol 1 on Horizontal adaptations to the EEA Agreement.
284. *See* S. Norberg et al., *The European Economic Area, EEA Law, A Commentary on the EEA Agreement* 687 (Stockholm: Fritzes, 1993).
285. *See also* 'Adaptation texts to EU acts upon incorporation into the EEA Agreement', *EFTA Bulletin June 2019, Legal Notes by the EFTA Secretariat on the EEA Agreement,* 50.

Committee Agreement. These two provisions mirror paragraph 4(b) of Protocol 1 to the EEA Agreement and entrust the Standing Committee with a function of mailbox and dispatcher in a process of exchange of information.

The remaining tasks of the Standing Committee cannot be classified in either of the above-mentioned two main categories. The most important of these tasks are the tasks which the Standing Committee is to carry out under the EFTA comitology procedures. In the EFTA pillar, some of these executive powers are entrusted to the EFTA Surveillance Authority. With a view to providing the EFTA States with the same status in connection to these executive powers as enjoyed by the EU institutions, Article 3 of Protocol 1 to the SCA provides for the setting-up of EFTA comitology committees in which representatives of the EFTA States can be heard by the EFTA Surveillance Authority.

332. Following the modification of the comitology procedures on the EU side with a view of putting into practice Article 291 TFEU, the Standing Committee modified its own comitology procedures.[286] The procedures before the EFTA comitology committees are set out in Decision No. 3/2012/SC[287] and No. 4/2012/SC[288] of the Standing Committee.

333. Finally, the Standing Committee also exercises functions in the context of the settlement of disputes between the EFTA States in the field of transport[289] and lays down certain procedures in the veterinary field.[290]

II. Organization and Composition

A. *General Aspects*

334. Each EFTA State has a seat in the Standing Committee (Article 4(1) of the Standing Committee Agreement). The EFTA Surveillance Authority may attend meetings as observer, and the Standing Committee may invite any other person to sit in the meeting as observer as well. Accordingly, at its first meeting, the Standing Committee concluded that Switzerland is to be granted a permanent observer status in it.

---

286. *See* Regulation (EU) No. 182/2011 of the European Parliament and of the Council of 16 Feb. 2011 laying down the rules and general principles concerning mechanisms for control by Member States of the Commission's exercise of implementing powers (OJ L 55, 28.2.2011, 13).
287. Decision of the Standing Committee of the EFTA States No. 3/2012/SC of 26 Oct. 2012 laying down procedures for committees assisting the EFTA Surveillance Authority in carrying out its functions under Art. 3 of Protocol 1 to the Agreement between the EFTA States on the Establishment of a Surveillance Authority and a Court of Justice (OJ L 36, 7.2.2013, 5).
288. Decision of the Standing Committee of the EFTA States No. 4/2012/SC of 26 Oct. 2012 designating committees to assist the EFTA Surveillance Authority in carrying out its functions under Art. 3 of Protocol 1 to the Agreement between the EFTA States on the Establishment of a Surveillance Authority and a Court of Justice and repealing certain Standing Committee Decisions (OJ L 36, 7.2.2013, 8).
289. *See* Art. 3(1)(k) of the Standing Committee Agreement.
290. *See* Art. 3(1)(f) of the Standing Committee Agreement.

335. The rules of procedure[291] contain provisions on the office of the President. From 2005, the office of President is rotating between the different EFTA States every six months, starting with Norway, followed by Liechtenstein and Iceland.

336. Article 4 of the Standing Committee Agreement foresees that the meetings can be held at the level of Ministers or High Officials. It is the latter that is the norm: the Standing Committee normally meets at the level of the ambassadors (Heads of Missions of the EFTA States to the EU). These are the same persons that represent the EFTA States in the EEA Joint Committee. Meetings at other levels will be held in the subcommittees or other bodies set up pursuant to Article 5(1) of the Standing Committee Agreement (Article 4(2) of the Standing Committee Agreement).

337. As the Standing Committee serves as a forum for the preparations of the meetings of the EEA Joint Committee, it meets, in principle, as often as the EEA Joint Committee (i.e., about eight times per year). Normally, it meets on the day preceding the meetings of the EEA Joint Committee.

338. The meetings of the Standing Committee are conducted in English and, in principle, all the documents for the meetings are drawn up in English. Possible decisions and recommendations of the Standing Committee, which shall be published in the EEA Section of, and the EEA Supplement to, the Official Journal of the European Union, are, in principle, to be adopted in the official languages of the EU and of the EFTA States (Article 13 of the rules of procedure). However, for practical purposes, these decisions are normally adopted in English only and translated thereafter. There is no explicit decision on the authenticity of the remaining languages.

339. On 6 December 2007, the Standing Committee adopted Decision No. 3/2007/SC on public access to EFTA documents.[292] According to this decision, the EFTA Secretariat makes available to the public by placement on its website the documents listed in the Annex to the decision. In addition, any person may request, subject to some exceptions, access to EEA-related documents drawn up or received by the EFTA Secretariat that are in the EFTA Secretariat's possession.

B. Voting Arrangements

340. Pursuant to Article 6 of the Standing Committee Agreement, the Standing Committee may take decisions or make recommendations to the EFTA States. The decisions shall be binding on all the EFTA States. With a few exceptions, both the recommendations and the decisions are to be taken in principle by a unanimous

291. Decision of the Standing Committee of the EFTA States No. 1/94/SC of 10 Jan. 1994 adopting the Rules of Procedure of the Standing Committee of the EFTA States (OJ, L 85, 30.3.1994, 72), as amended. The rules of procedure are available on the EFTA Secretariat's website: www.efta.int/legal-texts/committees.

292. The Decision is available on the EFTA Secretariat's website: www.efta.int/legal-texts/public-access-archives.

vote, which shall be considered as achieved if no EFTA State casts a negative vote. However, in practice the Standing Committee almost never proceeds to a vote. It prefers to take its decisions by consensus.

341. In certain, exhaustively enumerated situations, the Standing Committee may take decisions by a majority vote. The cases in which majority voting applies are mentioned in the Annex to the Standing Committee Agreement. In essence, they concern certain instances where the Standing Committee may adopt decisions in cases referred to it under an EFTA comitology procedure,[293] or other cases in which it should be avoided that no decision would be taken at all.

C. Subcommittees and Working Groups

342. Like the EEA Joint Committee, the Standing Committee may set up subcommittees and other bodies to assist it in accomplishing its tasks. It has done so along the same lines as the EEA Joint Committee, with a view to facilitating the elaboration of the position to be taken by the EFTA States in the respective subcommittees under the EEA Joint Committee.[294] Accordingly, there are five subcommittees dealing with free movement of goods, free movement of capital and services, free movement of persons, horizontal and flanking policies and finally legal and institutional matters (respectively called subcommittees I, II, III, IV and V). These subcommittees mirror the above-mentioned subcommittees of the EEA Joint Committee. Initially all these subcommittees met independently. However, it was later agreed that it would be useful to streamline the work of subcommittees I, II, III and IV, and they were administratively merged. While the subcommittees formally continue to exist, they meet under one chairperson in one single meeting and the reports are drawn up in one single joint report covering all the four subcommittees. The EFTA Secretariat coordinates and prepares the meetings of the subcommittees.

343. The mandate of these subcommittees is to prepare the consultations to be held in the Standing Committee pursuant to Article 2 of the Standing Committee Agreement. In addition, they are to carry out any other task delegated to them (Article 18 of the rules of procedure). Accordingly, most subcommittees meet at the same frequency as the Standing Committee and the EEA Joint Committee. Subcommittee V on legal and institutional matters has met less frequently. This can be explained by the fact that it is not as directly involved in the decision-making procedure of the Standing Committee and the EEA Joint Committee.[295]

---

293. The appendix to the Annex to the Standing Committee Agreement further specifies the cases of EFTA comitology procedure in which the EFTA States decide by majority.

294. The subcommittees are set up pursuant to Art. 5 of the Agreement on a Standing Committee of the EFTA States and Art. 18 of the Decision of the Standing Committee of the EFTA States No. 1/94/SC (Rules of Procedure of the Standing Committee).

295. *See* A. Entner-Koch and K. Isaksen, 'Subcommittee V and the legal work of the EFTA Secretariat in Brussels', *EFTA Bulletin* June 2019, 4.

344. The rules of procedure of the Standing Committee allow its subcommittees to establish working groups for individual tasks. However, the entry into force of a decision to establish a working group remains subject to approval by the Standing Committee. The same procedure must apply in case the mandate of a working group needs to be changed.

345. The working groups that have been established by the subcommittees each deal with a specific substantive matter under the EEA Agreement, such as financial services, transport, public procurement, environment, etc. Each working group has the right to establish expert groups. Currently, there are thirty Working Groups and twenty-three Expert Groups.

346. Of all these committees and groups only subcommittee V on legal and institutional matters has a mandate that can be considered as dealing with horizontal matters. Subcommittee V consists of legal experts within the Governments of the EFTA States and meets regularly to discuss issues on the subcommittee's own initiative or upon request by the Standing Committee. The EFTA Surveillance Authority attends subcommittee V meetings.

D. The ESA/Court Committee

347. The 'ESA/Court Committee', as commonly referred to, is the Committee of Representatives of the Contracting Parties[296] to the SCA. This Committee has the task of handling the review of the SCA and establishing the budgets of the two bodies, i.e., of the EFTA Surveillance Authority (ESA) and the EFTA Court. Their financial statements are also being accepted or rejected by this Committee. In addition, the ESA/Court Committee also appoints the judges of the EFTA Court, including ad hoc judges, and the members of the College of the EFTA Surveillance Authority, including its ad hoc members. The ESA/Court Committee can also issue decisions, e.g., on occupational activities of judges.

348. Members of the ESA/Court Committee are the ambassadors of the three EEA-EFTA States. They normally meet once or twice towards the end of the year, after the budgets have been presented.

§6. The EFTA Surveillance Authority

I. Tasks and Status

349. From the early days of the negotiations, it was clear that the EEA Agreement had to ensure that a surveillance mechanism corresponding to that of the European Commission be created for the EFTA States.[297] For that reason, Article 108 of

296. Iceland, Liechtenstein and Norway.
297. *See supra* Part II, Ch. 1, §2, III.

the EEA Agreement requires the EFTA States to establish an independent surveillance authority that shall monitor the application of the EEA Agreement in relation to the EFTA States in the same way as the European Commission monitors the implementation and application of the EEA Agreement within the EU. To this end, the EFTA Surveillance Authority ('the Authority') was established by the SCA.[298] Article 108 of the EEA Agreement also states that the procedures pertaining to the Authority shall be similar to those existing in the EU. Provisions implementing this obligation are to be found in the SCA. The operation of the Authority is governed by its Rules of Procedure.[299]

350. The Authority is an independent international institution. This status and its institutional set-up aim to ensure its independence vis-à-vis the EFTA States and also EFTA itself. Independence as regards EFTA was deemed necessary because EFTA, as such, is an intergovernmental organization of traditional character lacking the corresponding supranational structure of the EU.[300] Originally the plan was that the Authority should be placed in Geneva. However, when it became clear that Switzerland was not going to ratify the EEA Agreement, a decision was taken to place the Authority in Brussels – a location that has the advantage of allowing frequent meetings with the European Commission.

351. According to Article 5(1) SCA, the Authority has the following tasks: (a) It ensures the fulfilment, by the EFTA States, of their obligations under the EEA Agreement and the SCA itself. To this end, the Authority may pursue infringement procedures against EFTA States for their failures to comply with EEA law.[301] (b) It ensures the application of the EEA Agreement in the field of competition. In this respect, the Authority takes, for example, decisions in the areas of CSA.[302] (c) Finally, it monitors the application of the EEA Agreement by the other Contracting Parties. The latter task has been given to the Authority as it is in a better position to follow the application of the Agreement by the EU side, although it is in practice not equipped to carry out this task in a systematic way. Should the Authority detect problems in the way the EU side applies the EEA Agreement, it can raise the issue according to the general rules on cooperation and consultation laid down in Article 109 of the EEA Agreement. It can, furthermore, bring the matter up for discussion in the EEA Joint Committee. As the Authority's competence to monitor the other

298. Agreement between the EFTA States on the Establishment of a Surveillance Authority and a Court of Justice, OJ L 344, 31.1.1994, 3, as amended. *See* in particular Arts 4–21 SCA.
299. EFTA Surveillance Authority Rules of Procedure, adopted 7 Jan. 1994 and most recently amended by College Decision No. 004/21/COL of 3 Feb. 2021 (OJ L 179, 20.5.2021, 63).
300. *See* S. Norberg, 'The EFTA Court, One of the Two Main Components of the EEA Judicial Mechanism', in *The European Economic Area EC-EFTA* 9 (23) (Stuyck & Looijestijn-Clearie eds, Dordrecht: Kluwer 2000). The Authority has a headquarters agreement with the Belgian State. Moreover, according to Protocol 6 to the Surveillance and Court Agreement, the Authority possesses legal personality. This protocol also lays down rules concerning immunity of the Authority as such, just as it contains rules on immunity for the Members of the Authority (the College Members) and other servants of the Authority in relation to the EFTA States.
301. *See infra* Part II, Ch. 5, §1, I and §2, I.
302. *See infra* Part II, Ch. 5, §1, II, C.

Contracting Parties only flows from the SCA, and not the EEA Agreement itself, the Authority has had no specific powers against EU institutions or EU Member States conferred upon it.

352. According to Article 5(2) SCA, the Authority shall perform its surveillance tasks by (a) taking decisions and other measures in cases provided for in the EEA Agreement and the SCA; (b) formulating recommendations, delivering opinions and issuing notices or guidelines on matters dealt with in the EEA Agreement; (c) carrying out cooperation, exchange of information and consultations with the European Commission; and (d) carrying out the functions which, through the application of Protocol 1 to the EEA Agreement, follow from the acts referred to in the Annexes to the Agreement.

353. These latter functions entail that the Authority also performs a wide range of tasks of an administrative character, which match those performed by the European Commission. Generally speaking, these tasks relate to EEA rules the proper application of which is not only subject to the general surveillance function, but to more direct control by the Authority. The tasks often mean that the Authority, under procedures presupposing an exchange of information between the EFTA and EU sides, is to take measures that are to have an effect throughout the entire EEA. Typical tasks of this kind are the approval of certain administrative decisions taken by the EFTA States such as measures restricting the free circulation of goods in order to protect human health, or the refusal to recognize diplomas or licences. The Authority undertakes these kinds of tasks in most fields of activity. However, they are of particular importance in the sector of free movement of goods, notably in relation to technical regulations, standards, testing and certification and animal health. These tasks include, for instance, an assessment of the application of the provisions laid down in the acts relating to border inspection posts, fresh meat and meat products and fish. Most of these tasks are regulated in acts corresponding to directives and regulations.

354. Following the UK's departure from the EU, the EEA-EFTA States reached an agreement with the UK known as the Separation Agreement.[303] The Separation Agreement guarantees UK nationals and their family members living in the EEA-EFTA States many of the same rights that were previously protected by EEA law, including the right to work, study and travel freely between the UK and the EEA and to live in the EEA-EFTA States. The Authority has been tasked with overseeing the implementation and application in the EEA-EFTA States of Part Two of the Separation Agreement.[304] Part Two is entitled 'Citizens' Rights'. This means that the Authority is responsible for monitoring that the rights of UK nationals are respected in Norway, Iceland and Liechtenstein.

303. *See supra* Part II, Ch. 1, §2, V.
304. *See* Art. 44a SCA and Art. 2 of Protocol 9 SCA.

II. The College

355. The governing body of the Authority is the College. College Members can be compared to European Commissioners. Initially, it was the intention that the College should consist of seven members. However, since the accession of Sweden, Finland and Austria to what is now the EU, the College has been made up of three members. The College Members are appointed for renewable mandates of four years by common accord of the Governments of the EFTA States.[305] As with European Commissioners, College Members are to be chosen on the grounds of their general competence. In contrast to European Commissioners, however, the practice has hitherto been that notably high officials from the respective countries' foreign services, rather than politicians, have been appointed. This difference can be explained by the fact that the Authority is not entrusted with the task of formulating proposals for future EEA rules but solely functions as a supervisory organ; it is more technocratic than political. At the same time, the fact that College Members have in many cases been career civil servants or diplomats has been criticized by some.[306]

356. The College Members are, in language mirroring that found in Article 17(3) TEU concerning the European Commission, required to be completely independent in the performance of their duties. Article 8(1) SCA further enunciates that they shall neither seek, nor take, instructions from any Government or other body, and that each EFTA State undertakes to respect this principle and not to seek to influence the College Members in the performance of their tasks.

357. According to Article 8(2) SCA, the College Members shall not, during their term of office, engage in any other occupation, whether gainful or not. This requirement has been rendered more concrete by the Rules of Conduct adopted by the College itself.[307] Those Rules provide that College Members are to comply strictly with the prohibition in Article 8(2) SCA. 'Supplying a regular flow of press articles' is expressly considered an occupation and therefore precluded. College Members are permitted to accept speaking engagements and to teach on matters concerning European integration but are precluded from accepting any payments. The only exception in this regard concerns the publication of books, which is permitted with prior information of the President, and in respect of which royalties may be received. The Code of Conduct for members of Staff of the Authority expressly does not apply to College Members.

358. The EFTA States do not have the power to force College Members to step down. It is only College Members no longer fulfilling the conditions required for the performance of their duties or having been found guilty of serious misconduct that may be compulsorily retired by the EFTA Court, on application by the Authority.

305. Article 9 SCA.

306. Baudenbacher, 'Restoring the Balance in the European Economic Area', *European Law Reporter* (2021): 97.

307. Minutes of the College Meeting of 27 Mar. 1996, Doc No. 96-2152-I, COL020.000.34.

359. The President of the Authority represents the Authority as a whole publicly and oversees its administration. Meetings of the College are convened by the President, who is also responsible for the communication and publication of decisions of the Authority. The President is appointed among its Members for a period of two years by common accord between the Governments of the EFTA States (Article 12 SCA). Since the establishment of the Authority, the Presidency has practically always been held by a Norwegian.[308]

360. Pursuant to Article 14 SCA, the Authority acts by a majority of its College Members.[309] However, the decisions are normally taken by consensus. The Authority functions on the basis of the same principle of collegiate responsibility as the European Commission. Based on usually weekly meetings, the College takes decisions concerning, *inter alia*, the pursuit of infringement procedures or decisions in the field of State aid and competition. Meetings of the College are not normally public and deliberations are confidential.[310] In addition to the default procedure of taking decisions at College Meetings, decisions can also be adopted by Written Procedure[311] or in the form of Delegated Decisions,[312] by a single College Member acting pursuant to an empowerment. Decisions adopted by either one of these procedures are recorded in the minutes of a subsequent College Meeting.

361. According to the Authority's Rules of Procedure, the College assigns to each Member the responsibility for the preparation and implementation of its decisions in a particular field, referred to as a portfolio.[313] The College routinely empowers College Members to take, within their portfolios, clearly defined measures of management or administration and to adopt the definitive text of a decision, the substance of which has been determined by the College.[314] This division of tasks between the College Members does not curtail the collective responsibility of the College but merely means that each College Member can, in daily practice, focus on a particular area. In order to prevent individual College Members from unduly delaying the adoption of decisions (notably concerning infringement procedures) within their portfolios, the Rules of Procedure require any item that is still

308. The only exception consisted in the seventeen months during which the Icelandic College Member, Hannes Hafstein, held the Presidency, starting on 1 Jan. 2004.
309. *See also* Art. 8 of the Rules of Procedure.
310. Articles 9(2) and 10(1) of the Rules of Procedure. In addition, Art. 14(4) SCA contains a general provision on professional secrecy for both the College Members and the Authority's officials. This provision is modelled on the corresponding provision in Art. 339 TFEU and interpreted in accordance with the case law pertaining to that provision.
311. Article 12 of the Rules of Procedure.
312. Article 13 of the Rules of Procedure.
313. Article 3 of the Rules of Procedure. Information as to the division of portfolios can be found on the Authority's website. The President traditionally oversees the LEA as well as Administration departments and has substantive responsibility for State aid, being the portfolio of greatest practical importance for Norway.
314. Also officials may be empowered to take clearly defined measures of management or administration if this proves indispensable for the Authority to properly fulfil its tasks. These powers may not be subdelegated, except to the extent expressly laid down in the enabling decision. That being said, Art. 5 of the Authority's Rules of Procedure contains rules on deputizing.

pending more than six months after approval by the Director of Legal and Executive Affairs (LEA) to be placed on the draft agenda of the first College Meeting of every month.[315] In this way, it is only by unanimity that the item can be removed from the draft agenda again,[316] meaning that any one College Member can at least force a vote on the matter, which is then required to be recorded in the minutes of the College Meeting.[317]

III. The Organization

362. The budget of the Authority is established by the Governments of the EFTA States.[318] Contrary to the position of the EU, which operates on the basis of a multiannual financial framework spanning seven years, the Authority's budget is set on an annual basis. While, according to Article 14 SCA, the Authority has the competence to hire its staff, as this competence must be exercised within the budget framework set by the EFTA States, this has, in practice, a substantial influence on the Authority's ability to fulfil its functions. The Authority has never had substantially more than a hundred staff, i.e., less than 0.3% of the staff of the European Commission. Moreover, staff are employed on three-year fixed-term contracts, which are normally renewed once only, leading to significant staff turnover. In addition, a sizeable proportion of staff are employed on one-year contracts or as trainees, known as 'junior professionals'. Many EU nationalities are usually represented among the staff, approximately half of whom come from the EEA-EFTA States.

363. The Authority's organizational structure comprises four departments.[319] The Internal Market Affairs (IMA) and CSA directorates assemble the Authority's subject matter expertise in their respective purviews and are responsible for the day-to-day application and enforcement of EEA law in those areas. The LEA department supports the College Members in the adoption of formal decisions, the legality of which it reviews, and fulfils horizontal coordination duties regarding policy formulation and communication. LEA represents the Authority in court proceedings and also comprises the Authority's Communications Unit. All departments are supported by the Administration department with regard to matters such as human resources, financial planning, information technology and facility management.

364. The departments work in close cooperation. Before submitting a proposal for a decision to the College, the department preparing the proposal consults all other departments that are concerned in the matter. The LEA department must be consulted on proposals for legal instruments and measures which may have legal implications. The Administration department is consulted on proposals which may have budgetary implications.

---

315. Article 9(1) of the Rules of Procedure.
316. Article 9(4) of the Rules of Procedure.
317. Article 11 of the Rules of Procedure.
318. Article 47 SCA.
319. Article 4 of the Rules of Procedure.

365. The working language of the Authority is English. According to Article 20 SCA, individuals and economic operators are entitled to address and be addressed by the Authority in any official language of the EFTA States and the EU as regards notifications, applications and complaints, but most choose English. In contrast, communication with the EFTA States is carried out exclusively in English.

366. Access to documents held by the Authority is regulated under its Rules on Public Access to Documents.[320] Anyone can request public access to any document, and the requester is not obliged to state any reason for the public access request. The main rule is that documents should be publicly available. There are, however, some exemptions, which give the Authority a right to refuse disclosure of certain documents. Most of these exemptions are found in Article 4 of the Rules on Public Access to Documents.

§7. The EFTA Court

I. Organizational Issues

367. According to Article 108(2) of the EEA Agreement, the EFTA States shall establish a court of justice. By way of the SCA, the EFTA States have established the EFTA Court (Article 27 SCA). The organization of the Court is further detailed in its Rules of Procedure.[321]

368. The EFTA Court is an independent international institution – a status that was deemed necessary in order to ensure its independence from the EFTA States, taking into account the fact that EFTA, as such, is an intergovernmental organization of traditional character lacking the corresponding supranational structure of the EU. As stated in Article 1 of Protocol 7 SCA, the EFTA Court thus has legal personality as an international institution.

II. The Judges

369. Originally, the intention was that the Court should consist of seven members. When Switzerland decided not to join, the number was reduced to five and fell again to three, when Austria, Finland and Sweden joined the EU.[322] The same development also made the remaining EFTA States decide, in December 1994, to move

320. EFTA Surveillance Authority Rules on Public Access to Documents. Adopted on 3 Mar. 2021 by College Decision No. 015/21/COL (Date of entry into force: 8 Mar. 2021). The Rules are available on the Authority's website: www.eftasurv.int/esa-at-a-glance/publications/public-access-to-documents.
321. Rules of Procedure of the EFTA Court (OJ L 179, 20.5.2021, 13).
322. *See* Art. 28 SCA. Former president of the EFTA Court, T. Vilhjálmsson, 'EFTA-domstolen', in *Rettsteori og Rettsliv – Festskrift til Carsten Smith* 897 (899) (Lødrup et al. eds, Oslo: Universitetsforlaget 2002), argues that the number of judges has become too few compared to the kind of work that the Court has to perform.

the Court from Geneva (the historical place of the EFTA institutions) to Luxembourg. Since September 1996 the EFTA Court has thus been situated next to the CJEU. The Court remains permanently in session and judges and the registrar are required to reside at the place where the Court has its seat.

370. The formal requirements regarding the qualifications for being appointed as a judge in the EFTA Court are the same as those pertaining to judges in the CJEU (Article 30 SCA). Consequently, the judges shall be chosen from persons whose independence is beyond doubt and who possess the qualifications required for appointment to the highest judicial offices in their respective countries or who are 'jurisconsults' of recognized competence. There is no requirement as to the nationality of the judges. Indeed, the President of the EFTA Court, from 2003 until the end of 2017, was Carl Baudenbacher, a Swiss national. The appointments of the judges are decided by common accord of the Governments of the EFTA States and are for a term of six years. As in the CJEU, retiring judges are eligible for reappointment (Article 30 SCA). If, in the opinion of the two other judges, one of the judges is disqualified from acting in a particular case, the two other judges shall agree to replace him with an ad hoc judge chosen from a list established by common accord by the Governments of the EFTA States.

371. The judges themselves elect their President for a period of three years. The President may be re-elected (Article 30 SCA). The President since 1 January 2018 is Páll Hreinsson.[323] According to Article 9 of the Court's Rules of Procedure, the President shall direct the judicial business and the administration of the Court as well as preside at hearings and deliberations.

III. The Registrar and Other Officials and Servants of the Court

372. Pursuant to Article 11 of the Court's Rules of Procedure, the Court itself appoints its Registrar. The responsibilities of the Registrar are laid down in the Court's 'Instructions to the Registrar' and correspond largely to those of the registrars of the CJEU and the General Court.[324] In consequence, the Registrar has, under the authority of the President, the responsibility for, *inter alia*, the administration of the Court (including its Registry), its financial management, its accounts and, finally, certain procedural issues. The Court appoints the Registrar for a renewable three-year term. In addition to the Judges and the Registrar, the EFTA Court currently employs fifteen persons. Each judge is assisted by two legal secretaries and one secretary.

323. On 22 Nov. 2023, the Judges of the EFTA Court re-elected Páll Hreinsson as President for a third term ending on 31 Dec. 2026.

324. The Instructions were adopted by the EFTA Court on 7 Apr. 1994 and subsequently amended on 22 Aug. 1996. The few differences concerning the instruction to the respective registrars are summarized by, S. Norberg, 'The EFTA Court', in *European Courts, Practice and Precedents* 77 (116–117) (Plender ed., London: Sweet & Maxwell 1997).

IV. Privileges and Immunities

373. The privileges and immunities accorded by the EFTA States to the EFTA Court are laid down in Protocol 7 SCA. The first six articles, in Part I, of the protocol concern the Court itself, including its legal personality and various immunities in relation to jurisdiction and execution, the archives of the Court, its financial assets, exemption from taxes and custom duties and unhindered right to communication. In Part II, the following Articles 7–9 regulate the privileges and immunities of the judges, the registrar and other officials and servants of the Court. Finally, in Part III, Articles 10–13 address the circumstances under which the Court should waive the listed privileges and immunities.

374. Moreover, according to Article 44(2) SCA, the Court may conclude, with the government of the State in whose territory it is situated (i.e., Luxembourg), an agreement relating to privileges and immunities to be recognized and granted in connection with it. By a so-called Headquarters Agreement of 17 April 1996, the Court has been conferred status, privileges and immunities similar to those enjoyed by the CJEU. The Grand Duchy of Luxembourg thus, *inter alia*, recognizes the international legal personality and capacity of the Court. It ensures the inviolability of the premises of the EFTA Court and its archives. The Headquarters Agreement, furthermore, confers immunities on persons required to attend the Court for official purposes. It is explicitly stated that the privileges and immunities conferred by the Agreement have the sole purpose of securing the unhindered functioning of the Court and the complete independence of the persons concerned.

V. Procedural Issues

375. The Rules of Procedure of the EFTA Court are to a large extent based upon those of the CJEU. For instance, there is no possibility for dissenting opinions. However, on several points the rules concerning the EFTA Court differ from those concerning the CJEU.

376. First, the Court always delivers its judgments in plenum (Article 29 SCA and Article 82 of the Court's Rules of Procedure). Originally, when the Court was intended to have five members, it was felt that plenary decisions were preferable, at least until more experience had been gained. With the present number of three judges, the possibility for establishing chambers was removed.

377. Second, the EFTA Court does not have Advocates General.

378. Third, there exists no EFTA Court of First Instance similar to the General Court. When the Court was established, it was not considered that its workload would be such as to warrant two bodies, and experience has proven that prognosis correct. Partly for that reason, the procedure before the EFTA Court is quite fast, as compared with that before the EU Courts, cases usually taking less than a year to decide.

379. A fourth difference is that the Registrar shall notify the Governments of the EFTA States, the EFTA Surveillance Authority, the Union and the European Commission of any case before the Court (Article 20 of the Court's Statute). The corresponding provision in the CJEU statute only refers to cases under Article 267 TFEU (i.e., the procedure on preliminary rulings) and is, furthermore, limited to cases where a field covered by the EEA Agreement is concerned. The difference shows that the EFTA States felt it important that, in order to secure the homogeneous interpretation, the EU pillar should also be notified about all cases before the EFTA Court, regardless of whether the case takes the form of an advisory opinion, an infringement procedure or an action for annulment. EU Member States often submit observations in cases before the EFTA Court.

380. The working language of the EFTA Court is English (Article 29 of the Court's Rules of Procedure). This covers the entire procedure, including deliberations and decisions of the Court, just as English is used both in the written and oral procedure by the parties, the interveners, the EFTA Surveillance Authority and the EU institutions. In principle, this also applies to documents submitted to the Court, thus requiring the party in question to provide an English translation. The decision to opt for English only was taken in order to restrict the investment in linguistic resources and to shorten the duration of the proceedings. Moreover, the working language in EFTA had always been English, just as the negotiations on the EEA Agreement had been conducted in English.

381. Requests concerning advisory opinions may nevertheless be posed in the language of the national court asking for the opinion.[325] Moreover, both the requesting court and the parties to the dispute in the main proceedings may submit documents in the language in which that case is dealt with before that court. The same parties are, furthermore, entitled to address and be addressed by the Court in that language. The report for the hearing and the advisory opinion itself is given both in English and in the language of the referring court.

§8. EEA-EFTA Forum of Elected Representatives from Local and Regional Authorities

382. In 2009, the EFTA States set up an EEA-EFTA Forum of elected representatives from local and regional authorities (the Forum).[326] Its main aim is to involve municipalities and regions of the EFTA States in the EEA work and to facilitate regular consultations with the EU Committee of the Regions. The reason why such a forum had not been introduced by the EEA Agreement itself may in all likelihood be found in the fact that the EU Committee of the Regions was itself only established in 1994, that is, after the signing of the EEA Agreement. However, the Forum

325. Article 30(1) of the Court's Rules of Procedure.

326. Decision of the Standing Committee of the EFTA States No. 10/2009/SC of 3 Dec. 2009 establishing a Forum of Elected Representatives of Local and Regional Authorities of the EFTA Member States (not published in the OJ or in the EEA Supplements to the OJ).

was initially planned to be an EFTA body. But after Switzerland changed its position and did not participate as a full member it was decided to establish it as an EEA-EFTA body.

383. The Forum is composed of up to six members or alternate members from each EFTA State, which shall elect their Chairman from among themselves. Switzerland participates with the status of an observer. This being said, as Liechtenstein is not divided into regions and its local authorities have a limited need for regular consultations, Liechtenstein has for the time being decided not to participate in the Forum. In addition to the members or alternate members, representatives of the EEA-EFTA States, the Secretary-General of EFTA and experts of the regional and local authorities of the EEA-EFTA States may attend the meetings of the Forum and take part in its deliberations. Voting rights are, however, strictly limited to the members or alternate members.

§9. Financial Mechanisms (Cohesion Funds)

384. When the EEA Agreement was signed, the EEA-EFTA States agreed to contribute to reducing 'the social and economic disparities between their regions'.[327] For this purpose a Financial Mechanism, in EU terms: a cohesion fund was established. This, however, did not end after five years, as the wording of Article 2(5) of Protocol 38 to the EEA Agreement might suggest. Subsequently, another 'Financial Instrument' was established. In the period 1999–2003, the beneficiary states Greece, Ireland, Northern Ireland, Portugal and Spain received EUR 119.6 million. In 2004, with the enlargement of the EU and subsequently the EEA[328] by ten new Member States, the EFTA States and the EU agreed that the EFTA States should continue to contribute to the reduction of economic and social disparities between their regions. For that purpose they adopted Protocol 38a on an EEA Financial Mechanism. The contribution of the EFTA States, now also called 'EEA Grants', amounted to EUR 600 million over a period of five years, and Norway agreed to complement this amount by another EUR 567 million (the so-called Norway Grants). In 2007 Bulgaria and Romania were included as beneficiary states. Both the EEA and the Norway Grants were extended beyond the period 2009–2014, with the subsequent inclusion of Croatia as a beneficiary state in 2014. The amounts provided for this period are respectively EUR 988.5 million and EUR 800 million.[329] For the 2014–2021 period another Financial Mechanism was agreed between the EEA-EFTA States and the EU. Again, Norway has committed to an

327. Article 115 of the EEA Agreement.
328. Article 128(1) of the EEA Agreement.
329. *See* Art. 2 of Protocol 38b to the EEA Agreement and Art. 2 of the Agreement between the Kingdom of Norway and the EU on a Norwegian Financial Mechanism for the period 2009–2014. The Norwegian grants are directly managed by the Norwegian Ministry of Foreign Affairs.

additional bilateral mechanism ('the Norway Grants'). For the period of now seven years a total contribution of EUR 2.8 billion was set out.[330]

385. It is important to note that these funds are managed by the EEA-EFTA States alone and are not part of the EU budget in any way.

386. With a view to managing the EEA Grants, the Standing Committee of the EFTA States established a Financial Mechanism Committee.[331] Although having been established by the Standing Committee, the Financial Mechanism Committee cannot be considered being part of the Standing Committee's substructure in the same way as the subcommittees and working groups previously mentioned.[332]

387. The Financial Mechanism Committee is composed of one representative of each EFTA State, each representative having one vote. Pursuant to Article 5 of the Standing Committee Decision No. 4/2004/SC of 3 June 2004 establishing a Financial Mechanism Committee, the Financial Mechanism Committee takes its decisions by unanimous vote. Failing unanimity, each representative may bring the matter before the Standing Committee. This being said, if one representative opposes the award of a grant, the grant shall be considered as definitively rejected. The decision rejecting the grant may not be referred to the Standing Committee.

388. In its beginnings the Financial Mechanism was administered by a small number of people within the EFTA Secretariat. It goes without saying that the Financial Mechanism Committee, with the increase in beneficiaries and funds, could not on its own manage the full operations of the EEA Grants without some kind of support from a permanent body, as hundreds of projects have been awarded support through the EEA Grants. Therefore, the Standing Committee has established an Office for the EEA Financial Mechanism and the Norwegian Financial Mechanism[333] with the task of *inter alia* assisting in the management of the EEA and Norwegian Financial Mechanisms. The Office is administratively a part of the EFTA Secretariat. It, however, has a separate administrative budget, financed by the EEA and Norwegian Financial Mechanisms on a ratio based on their respective costs.[334]

330. *See* Art. 2 Protocol 38c to the EEA Agreement and Art. 2 of the Agreement between the Kingdom of Norway and the EU on a Norwegian Financial Mechanism for the period 2014–2021. On 1 Dec. 2023 the EEA-EFTA States and the EU reached an agreement on the contribution for the period 2021–2028.

331. *See* Decision of the Standing Committee of the EFTA States No. 4/2004/SC of 3 Jun. 2004 establishing a Financial Mechanism Committee (OJ L 54, 23.2.2005, 54). The mandate of the Financial Mechanism Committee, which was originally limited to the period up to 2009, was subsequently extended by Decision of the Standing Committee of the EFTA States No. 5/2010/SC of 9 Dec. 2010 amending Decision of the Standing Committee of the EFTA States No. 4/2004/SC establishing a Financial Mechanism Committee (OJ L 78, 24.3.2011, 57) to also include the management of the EEA Grants for the period 2009–2014.

332. *See supra* Part II, Ch. 3, §5, II, C.

333. *See* Decision of the Standing Committee of the EFTA States No. 1/2004/SC of 5 Feb. 2004 establishing an Office for the EEA Financial Mechanism and the Norwegian Financial Mechanism (OJ L 332, 30.11.2006, 34).

334. *See* Art. 1(6) of the Decision of the Standing Committee of the EFTA States No. 1/2004/SC.

Depending on whether the Office deals with a matter under the EEA Grants or the Norway Grants, it reports to the Financial Mechanism Committee or the Norwegian authorities. Currently there are about seventy people working in the Financial Mechanism Office (FMO).[335]

335. More information on the EEA and Norway Grants is available under the following website: www.eeagrants.org.

Chapter 4. The Decision-Making Process in the EEA

389. As has been indicated above,[336] the EEA Agreement is based on the principle of homogeneity. The same rules should apply in both the EU and in the EEA, in particular in the EFTA States. Accordingly, at the time of the signing of the EEA Agreement, the then existing relevant EC rules were, to a large extent, reflected in the EEA Agreement. However, as the internal market rules of the Community would further develop after the signing of the EEA Agreement, the homogeneity achieved in the negotiations for the EEA Agreement would disappear over time if no mechanism were found for a parallel development of the two legal orders. For the EEA Agreement to function, an institutional mechanism had to be set up for this parallel development to take place. In other words, the principle of homogeneity had to contain a dynamic element.

390. When designing this institutional mechanism, the negotiators faced several, to a certain degree conflicting, demands from either side. On the one hand, the Community required that its decision-making autonomy with regard to its internal rules be safeguarded. On the other hand, the EFTA States required participation in the decision-making process of the decisions to which they would subsequently be subjected. Finally, the EFTA States were not able to accept a transfer of decision-making power to a supranational body.[337]

391. The solution eventually adopted constitutes a compromise between the different requirements of the negotiating parties in the light of the principle of homogeneity. The key provisions of the solution are found in Articles 98–103 of the EEA Agreement.

392. First, the Community's decision-making autonomy remained intact. The EFTA States have neither been granted a vote in the EU decision-making process, nor has the greater recourse to qualified majority voting that has been enacted with various changes to the treaties on the EU side, been undermined by external obligations vis-à-vis the EFTA States. Subject to the requirements of Article 97 of the EEA Agreement,[338] the EU has remained free to develop its internal legislation, which is subsequently to be extended to the entire EEA.

393. Second, the EFTA States have been granted a certain degree of involvement in the EU decision-shaping process (as opposed to decision-making). At the important stages of the EU policy cycle, they have been granted the right to express

---

336. *See supra* Part II, Ch. 2, §1, I–II.
337. *See supra* Part II, Ch. 2, §2, II.
338. Article 97 of the EEA Agreement: 'This Agreement does not prejudge the right for each Contracting Party to amend, without prejudice to the principle of non-discrimination and after having informed the other Contracting Parties, its internal legislation in the areas covered by this Agreement: – if the EEA Joint Committee concludes that the legislation as amended does not affect the good functioning of this Agreement; or – if the procedures referred to in Art. 98 have been completed.'

their views and give advice on acts to be adopted by the EU institutions. This right was, and still is, one of the political and constitutional prerequisites for the EFTA States' acceptance of the Agreement.

394. Third, for a new piece of EU legislation to be applicable in the EEA, it has to be formally incorporated into the EEA Agreement. With a view to so doing, the EEA Joint Committee amends Annexes or Protocols to the EEA Agreement by including a reference to the EU act in the relevant Annex or Protocol. Accordingly, the adoption of an EU act in the EU pillar does not ipso facto lead to a modification of the EEA rules. The EFTA States' opposition to a transfer of decision-making power to a supranational body was thus respected.

395. Finally, the principle of homogeneity is reflected in Article 102(1) of the EEA Agreement, which provides that the EEA Joint Committee takes a decision concerning the amendment of an Annex to the EEA Agreement, in order to 'guarantee the legal security and the homogeneity of the EEA'. The introduction of the principle of homogeneity at this point does not transform that principle into a legal obligation for the EFTA States to take over, unconditionally, all EU acts that might be considered relevant for the functioning of the EEA Agreement. It serves more as a political guiding principle. Accordingly, the EEA Joint Committee remains free, in principle, not to incorporate an EU act that would fall within the scope of the EEA Agreement.

396. When including this solution into the structure of the EEA Agreement, the Contracting Parties preferred the term 'decision-making' as it was considered much less sensitive than the term 'law-making' and, thus, would be much less likely to create difficulties in the ratification procedures in the EFTA countries. Moreover, as one scholar put it, the term 'law-making' would have been incorrect anyway; not only is the entire complex and scarcely transparent procedure little more than 'collective and reactive' ex-post facto implementation of EU law in the EEA, it does not normally even involve a substantive decision-making procedure.[339] Indeed, EEA law can only reflect the substance of EU law, subject to certain adaptations. It cannot constitute completely independent rules that have no counterpart in EU law. For that reason, it has been argued in legal literature that the EEA decision-making to a large extent consists of a one-way process in which the EFTA States follow their EU counterparts.[340]

339. F. Weiss, 'The Oporto Agreement on the European Economic Area – A Legal Still Life', *Yearbook of European Law* 12 (1992): 385.

340. F. Sejersted, 'Between Sovereignty and Supranationalism in the EEA Context – On the Legal Dynamics of the EEA Agreement', in *The European Economic Area – Norway's Basic Status in the Legal Construction of Europe* 43 (44) (C. Müller-Graff & E. Selvig eds, Berlin: Berlin Verlag A. Spitz 1997). *See similarly* S.L. Jervell, *Lovgivningen i EØS* 81 (Oslo: Cappelens Forlag 2001), who summarizes the political power-balance in the Agreement as follows: In EEA law it is the EU pillar that is responsible for the dynamic evolvement while the EFTA pillar is responsible for homogeneity. The EU makes the rules and the EFTA accepts and implement them.

397. The set-up of the solution as it is introduced into the EEA Agreement highlights two aspects of the above-mentioned compromise. On the one hand, it lays down the different processes pursuant to which the EFTA States may participate in the decision-shaping process of the EU. On the other hand, it sets out in detail the process following which EU legislation could become a part of the EEA legal order. Therefore, the ensuing analysis not only covers the decision-making procedure stricto sensu, but also includes the rules on the EFTA States' participation in the EU decision-shaping process.

§1. Participation in Decision-Shaping

398. The level of participation of the EFTA States in the EU decision-shaping process varies according to the phase of the decision-shaping process concerned. Three phases can be distinguished: (1) the policy development; (2) the policy making; and (3) the policy implementation phase.[341]

I. Participation in the Policy Development Phase

399. The policy development phase is the phase in which the European Commission develops its strategies and discusses the possibility of future measures. At this stage, no decision has yet been taken on a proposal to be submitted to the European Parliament and the Council.

400. Article 99(1) of the EEA Agreement provides that:

> as soon as new legislation is being drawn up by the EC Commission in a field which is governed by this Agreement, the EC Commission shall informally seek advice from experts of the EFTA States in the same way as it seeks advice from experts of the EC Member States for the elaboration of its proposals.

401. The aim of that provision is, *inter alia*, to give the European Commission the best possible means to reflect special circumstances in, and considerations pertaining to, the EFTA States when drafting the proposed act.[342] It also gives the EFTA States the possibility to start the preparations for the implementation of the proposed act as early as possible, which facilitates the entry into force of the act in the EFTA States as closely as possible in time to that in the EU.[343] The experts are formally not representing their respective states. In practice, experts of the EFTA States actively participate in the meetings where the Commission consults the experts of the EU Member States.

341. For an overview, *see also* G. Baur, 'Chancen und Grenzen des decision shaping', in Müller & Schroeder (eds), *25 Jahre Europäischer Wirtschaftsraum* (2020): 17–32.

342. *See* S.L. Jervell, *Lovgivningen i EØS – Beslutningsprosessen, gjennomføringen og konsekvensene* 34 (Oslo: Capellen Akademisk Forlag 2002).

343. *See* M. Dystland, F. Finstad & I. Sørebø, in Arnesen et al. (eds), *Agreement on the European Economic Area, A Commentary* (2018): 799.

402. The participation of the EFTA States' experts in the decision-shaping process of the EU should not be confused with the public consultations that the Commission carries out during the policy-shaping phase. Indeed, Article 99(1) of the EEA Agreement has been drawn up as a privileged access of the EFTA States' experts to the Commission, while the public consultation process is open to the general public.

403. The right of participation set out in Article 99(1) of the EEA Agreement extends only to areas which are covered by the EEA Agreement. At the time of negotiation and, to a slightly lesser extent, entry into force of the EEA Agreement, it was fairly easy to determine whether new legislation would be covered by the EEA Agreement or not. The EEA Agreement is a very close reproduction of the provisions of the EC Treaty as it stood at the time. Therefore, the EEA Agreement presumably covered any legislation that would have as a legal basis a provision of that treaty that is reproduced in the EEA Agreement.

404. Already before the Lisbon Treaty that presumption had become less and less accurate. Indeed, with the successive modifications of the EU primary law and the widening competence by the Treaties of Maastricht, Amsterdam and Nice,[344] certain 'grey areas' had emerged. It may not always be entirely clear whether and if, to what extent, new legislation concerns an area covered by the EEA Agreement. As a consequence, with a view of determining whether the EFTA States have a right in the shaping of a certain piece of future legislation, the Contracting Parties will need to assess the EEA relevance at an early stage.

II. Participation in the Policy Decision Phase

405. The policy decision phase starts with the submission of the Commission proposal for a new piece of legislation to the Council and/or the European Parliament. For this situation, Article 99(2) of the EEA Agreement foresees that the Commission is to transmit copies of the proposals to the EFTA States as soon as it transmits its proposal to the EU Council.

406. The act of submitting a proposal to a branch of the legislator is an action which the general public and, hence, also the EFTA States can easily identify. The EFTA States will therefore have no difficulty in identifying the acts, to the shaping of which they might want to contribute. In practice, the EFTA States rely mostly on

344. As the EEA Agreement is a public international law agreement binding the EFTA Member States on the one hand and the EU and its Member States on the other hand, the EU cannot by agreeing on changes to the EU Treaties unilaterally modify the terms and conditions under which the EEA Agreement operates. This being said, some of the changes brought by the TFEU might have a practical impact on the functioning of the EEA Agreement. This is the case, for instance, of the merging of the pillars: Because future EU legislative acts will increasingly cover matters which have hitherto been covered by the previous different pillars of the EU structure, new EU legislation might be subject to a more detailed analysis of its EEA relevance and the EFTA States might have to ask more frequently for adaptations thereto.

the services of the EFTA Secretariat, which closely follows any developments on the EU side. As soon as the EFTA Secretariat identifies a new proposal that is likely to be incorporated into the EEA Agreement at a later stage, it informs the EFTA States accordingly.

407. Once the EFTA States have become aware of a proposal for new legislation, they can request a preliminary exchange of views on the matter within the EEA Joint Committee. Although this was once considered to be an essential element of the political compromise concerning the EFTA States' involvement in the EU's legislative process, this preliminary exchange of views does not occur very often. Moreover, when it happens, the exchange of views does not so much concern the substance of the legislation but rather whether the measures contemplated by the Commission will affect the very structure of the EEA Agreement. More practical is that the EFTA States invite the Commission to discuss proposals at Working Group meetings.[345]

408. After the European Commission's proposal for a new piece of legislation has been submitted to the EU Council, and during the whole phase preceding the decision on the proposal, the Contracting Parties are to consult each other again, in the EEA Joint Committee, at the significant moments at the request of one of them (Article 99(3) of the EEA Agreement). That provision also provides for a continuous information and consultation process.

409. Whether or not this continuous information and consultation process actually takes place, depends to a large extent on the issues involved. Subject matters that are sensitive for the EFTA States, will, of course, be more closely followed by them. On the other hand, if the relevant subject matters are sensitive for the EU, the quality of the information and consultation process might sometimes be negatively affected. The Commission is reluctant to complicate the picture on the EU side by discussing issues that are already sensitive inside the EU.

410. Over the years, a practice has evolved that the Contracting Parties do not discuss the issues in the EEA Joint Committee, but instead exchange information in writing. Indeed, the standard method of making EFTA's position known to the EU is to send written comments to the Commission Services concerned.[346] In the subsequent meetings of the EEA Joint Committee, the Contracting Parties usually take note of the fact that the EFTA States have sent a comment to a proposal. A more detailed exchange of views virtually never takes place in that forum.

411. This being said, one should not conclude from the foregoing that an exchange of views does not take place at all. Indeed, after a comment has been sent

345. *See* M. Dystland, F. Finstad & I. Sørebø, in Arnesen et al. (eds), *Agreement on the European Economic Area, A Commentary* (2018): 800–801.

346. An overview of such EEA EFTA Comments can be found on the website of the EFTA Secretariat (www.efta.int). In 2021, the EFTA States sent eight such comments, and in 2022 six.

to the Commission, the officials of the EFTA side follow the matter up and also put into effect Article 99(3) of the EEA Agreement, although in a less formal manner than originally foreseen.

III. Participation in the Policy Implementation Phase

412. Article 100 of the EEA Agreement sets out the EFTA States' involvement in cases of the so-called comitology procedure, where a committee is to assist the Commission in the exercise of its executive powers. In addition, the matter was the subject of a 'declaration by the European Community on the Participation of the EFTA States' Experts in EEA-Relevant EC Committees in Application of Article 100 of the Agreement', included in the Final Act adopted by the plenipotentiaries of the signatory parties to the EEA Agreement on 2 May 1992.[347]

413. The procedures in question can be separated into two categories. A first category encompasses the EFTA States' participation in the preparation of delegated acts adopted by the Commission under Article 290 TFEU. The second category, which can be separated into two issues, concerns the Commission's implementing acts under Article 291 TFEU.

A. *Involvement in the Preparation of Delegated Acts*

414. Since the entry into force of the TFEU, an EU act may delegate to the Commission the power to adopt a non-legislative act of general application to supplement or amend certain non-essential elements of the legislative act (Article 290 TFEU).

415. It appears that the acts adopted under this provision cannot be clearly subsumed under any of the provisions of the EEA Agreement concerning decision-shaping: On the one hand, acts adopted under Article 290 TFEU can supplement or amend a legislative act and should therefore be dealt with under EFTA participation in the policy decision phase. On the other hand, the provisions of the EEA Agreement on EFTA participation in the policy decision phase are designed on the premise that the Commission submits a proposal for the measure to be adopted to the Council, which is not the case under Article 290 TFEU. In addition, the acts that will be adopted under this provision tend to correspond to acts that were previously covered by the regulatory procedure with scrutiny and, hence, fell within the ambit of Article 100 of the EEA Agreement.

416. However, there are good arguments in favour of arguing that these acts will be dealt with by applying Article 99(1) of the EEA Agreement *mutatis mutandis*: Pursuant to this provision:

347. *See* item No. 29 on the list of declarations of which the plenipotentiaries have taken note.

> as soon as new legislation is being drawn up by the EC Commission in a field which is governed by this Agreement, the EC Commission shall informally seek advice from experts of the EFTA States in the same way as it seeks advice from experts of the EC Member States for the elaboration of its proposals.

Therefore, reference can be made to the explanations on EFTA participation in the policy development phase.[348]

B. Involvement in the Adoption of Implementing Acts

417. As set out above, EFTA participation in the elaboration of implementing acts can be separated in two issues: A first issue concerns the general question as to the degree of EFTA participation in the comitology committees. A second issue then arises in connection with EFTA participation in the so-called appeal committees.

1. Involvement in the Committees

418. Article 100(1) of the EEA Agreement sets out the conditions for involvement of the EFTA States in the 'comitology committees'. The provision states the following:

> The EC Commission shall ensure experts of the EFTA States as wide a participation as possible according to the areas concerned, in the preparatory stage of draft measures to be submitted subsequently to the committees which assist the EC Commission in the exercise of its executive powers. In this regard, when drawing up draft measures the EC Commission shall refer to experts of the EFTA States on the same basis as it refers to experts of the EC Member States.

419. At first sight, this provision repeats in its second sentence, what it stated in the first, namely that the EFTA States' experts are involved in the 'preparatory stage of draft measures' and 'when drawing up draft measures'. The degree of involvement, however, differs. While in the preparatory stage of draft measures, the EFTA States' experts enjoy a participation as wide as possible, the European Commission shall refer to experts of the EFTA States on the same basis as it refers to experts of the EU Member States when drawing up draft measures.

420. As the Contracting Parties decided on different degrees of involvement of the EFTA States' experts, depending on whether the preparatory stage of the draft measures was concerned or whether the Community was drawing up draft measures, the two sentences must cover two different situations. When trying to identify the difference between the two situations, recourse can be made to the

348. *See supra* Part II, Ch. 4, §1, I.

aforementioned Declaration by the (then) EC, which concerns 'the participation of the EFTA States' experts in EEA-relevant EC Committees in application of Article 100 of the Agreement'.

421. In practice, the EFTA States have been invited to participate in virtually all EEA-relevant comitology committees.[349] Only in some isolated cases has it happened that the EFTA States' participation in the comitology committees has been denied.

422. The level of involvement of the EFTA States' experts consists of full participation without the right to vote.[350] Formally, this, of course, puts the EFTA States' experts in a very different situation from those of the EU Member States. However, in practice, the distinction 'without the right to vote' is of less significance, as in most cases, there is actually no vote.

2. Involvement in the Appeal Committees

423. When an examination procedure committee gives a negative opinion or, in some cases issues no opinion, the Commission is required to submit its draft implementing act to an appeal committee if it intends to adopt the measure in question.

424. These appeal committees have not been foreseen by the EEA Agreement, which merely refers to committees assisting the Commission in the exercise of its executive powers. However, there can be no doubt that these appeal committees are nothing more than a second degree of committees assisting the Commission in the exercise of its executive powers. Therefore, it can be assumed that the EFTA States' participation in the policy implementing phase should also extend to the appeal committees.

IV. Assessment of the EFTA States' Involvement in the EU's Policy Cycle

425. An assessment of the EFTA States' participation in the EU decision-shaping and decision-making process leads to differing conclusions depending on the policy cycle in question.

426. While the influence of the EFTA States in the policy development phase is potentially important, it is much less so in the policy decision phase.[351] The difference between the two can be explained by the fact that exercising influence in the

349. This practice was summarized by a draft report on comitology and the EEA of the EEA Joint Parliamentary Committee of 1 Jun. 2001. *See* Doc No. M/20/R/029 – PE 304.327.
350. While in some cases the EFTA States' experts have been requested to leave the room when the committee moves to a vote, in other cases they simply did not cast a vote.
351. *See* S.L. Jervell, *Lovgivningen i EØS – Beslutningsprosessen, gjennomføringen og konsekvensene* 35 et seq. and 72 et seq. (Oslo: Capellen Akademisk Forlag 2002).

policy development phase is, to a large extent, based on informal participation in processes where the formal differences of the status between non-EU States and EU Member States are less apparent. Indeed, the Commission is free to carry out a consultation of the experts of the EU Member States or not. In the policy decision phase, in turn, it is the EU Member States that are the main actors. As stated by a former President of the CJEU: 'As soon as the traditional horse-trading and making up of package-deals starts then the influence of the EFTA States stops. From then on, all political inputs will come from the Member States of the EU and from the European Parliament.'[352] In addition, it appears that it is easier to influence a measure, the content of which is not yet determined, than to endeavour to have an official draft measure modified. Accordingly, the earlier the EFTA States put forward their positions and participate actively in the process, the more likely it is that they will yield results.[353]

427. Regarding the policy implementation phase, EFTA States' potential influence is considerable. Through their participation in a 'comitology committee', the EFTA States can contribute to the shaping of the measures implementing a certain piece of legislation. This not only holds true for the work in the basic committees but also for the work in the appeal committees. The EFTA States' participation in the comitology committees is of great practical importance, as a high proportion of the acts incorporated into the EEA Agreement involve such committees.[354]

428. Similarly, the influence of the EFTA States in the elaboration of delegated acts may be considered as potentially important. In fact, in this case, EFTA's participation may be largely based on the same premises as in the policy development phase.

§2. Cooperation with a View to Ensuring the Good Functioning of the EEA Agreement

429. Pursuant to Article 3 of the EEA Agreement, the Contracting Parties shall facilitate cooperation within the framework of the EEA Agreement. Article 99(4) of the EEA Agreement is an expression of this general duty to cooperate. It states that the 'Contracting Parties shall cooperate in good faith during the information and consultation phase with a view to facilitating, at the end of the process, the decision-taking in the EEA Joint Committee.'

352. *See* Ole Due, 'The EFTA Court and its Responsibility to the European Court of Justice', in *The Fifth Nordic Conference on EFTA and the European Union* 52 (58) (Sundström ed., Helsinki: Yliopistopaino 1994).
353. S.L. Jervell, *Lovgivningen i EØS – Beslutningsprosessen, gjennomføringen og konsekvensene* 39 (Oslo: Capellen Akademisk Forlag 2002).
354. In the years 2017 and 2018, a total of 947 EU acts were incorporated into the EEA Agreement. Out of these, less than 10% were adopted by the European Parliament and the Council. The rest of the acts were mainly Commission delegated or implementing acts. *See* K. Isaksen, 'The Process of Incorporating EU Acts into the EEA Agreement', in Müller & Schroeder (eds), *25 Jahre Europäischer Wirtschaftsraum* (2020): 57.

430. Another provision that is an expression of the general principle of cooperation is Article 101 of the EEA Agreement concerning the participation of the EFTA States in committees, which are covered neither by Article 81 of the EEA Agreement nor by Article 100 of the EEA Agreement. Due to the importance of cooperation in such committees, the Contracting Parties felt the need to spell out this obligation explicitly.

431. The Contracting Parties have determined that the EFTA States should participate in a number of committees and added a number of other committees thereafter. The committees in question are not directly related to one of the phases of the EU policy cycle. Their main aim is to bring together experts from the Contracting Parties, with a view to ensuring optimal implementation of the acquis communautaire in the Contracting Parties.

432. The list of the committees concerned can be found in Protocol 37 to the EEA Agreement.[355] However, the hitherto applied practice makes it clear that the name of the body, as such, is not determinative for a body to be added to the list of Protocol 37 to the EEA Agreement. The Contracting Parties have added a number of bodies to that list that do not bear the denomination 'committee'. Among others, the Contracting Parties have agreed to include the Radio Spectrum Policy Group,[356] the group of coordinators for the recognition of professional qualifications,[357] the Security Board for the European GNSS Systems[358] as well as the European Cybersecurity Certification Group.[359] All that counts is the fact that the association of the EFTA States could be considered as having a positive effect on the functioning of the EEA Agreement.

433. Protocol 37 to the EEA Agreement only contains the list of the committees in which the EFTA States are to participate. The terms under which they are to participate are set out in the relevant sectoral Protocols or Annexes. Accordingly, the listing of the body in question in Protocol 37 to the EEA Agreement is insufficient if one intends to determine the terms and conditions of the EFTA States' participation in those bodies.

434. The listing or non-listing of a body in Protocol 37 to the EEA Agreement, as well as in the relevant sectoral protocol or annex, is without prejudice to the fact that the EFTA States can always rely on Article 99(1) of the EEA Agreement to request their participation in the body in question, in case the Commission seeks

355. Notwithstanding the fact that Art. 101 of the EEA Agreement can be considered an expression of the general duty to cooperate, the EFTA States only have a right to participate in those Committees which are explicitly mentioned in Protocol 37 to the EEA Agreement.
356. Decision of the EEA Joint Committee No. 9/2004 of 6 Feb. 2004 (OJ L 116, 22.4.2004, 56; EEA Supplement No. 20, 22.4.2004, 12).
357. Decision of the EEA Joint Committee No. 142/2007 (OJ L 100, 10.4.2008, 70 and EEA Supplement No. 19, 10.4.2008, 70).
358. Decision of the EEA Joint Committee No. 159/2009 (OJ L 62, 11.3.2010, 65 and EEA Supplement No. 12, 11.3.2010, 63).
359. Decision of the EEA Joint Committee No. 22/2023 (OJ L, 19.10.2023, 1).

advice from that body for the drawing up of new legislation in a field governed by the EEA Agreement. The fact that, according to Article 99(1) of the EEA Agreement informal consultation of the EFTA States' experts is provided simply means that these experts should be allowed to participate informally in the body in question, rather than formally.

§3. Decision-Making in the EEA

435. The decision-making procedure in the EEA is based on the premise that by entering into the EEA Agreement, the EFTA States have not transferred any legislative competences to a supranational body. Therefore, if an act adopted by the EU legislative bodies is to apply in the whole EEA, the EEA Agreement will have to be amended.

436. This being said, it would have been inconceivable to reconvene all Contracting Parties for agreeing on the incorporation of an EU act into the EEA Agreement each time the EU bodies had adopted an act of EEA relevance. Taking into account the volume of internal market legislation adopted by the EU bodies, the EEA Agreement would quickly have become paralysed.[360] For that reason, the Contracting Parties designed a procedure for modifying Annexes and certain Protocols to the EEA Agreement. That procedure is laid down in Articles 102 of the EEA Agreement et seq.

437. The provision that gives the EEA Joint Committee the competence to modify the EEA Agreement following the procedure is, in most of the cases, Article 98 of the EEA Agreement. Regarding decisions amending Protocol 31 to the EEA Agreement, the legal basis is Article 98 of the EEA Agreement in conjunction with Article 86 of the EEA Agreement.

I. Scope of the Procedure for Amendments of the EEA Agreement

438. Pursuant to Article 102(1) of the EEA Agreement, 'the EEA Joint Committee shall take a decision concerning an amendment of an Annex to this Agreement'. The wording of this provision refers to amendments of Annexes to the EEA Agreement only. The question thus arises as to what extent the provisions of Article 102 of the EEA Agreement can be considered as applicable in the context of amendments to Protocols to the EEA Agreement. This is of particular importance, as certain Protocols to the EEA Agreement contain references to EU acts in a similar way as do the Annexes to the EEA Agreement (Protocol 21 to the EEA Agreement on the implementation of competition rules to undertakings), or reproduce almost

360. At the time of signing, the EEA Agreement referred to 1,875 acts. Since 1994, more than 10,000 acts have been incorporated by decisions of the EEA Joint Committee. According to the Annual Report of the EEA Joint Committee 2022, in 2022, the EEA Joint Committee adopted 354 decisions incorporating 628 legal acts.

exactly, the substance of certain EU acts (Protocol 24 to the EEA Agreement on cooperation in the field of control of undertakings).

439. The answer to the question could be found in Article 98 of the EEA Agreement. This provision treats certain Protocols and Annexes to the EEA Agreement identically, when it deals with the competence of the EEA Joint Committee to adopt amendments and explicitly refers to Article 102 of the EEA Agreement. The procedure of Article 102 of the EEA Agreement could thus apply for the amendments, not only of the Annexes to the EEA Agreement but also for the Protocols of the EEA Agreement, which are mentioned in Article 98 of the EEA Agreement. On the other hand, it has been argued that Article 102 of the EEA Agreement would not apply to amendments of these Protocols, since the content of some of the provisions of Article 102 of the EEA Agreement is very specific to amendments of annexes.[361] The main part of the EEA Agreement and the Protocols not mentioned in Article 98 of the EEA Agreement cannot be amended by the EEA Joint Committee.

II. Different Stages of the Procedure Leading to an Amendment of the EEA Agreement

440. According to Article 102 of the EEA Agreement, the EU is to inform the other Contracting Parties in the EEA Joint Committee, as soon as possible, of the adoption of an EU act of EEA relevance.[362] The EEA Joint Committee then is to assess the part of an Annex to the EEA Agreement that would be directly affected by the EU act in question, and the Contracting Parties would make all efforts to arrive at an agreement on matters relevant to the EEA Agreement. Substantial discussions, however, are rare in the EEA Joint Committee. Most of the time, the information, discussions, assessments or negotiations take place outside the EEA Joint Committee. Accordingly, the procedures that precede the EEA Joint Committee are of utmost importance to the successful management of the EEA.

A. *The Procedure Preceding the Discussions in the EEA Joint Committee*

441. The procedure preceding the discussions in the EEA Joint Committee involves experts, from both the EFTA side and the EU side, who communicate with each other in the subcommittees to the EEA Joint Committee, and in an informal manner.

---

361. *See* S.L. Jervell, *Lovgivningen i EØS – Beslutningsprosessen, gjennomføringen og konsekvensene* 39 (Oslo: Capellen Akademisk Forlag 2002).

362. In a pre-internet world this information procedure might have been practical, but it is no longer considered necessary.

1. Procedures to Be Followed in the EFTA Pillar

442. The EFTA States have set up a multi-layered structure of committees and groups and have set out detailed procedures for the process of incorporating EU legal acts into the EEA Agreement. The structure and procedures seek to balance on the one side the need for timely incorporation against on the other side the need for experts in the EFTA States to have sufficient time to assess EEA relevance, the need for adaptations and to prepare for the implementation.[363]

443. The volume of acts being processed and prepared for incorporation at any given time is high, and the EFTA Secretariat is coordinating this process.[364] The details of the process on the EFTA side can be found in the Decision of the Standing Committee of the EFTA States from 2014.[365] The EFTA States updated the procedures in 2014 as a result initiated in 2013 with the aim of looking into ways of processing and incorporating EEA-relevant acts in a more efficient manner. The decision describes in detail the various steps of the process and specifies indicative deadlines by which the various steps are to be carried out. As a starting point, the intensity of the scrutiny and the deadlines depend on the complexity of the legal act in question.

444. The procedure on the EFTA side starts in most cases after the publication of EU acts that are presumed to be covered by the EEA Agreement in the Official Journal of the European Union. For Commission implementing acts, the procedure starts when the acts have been published in the Comitology register following a positive vote in the relevant Committee. For Commission delegated acts, the incorporation process starts when the acts have been published in the Commission register after having been formally sent to the European Parliament and Council for scrutiny.[366] The purpose of starting the process early in case of implementing and delegated acts is to speed up the incorporation process. In this context, it should be reiterated that, at least for Commission implementing acts, the EFTA States are fully participating in the Committees, except for the right to vote and are as such directly involved in the adoption of these acts from an early stage, in contrast to other EU acts.[367] It is the EFTA Secretariat that constantly monitors the Official Journal and other registers of the EU, with a view to identifying EEA-relevant acts.

445. EU legal acts of relevance to the Internal Market are generally labelled by the EU as 'Text with EEA relevance'. This labelling is however not legally binding

363. *See* K. Isaksen, 'The Process of Incorporating EU Acts into the EEA Agreement', in Müller & Schroeder (eds), *25 Jahre Europäischer Wirtschaftsraum* (2020): 58.
364. As of 5 Apr. 2023, there were 612 legal acts in the process of being incorporated, where the compliance date in the EU had passed, compared to 574 acts on 12 Oct. 2022, *see* Progress report of the EEA Joint Committee 22 May 2023 (EEE 1603/23).
365. Standing Committee Decision No. 1/2014/SC of 8 May 2014.
366. *See* K. Isaksen, 'The Process of Incorporating EU Acts into the EEA Agreement', in Müller & Schroeder (eds), *25 Jahre Europäischer Wirtschaftsraum* (2020): 60.
367. In addition, Commission implementing and delegated acts are normally straightforward, technical legal acts that do not raise any specific challenges for the implementation in the EFTA States.

on the EFTA States and does not always mean that the act should be incorporated into the EEA Agreement. First, it might happen that the EU erroneously labels an act as being of EEA relevance or omits to label an act as being of EEA relevance although, after a final evaluation, it turns out to be EEA relevant. Second, acts addressed to individual Member States or individual legal entities in the EU would in areas covered by the EEA Agreement normally be labelled as EEA relevant. However, as such acts do not have general application, they are as a starting point not incorporated into the EEA Agreement.[368] Therefore, the EFTA States themselves have to assess the EEA relevance of the act in question.

446. To this end, the EFTA Secretariat informs the EFTA States about the adoption of any EU legislation, which could be of interest for the EFTA States. The information is provided in a structured form. Within one week of registration of an act that has been published in the Official Journal or another register, the EFTA Secretariat sends it to the relevant EFTA Working Group, suggesting which part of an Annex to the Agreement would be directly affected by the new act in question, as well as a preliminary assessment of the EEA relevance and the possible need for adaptations. At the same time, the EFTA Secretariat also proposes one of the three procedures for incorporation of the act: fast-track, simplified procedure or standard procedure.[369] At this point, the EFTA Secretariat raises the question of whether the future decision of the EEA Joint Committee will be binding on one or more of the EFTA States only after the fulfilment of constitutional requirements.[370]

447. The fast-track procedure was introduced by the EFTA Standing Committee in 2014 in response to the high number of acts awaiting incorporation into the EEA agreement.[371] The procedure is intended to be used for straightforward acts that by their nature do not raise any challenges, do not need any adaptations and do not call for constitutional requirements.[372] The EFTA States have a six-week deadline to oppose the use of the fast-track procedure, and in such a case, the standard procedure is initiated. If no opposition is received within the deadline, the EFTA Secretariat moves on to draft a Joint Committee Decision for the incorporation of the act.[373]

448. The simplified procedure is used for certain legal acts in the veterinary and food areas, particularly for acts concerning safeguard and protective measures. For some acts in these areas, it is essential that they enter into force and are applied

368. *See* K. Isaksen, 'The Process of Incorporating EU Acts into the EEA Agreement', in Müller & Schroeder (eds), *25 Jahre Europäischer Wirtschaftsraum* (2020). 60.

369. *Ibid.*

370. *See supra* Part II, Ch. 2, §2, II, A.

371. *See* Handbook on EEA EFTA procedures for incorporating EU acts into the EEA Agreement, October 2016, Second Edition, 5. The fast-track procedure is described in detail in the Annex to Decision of the Standing Committee of the EFTA States No. 1/2014/SC, point 2.2.1.

372. *See* K. Isaksen, 'The Process of Incorporating EU Acts into the EEA Agreement', in Müller & Schroeder (eds), *25 Jahre Europäischer Wirtschaftsraum* (2020): 61.

373. The fast-track procedure is used for approximately 50% of the acts incorporated into the EEA Agreement, *see* K. Isaksen, 'The Process of Incorporating EU Acts into the EEA Agreement', in Müller & Schroeder (eds), *25 Jahre Europäischer Wirtschaftsraum* (2020): 61.

simultaneously in the whole of the EEA. The legal basis for the simplified procedure in the veterinary and food areas can be found in Annex I to the EEA Agreement and is as such based on an agreement between the EFTA States and the EU.[374] According to the simplified procedure, the EFTA States simultaneously take measures corresponding to those taken by the EU, and consequently, for acts subject to this procedure, there is no decision by the Joint Committee.[375]

449. For the remaining cases, where neither the fast-track nor the simplified procedure is applied, the standard procedure is used. In these cases, the EFTA States have a sixteen-week deadline to assess EEA relevance and if the incorporation of an EU act raises any challenges that might require an adaptation.

450. Based on the information submitted by the EFTA States, the EFTA Secretariat drafts a Joint Committee Decision. The general rule is that decisions amending an Annex of the EEA Agreement shall be taken separately in relation to each individual EU act, unless otherwise agreed.[376] In practice, decisions often group several acts together if they have the same legal basis or if there are other reasons for grouping them.

451. The EFTA Secretariat draws up the draft Joint Committee Decisions based on a template consisting of recitals and articles.[377] In most cases, the recitals are not very elaborate but merely refer to that a certain EU act is to be incorporated into the EEA Agreement and that therefore an Annex should be amended accordingly. In some cases, however, the recitals can be more elaborate, especially in decisions containing adaptations, and hence be of relevance for the interpretation of that decision.[378]

Upon clearance of the draft Joint Committee Decision by the EFTA States in the subcommittee, the Secretariat sends it to the Secretariat-General of the Commission. As long as one of the EFTA States opposes the incorporation of an act into the EEA Agreement, the act cannot be incorporated.

---

374. *See* paras 7 and 8 of the introductory part of Annex I, Ch. I to the EEA Agreement, as well as the adaptation texts in points 13 and 41 of Annex I, incorporating Regulation (EU) 2016/429 ('Animal Health Law') and Regulation (EC) No. 178/2002 ('General Food Law Regulation'), respectively.
375. Since 1994, more than 1,000 acts have been incorporated into the EEA Agreement by simplified procedure in the veterinary and food area.
376. *See* Decision of the EEA Joint Committee No. 1/94 of 8 Feb. 1994 adopting the Rules of Procedure of the EEA Joint Committee, Art. 9 (Rules of Procedure of the EEA Joint Committee), OJ L 085, 30.3.1994, 60.
377. Rules of Procedure of the EEA Joint Committee, Art. 8. Occasionally, the question of deviating from the template on an ad hoc basis has been raised, especially from parts of the EU with less experience in dealing with the EEA Agreement, such as the Council. However, in most cases this has been avoided, as deviating from the template could potentially create legal uncertainty, as regards the significance of alternative drafting, in a structure where there are hundreds of Joint Committee Decisions each year.
378. *See* K. Isaksen, 'The Process of Incorporating EU Acts into the EEA Agreement', in Müller & Schroeder (eds), *25 Jahre Europäischer Wirtschaftsraum* (2020): 62.

2. Procedures to Be Followed in the EU Pillar

452. The process in the EU Pillar is coordinated by the Secretariat-General of the Commission. Once the Commission has received a draft decision of the EEA Joint Committee from the EFTA States, it will run it through inter-service consultation, sharing the draft with the relevant Commission Directorates-Generals (DGs), with a view to determining whether the EU side would be ready to adopt the decision of the EEA Joint Committee. In most cases, where the draft decision does not contain any substantive adaptations to the EU act to be incorporated, there will be no difficulties.[379] Difficulties that might arise in these situations are almost exclusively of a technical nature and will normally be resolved in informal discussions between the responsible officials of the Commission and the EFTA side.

453. When a Joint Committee Decision simply extends EU acts to the EEA, subject to technical adjustments, the Commission is competent to adopt a position on behalf of the EU. This is the situation in the vast majority of cases. In some instances, however, completion of inter-service consultation within the Commission is not sufficient to be authorized to adopt a decision of the EEA Joint Committee. Article 1(2) and (3) of Council Regulation (EC) No. 2894/94 of 28 November 1994 concerning arrangements for implementing the Agreement on the EEA[380] provide that in cases where the draft decisions of the EEA Joint Committee do not simply extend EU acts to the EEA, subject to technical adjustments, it is the EU Council that adopts the EU's position. Substantive adaptations would in the terminology of Regulation No. 2894/94 be adaptations that are 'more than mere technical adjustments'. Such adaptations could concern the institutional set-up of the EEA Agreement or introduce exemptions due to a specific situation in an EFTA State.[381]

In essence, two categories of Decisions of the EEA Joint Committee fall within the EU Council's competence. On the one hand, the Council has reserved its competence in relation to any decision of the EEA Joint Committee that goes beyond a mere extension of EU legislation (including the provision of the necessary technical adaptations thereto) and in so doing introduces changes which are more than mere technical adjustments. On the other hand, the Council adopts the EU's position whenever the decision of the EEA Joint Committee is not to extend EU legislation to the EEA. This situation concerns mainly all the decisions of the EEA Joint Committee on the participation of the EFTA States in an EU activity under Protocol 31 to the EEA Agreement (on cooperation outside the four freedoms). This additional procedure created by the need of an EU Council Decision on the EU's position can cause delays of up to several months in the incorporation of the EU acts into the EEA Agreement.[382] This being said, there are only a few instances in which a quick

379. The distinction between technical and substantive adaptations is not always clear, and an assessment is made in each individual case by the Commission's Legal Service.

380. OJ L 305, 30.11.1994, 6.

381. *See* K. Isaksen, 'The Process of Incorporating EU Acts into the EEA Agreement', in Müller & Schroeder (eds), *25 Jahre Europäischer Wirtschaftsraum* (2020): 63.

382. While in some cases, such delays are not problematic, it may cause difficulties in others. However, the EU Council has proven to be capable of adopting its position very quickly in situations where

adoption of the EU's position is so crucial as to put in question the additional procedure before the EU Council. One of the fields concerned is cooperation outside the four freedoms: the EU Council reserves the right to adopt the EU's position for decisions of the EEA Joint Committee, providing for the participation of the EFTA States in certain EU activities. Indeed, the participation of the EFTA States in these activities needs to be ensured before the funds available to the participants under these activities are disbursed.

454. As regards voting, the Council shall act by the majority laid down in the provision adopted as the legal basis for the act that is to be incorporated into the EEA Agreement, as set out in Article 1(3)(a) of Regulation No. 2894/94. In practice, the draft Council Decision is discussed by the Council's EFTA Working Party, sometimes in the presence of relevant Commission Services. Following its approval, the EFTA Working Party submits the draft Council Decision to the Committee of Permanent Representatives (Coreper). Once Coreper approves the draft Council Decision, it is sent to any Council formation for formal approval.[383]

B. The Procedure Within the EEA Joint Committee

455. After the completion of the procedures in the two pillars, officials of the Commission and the EFTA Secretariat meet with a view to making the final adjustments to the draft decisions and to determining the exact text to be adopted by the EEA Joint Committee. Draft decisions, which at this stage do not cause particular difficulties, will be placed on the agenda of the next meeting of the EEA Joint Committee for adoption.

456. The procedure foreseen within the EEA Joint Committee is governed by two main considerations. First, the principle of homogeneity speaks in favour of taking the decisions of the EEA Joint Committee as closely as possible in time to the adoption of the EU act with a view to allowing simultaneous application of the EU act and the decision of the EEA Joint Committee. Second, the procedure needs to make sure that a lack of agreement regarding the amendment of an Annex between the two pillars can be overcome as soon as possible.

---

the EU's interest was at stake: When it came to the incorporation of Council Regulation (EC) No. 139/2004 of 20 Jan. 2004 on the control of concentrations between undertakings, the Council managed to adopt its position within a few weeks.

383. The question of the substantive legal basis for the Council to adopt a position on behalf of the EU on the EEA Joint Committee came up in Case C-431/11 *United Kingdom v. Council*, EU:C:2013:589. This case concerned an action for annulment by the United Kingdom of a Council Decision establishing the position to be taken by the EU within the EEA Joint Committee concerning an amendment to Annex VI (Social Security) and Protocol 37 to the EEA Agreement.

1. Considerations Related to the Principle of Homogeneity

457. Pursuant to Article 102(1) of the EEA Agreement, the EEA Joint Committee shall take a decision concerning an amendment of an Annex to this Agreement as closely as possible to the adoption, by the EU, of the corresponding new EU legislation, with a view to permitting a simultaneous application of the latter, as well as of the amendments of the Annexes to the Agreement. The main purpose of this rule is to guarantee the legal security and the homogeneity of the EEA, both substantively and with regard to when the different rules enter into force.

458. With respect to the timing of the amendment of an Annex to the EEA Agreement, the ideal timing is indicated by Article 102(1) of the EEA Agreement itself. The amendment should be adopted at a moment where the simultaneous application of the rule in question in the EEA and in the EU is still ensured.

459. In practice, simultaneous application of the EEA rules and the acquis communautaire is generally impossible where EU Regulations are concerned. Indeed, the fact that an EU Regulation will often be applicable as of the date of its entry into force (which occurs normally twenty days after its publication in the OJ, *see* Article 297 TFEU) implies that the EEA Joint Committee would have to incorporate the act within twenty days of the publication of the EU Regulation in the EU. Even with the best of intentions, this would not be feasible, taking into account that EEA Joint Committee meets only eight times per year.[384]

460. Even if the EU act foresees a delayed date of application, typically for directives, the goal of simultaneous application of EEA rules and acquis communautaire can sometimes be too ambitious. The procedures preceding a decision by the EEA Joint Committee can be time-consuming on both the EFTA side as well as on the EU side.

2. Overcoming a Lack of Agreement on Amending an Annex Between the Contracting Parties

461. For cases of difficulties, the EEA Agreement calls upon the Contracting Parties to make all efforts to arrive at an agreement on matters relevant to the EEA Agreement. In particular, Article 102(3) of the EEA Agreement requires the EEA Joint Committee to make every effort to find a mutually acceptable solution when a serious problem arises in any area, which, in the EFTA States, falls within the competence of the legislator. The EEA Agreement distinguishes between different levels of effort, depending on whether or not the substance matter falls within the competence of a legislator in one or more of the EFTA States. However, in practice such differentiation has never taken place.

384. *See supra* Part II, Ch. 3, §2, II, C.

462. Should the Contracting Parties not be able to reach an agreement on a matter concerning an amendment of an Annex to the EEA Agreement, a mechanism is foreseen that places upon the Contracting Parties an additional incentive to reach an agreement. This additional incentive consists of the threat of suspension of a part of an Annex to the EEA Agreement. However, before this additional incentive can be used, the EEA Joint Committee shall examine all other possibilities for maintaining the good functioning of the EEA Agreement. In particular, Article 102(4) of the EEA Agreement foresees that the EEA Joint Committee shall examine the possibility to take notice of – and thus accept – the equivalence of divergent legislation.

463. In view of the serious consequences looming at the end of the procedure (the suspension of a part of an Annex to the EEA Agreement), the procedure set out in Article 102(4) and (5) of the EEA Agreement determines the starting point thereof. Article 102(4) of the EEA Agreement requires the Contracting Parties to take a decision regarding the amendment of an Annex to the EEA Agreement within 'six months from the date of referral to the EEA Joint Committee'. In practice, it seems insufficient to discuss the matter in the EEA Joint Committee; a Contracting Party needs to expressly mention that it considers the procedure set out in Article 102(4) of the EEA Agreement to be running.[385] This approach has the merit of guaranteeing the legal security of all the Contracting Parties involved, to the extent that no Contracting Party would be able to claim that it had not considered that the matter had already been referred to the EEA Joint Committee for the purposes of the application of Article 102(4) of the EEA Agreement.[386]

464. If at the end of the period of six months, the EEA Joint Committee has not taken a decision on the amendment of the Annex in question, that part of the EEA Agreement shall be regarded as provisionally suspended after the lapse of another six months at least. However, the suspension is conditional upon the part to be suspended being determined beforehand. Article 102(5) of the EEA Agreement provides that 'the affected part' of the EEA Agreement, 'as determined in accordance with paragraph 2 [of Article 102 of the EEA Agreement]', is to be regarded as provisionally suspended. Article 102(2) of the EEA Agreement, in turn, provides that the part of an Annex to this Agreement, which would be directly affected by the new legislation, is assessed in the EEA Joint Committee.

465. A combination of these two paragraphs shows that the affected part of the EEA Agreement should not be considered as constituting an entire Annex to the EEA Agreement. This holds all the more true, as the part in question needs to be 'directly' affected by the new legislation. Should the negotiators of the EEA Agreement have intended the contrary, they would have specified that the Annex in question, rather than the affected part of an Annex to the EEA Agreement, should be

385. *See also* M. Dystland, F. Finstad & I. Sørebø, in Arnesen et al. (eds), *Agreement on the European Economic Area, A Commentary* (2018): 817; H. Fredriksen & G. Mathisen, *EØS-rett 4. utgave* 232–233 (Oslo: Fagbokforlaget 2022).

386. *See* G. Baur, 'Decision-Making Procedure and Implementation of New Law', in Baudenbacher (ed.), *The Handbook of EEA Law*, 71.

considered suspended. Which part of the EEA Agreement is to be suspended will have to be determined in accordance with Article 102(2) of the EEA Agreement. However, the EEA Joint Committee does not assess which part of an Annex to the EEA Agreement would be directly affected by the new legislation, before the Decision of the EEA Joint Committee incorporating the EU act in question is actually adopted.

466. There are two known examples of the use of Article 102(4) of the EEA Agreement, but the suspension of a part of an Annex to the EEA Agreement as provided for by Article 102(5) of the EEA Agreement has never occurred.[387]

In conclusion, the suspension of a part of an Annex to the EEA Agreement, due to disagreement regarding the amendment of an Annex, remains, to a large extent, hypothetical. If, however, one day, a part of an Annex to the EEA Agreement were to be suspended, it would not be the end of the story. On the one hand, the Contracting Parties would have to pursue their efforts to agree on a mutually acceptable solution (Article 102(5) of the EEA Agreement). On the other hand, and more importantly, the practical consequences of the suspension would have to be discussed in the EEA Joint Committee (Article 102(6) of the EEA Agreement). The issue would therefore remain on the agenda of the EEA Joint Committee.

467. Regarding the practical consequences of the suspension, any rights and obligations that individuals or economic operators have already acquired under the EEA Agreement shall remain unaffected (Article 102(6) of the EEA Agreement). Although the characteristics of vested rights may have to be assessed on a case-by-case basis depending on which part of which Annex to the EEA Agreement is suspended, there seems to be an intention to clearly limit the negative effects of a suspension.

387. *See* M. Dystland, F. Finstad & I. Sørebø, in Arnesen et al. (eds), *Agreement on the European Economic Area, A Commentary* (2018): 817.

Chapter 5. The Enforcement Mechanism

§1. SURVEILLANCE

468. As mentioned *supra* in Chapter 3, the enforcement of the EEA Agreement is organized according to a two-pillar structure. On the one hand, the European Commission ensures the correct application of the Agreement in the EU Member States. On the other hand, the EFTA Surveillance Authority ('the Authority') is entrusted with a correct application of the Agreement in the EFTA pillar. This chapter deals solely with the enforcement mechanism in the EFTA pillar.[388] As will be seen, the procedural framework in the two pillars is closely aligned and many of the mechanisms operate in practice in an identical way.

I. General Surveillance of the Transposition and Application of the EEA Agreement

A. *The Authority's Enforcement Policy*

469. As mentioned *supra* in Chapter 3, the competences of the Authority are mirroring those of the European Commission as regards surveillance, but unlike the Commission, the Authority is not a political body entrusted with the task of proposing or formulating rules. Against this background, and because of the limited resources, it could be argued that the Authority does not have a comprehensive enforcement policy, at least not comparable to that of the Commission. There is, however, in the interest of homogeneity, cooperation and alignment with the enforcement policy of the Commission. In view of its resource constraints, the Authority is moreover routinely closing large numbers of cases where it is not possible to allocate the resources required.[389] For the same reasons, even where the Authority does identify a systematic failure to comply with EEA law on the part of an EFTA State, investigations can take years.

470. In principle, according to Article 31 SCA, if the Authority considers that an EFTA State has failed to fulfil an obligation under the EEA Agreement or the SCA, it shall, unless otherwise provided for in the SCA, deliver a reasoned opinion on the matter after giving the State concerned the opportunity to submit its observations. If the State concerned does not comply with the reasoned opinion within the period laid down by the Authority, the latter may bring the matter before the EFTA Court.[390] This provision mirrors the competence given to the Commission in Article 258 TFEU and constitutes the Authority's main enforcement tool as regards the EFTA States. The surveillance tasks of the Authority, therefore, correspond, by and large, to those of the Commission. This implies, *inter alia*, that the Authority

---

388. Case T-115/94 *Opel Austria GmbH v. Council* [1997] ECR II-39, para. 108.
389. EFTA Surveillance Authority Decision No. 237/22/COL of 15 Dec. 2022 closing sixty cases following a prioritization exercise.
390. *See infra* Part II, Ch. 5, §2, I.

has the same wide discretion as the Commission as to whether or not pursue possible infringements.[391] Infringement procedures can either be initiated ex officio or by way of a complaint.

471. There are some noticeable differences between the pillars as regards the enforcement activity.[392] For example, the cases of the Authority have, to a relatively larger extent than the European Commission, been focussed on the tardy incorporation of secondary legislation into the legal orders of the EFTA States. In particular where no transposition at all takes place, these infringements are easy to detect. A practical reason for assiduously pursuing these cases stems from the absence of direct effect of non-incorporated acts in the EEA, meaning that individuals are not able to assert their rights due to non-implementation, hampering private enforcement.[393] Non-incorporation is thus more disruptive of the internal market in the EFTA pillar than in the EU pillar. The relative numerical preponderance of cases concerned with late incorporation into national legal orders is accentuated by consistent delays arising in Iceland. An up-to-date overview of the situation can be gleaned from the Internal Market Scoreboards regularly published by the Authority.

472. According to Article 109 of the EEA Agreement, the Authority is to work in close cooperation with the European Commission. Following the basic aim behind that provision, the Authority aims to ensure that the two institutions apply the common rules in a harmonious way, thus avoiding that the split of competence between them leads to different interpretations and uneven enforcement practice.[394] In any event, the Authority does not have the resources to duplicate or second-guess the assessments of the Commission, so that the Authority has tended to prioritize the same enforcement issues as the European Commission.[395] The Authority, therefore, follows the European Commission when deciding what areas of EEA law to

---

391. *See*, for example, Order of the EFTA Court of 23 Oct. 2013 in Case E-2/13, *Bentzen Transport v. EFTA Surveillance Authority* [2013] EFTA Court Report, 802, para. 40, and further, the Order of the EFTA Court in Case E-13/10 *Aleris Ungplan AS v. EFTA Surveillance Authority* [2011] EFTA Court Report, 3.
392. For more detail, *see* Zatschler, C. 'Priority', in *The Fundamental Principles of EEA Law* (Baudenbacher ed., Springer 2017).
393. As explained in *infra* Part II, Ch. 2, §2, Art. 7 of the EEA Agreement distinguishes itself from the situation in EU law in that EEA Acts corresponding to EU regulation are not, by virtue of EEA law, automatically applicable in the national legal order.
394. In case of disagreement between the two bodies on the action to be taken in relation to a complaint, or the result of an examination, the matter may be referred to the EEA Joint Committee, which shall deal with it in accordance with the rules on settlement of disputes in Art. 111 of the EEA Agreement. That mechanism has rarely been used, *see infra* Part II, Ch. 6. The fact that the Commission might not have initiated infringement proceedings against an EU State for maintaining in force a national legislation that resembles a legislation in an EFTA State against which the Authority has taken action cannot, of course, justify a breach nor in itself be seen as an indication that the legislation in the EFTA State is in conformity with EEA law, *see* Case E-1/03 *EFTA Surveillance Authority v. Iceland* [2003] EFTA Court Report, 143.
395. For example, by EFTA Surveillance Authority Decision No. 008/21/COL of 10 Feb. 2021, it was decided to deprioritize the treatment of complaints in the area of gambling. With its decision, the Authority aligned itself with the European Commission, which in December 2017 took a similar approach.

investigate systematically. It also occasionally starts investigations as a result of a 'tip-off' from the Commission. Conversely, the Authority will normally refrain from bringing actions concerning legal questions where the European Commission has decided that the corresponding EU rule is not sufficiently clear, which may be seen as regrettable to the extent that in some respects at least priorities in EFTA States are different compared to EU States. Thus, although formally not bound by the enforcement policy of the Commission, the Authority in practice follows the aim of uniform surveillance throughout the EEA that lies behind Article 109 of the EEA Agreement.

473. Different voices are heard in relation to the assessment of the Authority's enforcement policy. In the EFTA States, the Authority had sometimes been accused of being less flexible and harder in its enforcement practice than the European Commission towards the EU Member States. As independent experts demonstrated, such criticism is unwarranted.[396] Not least due to budgetary constraints, the Authority opens fewer cases than the Commission. On the contrary, the Authority seems more willing to solve cases informally than the Commission. Maybe for that reason, voices from the EU side occasionally point out that the Authority exercises its tasks in a spirit of cooperation and conciliation with the EFTA States and that its position represents more that of a 'friendly persuader' than that of a 'hard-hitting controller'.[397] The question has been raised whether the stance of the Authority might be influenced by the fact that the College Members of the Authority are often civil servants from the EFTA States.[398]

474. It has also been argued that since the Authority has no role to play in the legislative process but is only established to monitor the compliance of the EFTA States with their obligations under the EEA Agreement, the Authority's room for manoeuvre in exercising its discretion as to whether or not to bring an action for infringement against an EFTA State before the EFTA Court should actually be more limited than that of the Commission.[399] The credibility of the Authority and the enforcement mechanism in the EFTA pillar requires that the Authority does not follow a substantially more lenient practice than the Commission. It has in that context also been suggested that the credibility of both the Authority and EFTA Court might be best served by being reticent in bringing 'test-cases' before the EFTA Court thereby putting this Court at risk of later coming into conflict with the CJEU.[400]

396. *See* H.P. Graver & U. Sverdrup, *ESA og Norge* (Oslo: NHO 2002).
397. *See*, for example, J. Forman, 'The EEA Agreement Five Years on: Dynamic Homogeneity in Practice and Its Implementation by the Two EEA Courts', *Common Market Law Review* (1999): 751 (767 and 779).
398. Baudenbacher, *The EFTA Court in Action* 12–13 (Stuttgart: German Law Publishers 2010).
399. *See* S. Norberg, 'The EFTA Court', in *European Courts, Practice and Precedents* 77 (127) (Plender ed., London: Sweet & Maxwell 1997).
400. M. Everson, M. Wahl & S. Woolcock, *Navigating by the Stars* 33 (Brussels: Centre for European Policy Studies, 2002), claim that when, 'on rare occasion when ESA [i.e., the EFTA Surveillance Authority] might be in a position to set a precedent not yet covered by the EU *acquis*, the Commission has called for and obtained restraint from ESA'. That description is not accurate. First, it

475. Where the Authority is investigating the national legislation in an EFTA State, and a similar question concerning the same legislation is referred to the EFTA Court by way of an advisory opinion according to Article 34 SCA, the Authority often awaits the advisory opinion of the EFTA Court before it brings an infringement action before the Court and instead seeks to influence the judgment by way of an intervention. Where a question similar to the one under scrutiny by the Authority is pending before a national court in an EFTA State, the Authority has often been reticent to make use of the possibility of intervening in these national proceedings even where that possibility exists, even though that would be useful, in particular, if the national court has not yet taken any final stance as to whether the case should be referred to the EFTA Court. If, contrary to a national court's decision, the Authority is of the opinion that the national legislation is, in fact, contrary to the Agreement, the circumstance that a national court has arrived at the opposite conclusion would hardly carry much weight in the Authority's decision as to whether or not to bring the matter before the EFTA Court by way of an infringement case; if anything, a conflicting judgment of a national court would normally be prone to make the matter more pressing.

B. The Role of Complainants

476. The rules pertaining to complainants are broadly the same as the ones applicable in the EU. Thus, a complainant does not need to demonstrate any direct and individual concern in order to complain. On the other hand, a complainant cannot force the Authority to open a case. According to Article 109(3) of the EEA Agreement, the European Commission and the Authority shall receive any complaint concerning the application of the EEA Agreement. As in the EU legal order, complainants to the Authority do not, in cases of so-called normal supervision, have a status as a party to the proceedings between the Authority and the EFTA State concerned. The complainant, therefore, does not have a right to access the correspondence between the Authority and the EFTA State that goes further than the rights of the general public. A complainant would also have no standing to bring an action for passivity against the Authority if it decides not to go ahead with infringement proceedings.[401] That notwithstanding, the Authority follows the practice of the European Commission whereby complainants are given reasons, if its services intend to close the case.

477. Even where a case is based on a complaint, the Authority's primary focus will not usually be to ensure that the specific complaint is solved. Rather, the

actually happens quite often that the Authority is faced with legal questions where there is no practice from the EC pillar to rely on. Second, it is not practice of the Commission to ask the Authority to defer from taking action in such cases.

401. Nor can such an action be brought in the form of an action against the Authority's decision to close the case, *see* Case E-13/10 *Aleris Ungplan AS v. EFTA Surveillance Authority*, Order of 31 Jan. 2011.

Authority seeks to ensure that the EFTA State concerned brings its national provisions into line with the obligations arising from the EEA Agreement. Complaints are thus primarily a valuable source of information for the Authority. It is often through complaints that the Authority is made aware of potential infringements of the Agreement. For that reason, the Authority continues to encourage citizens and undertakings to contact the Authority if they feel that their rights have been breached, even if its resources do not permit to progress all the breaches that are brought to its attention. Moreover, approaching the Authority to vindicate rights of individuals does not entail any fee just as it often will be an advantage for the complainant not to be a party to the case, and even to remain anonymous during the investigation and any possible later infringement case. A major advantage of the complaint mechanism is that it allows infringements to be tackled that would otherwise not normally be pursued through private enforcement at national level, e.g., for financial reasons.

C. *Indirect Supervision via the EU Pillar*

478. The two surveillance authorities are entitled to participate in cases before the courts of the other pillar. For the Authority, Article 40(3) of the Statute of the Court of Justice permits the Authority to intervene in cases before the EU Court where one of the fields of application of the EEA Agreement is concerned. This possibility is most obviously useful where a case before the CJEU raises issues of EU law which are similar to those that have arisen in an EEA case pending before the Authority. For example, in *Lindman*,[402] concerning taxation of lottery gains, the CJEU was asked to assess the compatibility of Finnish legislation with Article 49 EC Treaty (now Article 56 TFEU). As that provision corresponded to Article 36 of the EEA Agreement and since the Finnish legislation was, for all practical purposes, similar to Norwegian provisions against which the Authority had issued a reasoned opinion, the Authority (and Norway) intervened in the case before the CJEU.

479. The Authority has presented observations in over hundred cases before the EU Courts and this is important for ensuring homogeneity with EU law. The Authority intervenes in both references for preliminary rulings and direct actions.[403] The practice of the Authority is to, as a rule, present its observations when the case before the CJEU raises fundamental questions of EEA law.[404] It will normally also

402. Case C-42/02 *Lindman* [2003] ECR I-13519.

403. Intervention has never been controversial in annulment cases before the General Court brought by private parties and in appeal cases before the CJEU; *see*, e.g., Case C-124/01 P *Commission v. EDF*, Order of 2 Sep. 2010. In contrast, during an interlude of some ten years, the Authority was prevented from intervening in infringement cases brought by the Commission against an EU Member State under Art. 258 TFEU as the then President of the Court of Justice interpreted Art. 40 of the Statute restrictively, *see* Case C-492/09 *Commission v. Portugal*, Order of 15 Jul. 2010, and C-542/09 *Commission v. Netherlands*, Order of 1 Oct. 2010. The situation was rectified expressly by an order of the President of the Court of Justice of 18 Dec. 2020 in Case C-328/20 *Commission v. Austria*, EU:C:2020:1068.

404. *See*, e.g., Case C-897/19 PPU *Ruska Federacija*, EU:C:2020:262.

make its view heard if the case raises issues of EU law that are similar to those that have arisen in an EEA case pending before the Authority or even to ensure consistency between the case law of the CJEU and the EFTA Court where a matter pending before the CJEU has already been adjudicated by the EFTA Court.[405] Moreover, the Authority presents observations in cases before the CJEU where similar problems are likely to arise in the EFTA pillar, even if the Authority has not yet been faced with an identical issue in its dealings with the EFTA States. Sometimes, the mere fact that a pending case raises a particularly interesting question of EU and EEA law has, in itself, prompted the Authority to intervene.[406] The Authority does not normally intervene in cases where the relevant EU rule does not have any counterpart in EEA law, though procedural – rather than substantive – aspects may of themselves prompt an intervention.[407]

II. Special Surveillance

A. Public Procurement

480. The opening-up of the EEA public procurement markets is an important feature in the realization of the internal market. The main objectives of the provisions in the EEA Agreement on public procurement are to ensure that public funds are spent in the most effective manner, according to the principle of 'best value for money', and to enhance cross-border competition for public contracts in the EEA. The EEA public procurement rules oblige public entities within the EEA to apply certain procedures when buying goods, services or works with a value exceeding given thresholds.[408] These procedures must guarantee transparency and equal treatment of all potential suppliers in the EEA and allow them equal access to public contracts in other EEA States. As a rule, such contracts are announced in the Tenders Electronic Daily (TED).[409] It is the Authority's task to monitor compliance by the contracting authorities in EFTA States with the public procurement rules. This role is intended to secure equal treatment of all suppliers, service providers and works contractors, established within the EEA, who wish to tender for contracts.

481. Article 65(1) of the EEA Agreement and Annex XVI to the EEA Agreement contain the entirety of the EU public procurement acquis.[410] The legislation distinguishes between the 'classic sector' and the 'utilities sector'. The

405. *See*, e.g., Case C-646/15 *Trustees of the P Panayi Accumulation & Maintenance Settlements* EU:C:2017:682 and Case C-8/23 *Conseil national de l'ordre des Médecins*.
406. *See*, e.g., Case C-566/15 *Erzberger*, EU:C:2017:562 and Case C-320/16 *Uber France*, EU:C:2018:221.
407. *See*, e.g., Case C-15/16 *Baumeister*, EU:C:2018:464 concerning access to documents and the concept of 'confidential information'.
408. The threshold values are published in the Official Journal of the European Union and updated every two years. Last time published in: OJ C 143, 31.3.2022, 8.
409. https://ted.europa.eu.
410. With the exception of Regulation (EU) 2022/2560 of the European Parliament and of the Council of 14 Dec. 2022 on foreign subsidies distorting the internal market ('the Foreign Subsidies

classic sector refers to all sectors except those that are explicitly excluded. Specific rules apply to the 'utilities sector', which covers water, energy, transport and postal services. However, public procurement law may not apply to the utilities sector if it can be demonstrated that the activity at stake is directly exposed to competition on markets to which access is not restricted. EFTA States or, where national legislation provides for it, the contracting authorities may therefore submit a request to the Authority aimed at establishing fulfilment of these conditions.[411] Such a request may be accompanied by a reasoned and substantiated position adopted by an independent national authority competent in the activity concerned (e.g., a national competition authority or national telecommunications regulator), which thoroughly analyses the conditions for the possible applicability of an exemption. During the formal procedure, i.e., once the request has been submitted, the Authority may request information from national authorities, competitors and other third parties based on the instruments available to it in the area of EEA competition law.[412] The procedure also foresees cooperation with the European Commission where necessary. The Authority will then carry out the necessary competition assessment[413] within a deadline of generally 90 or 130 working days[414] and finally decide whether it can exempt certain activities from the application of public procurement law.[415] This administrative procedure is free of charge.

482. The 'concessions sector' is the latest to be regulated at the EEA level. The 2004 Public Procurement Directives only partially covered concessions[416] and the absence of clear EEA rules led to legal uncertainty as well as obstacles to the free

---

Regulation'), OJ L 330, 23.12.2022, 1, which contains certain public procurement elements. The Foreign Subsidies Regulation has so far not been incorporated into the EEA Agreement, due to its 'third country trade policy' dimension.

411. Requests or enquiries should be sent to: registry@eftasurv.int.

412. In the interests of effective administration, the Authority recommends applicants to conduct 'pre-notification discussions' with the Authority, where the matter would be discussed informally. During these informal discussions, the Authority would inform the potential applicant about the information to be provided and discuss with them the competition situation in the respective sector. The Authority would further assess whether a specific draft request would comply with the legal requirements and discuss the likelihood of success to avoid unnecessary work.

413. Detailed rules applicable to the procedure for granting an exemption are contained in Commission Implementing Decision (EU) 2016/1804 of 10 Oct. 2016 (OJ L 275, 12.10.2016, 39), which the Authority applies *mutatis mutandis*.

414. With potential extensions depending on the specific circumstances of the case.

415. For example: EFTA Surveillance Authority Delegated Decision No. 42/19/COL of 17 Jun. 2019 exempting the operation of public bus transport services in Norway from the application of Directive 2014/25/EU (OJ L 259, 10.10.2019, 75); EFTA Surveillance Authority Decision No. 277/15/COL of 6 Jul. 2015 exempting certain logistics services of Posten Norge AS from the application of Directive 2004/17/EC (OJ L 92, 7.4.2016, 68); EFTA Surveillance Authority Decision No. 178/13/COL of 30 Apr. 2013 exempting the exploration and the extraction of crude oil and natural gas on the Norwegian Continental Shelf from the application of Directive 2004/17/EC (OJ L 249, 19.9.2013, 16); EFTA Surveillance Authority Decision No. 189/12/COL of 22 May 2012 exempting the production and wholesale of electricity in Norway from the application of Directive 2004/17/EC (OJ L 287, 18.10.2012, 21).

416. Concerning the difference between 'works concessions' and 'service concessions', *see* EFTA Court judgment of 21 Mar. 2018 in Case E-4/17, *EFTA Surveillance Authority v. the Kingdom of Norway* ('the Kristiansand case').

provision of services. In response, Directive 2014/23/EU was adopted,[417] introducing a legal framework for public authorities and economic operators to ensure non-discrimination and fair access to markets and EEA-wide competition for high-value concessions.[418]

483. As stated in Article 65(1) of the EEA Agreement, the public procurement rules apply to all products and to services, unless otherwise specified. Hence, products falling outside the product scope of Article 8(3) of the EEA Agreement (containing specific provisions on product coverage) and products mentioned in Article 123(b) of the EEA Agreement (products intended for specifically military purposes)[419] are not subject to the EEA procurement rules. Concerning the territorial application of the EEA public procurement rules, the EFTA Court found that the scope of application of Directive 2014/24/EU of the European Parliament and of the Council of 26 February 2014 on public procurement was not subject to any specific geographical limitation.[420] Consequently, the geographical scope of the EEA Agreement does not preclude EEA law from having effects outside the territory of the EEA.

484. In order to attain the goal of a liberalized public procurement market within the EEA, the substantial rules will have to be effectively enforced. The enforcement is mainly done nationally and remedies for breaches of EEA public procurement rules must be sought primarily before the national courts. This is covered by the 'Remedies Directive'.[421] The EFTA Court held that the Remedies Directive is an instrument of minimum harmonization. For example, Article 2(1)(c) of the Remedies Directive requires EEA States to ensure that the measures taken concerning the review procedures include provision for powers to award damages to persons

417. OJ L 94, 28.3.2014, 1.

418. Concession contracts are used by public authorities to deliver services or build infrastructure. Concessions involve a contractual arrangement between a public authority and an economic operator (the concession holder). The latter provides services or carries out works and is remunerated by being permitted to exploit the work or service.

419. However, Directive 2009/81/EC on defence and security procurement (OJ L 216, 20.8.2009, 76) has been included into Annex XVI to the EEA Agreement and is binding on the EFTA States since 1 Feb. 2014, with the exception of Liechtenstein, to which the Directive does not apply.

420. In the EFTA Court judgment of 16 Jul. 2020 in Case E-8/19, *Scanteam AS v. the Norwegian Government*, the Court decided that Directive 2014/24/EU was applicable to procurement procedures undertaken by a foreign mission of an EFTA State in a third country outside the EEA.

421. The 'Remedies Directive' for the public sector forms part of the EEA Agreement: Act referred to in point 5 of Annex XVI EEA Agreement (Council Directive 89/665/EEC on the coordination of the laws, regulations and administrative provisions relating to the application of review procedures to the award of public supply and public works contracts (OJ L 395, 30.12.1989, 33), as amended by Directive 2007/66/EC of the Parliament and the Council of 11 Dec. 2007 (OJ L 335, 20.12.2007, 31), and as amended by Directive 2014/23/EU of the European Parliament and of the Council of 26 Feb. 2014 (OJ L 94, 28.3.2014, 1; as corrected by OJ L 114, 5.5.2015, 24)). Equally, the 'Remedies Directive' for the utilities sector also forms part of the EEA Agreement: Act referred to in point 5a of Annex XVI EEA Agreement (Council Directive 92/13/EEC coordinating the laws, regulations and administrative provisions relating to the application of Community rules on the procurement procedures of entities operating in the water, energy, transport and telecommunications sectors, OJ L 76, 23.3.1992, 14, as amended).

harmed by an infringement. However, neither Article 2(1)(c) nor any other provision of the Remedies Directive lays down specific conditions for the award of damages. In a case concerning a damages claim raised by Fosen-Linjen AS, a Norwegian undertaking providing ferry services, against AtB AS, a company administering public transport services in the Norwegian county of Sør-Trøndelag, following the cancellation of a tender procedure for the procurement of ferry services, the EFTA Court held that Article 2(1)(c) of the Remedies Directive does not require that any breach of the rules governing public procurement in itself is sufficient to award damages for the loss of profit to persons harmed by an infringement.[422] The dispute in the national proceedings had already given rise to a request to the Court for an advisory opinion from the Frostating Court of Appeal and to the Court's judgment in Case E-16/16 (*Fosen-Linjen I*).[423] In that judgment, the Court held that a simple breach of public procurement law is in itself sufficient to trigger the liability of the contracting authority to compensate the person harmed for the damage incurred, pursuant to Article 2(1)(c) of the Remedies Directive, provided that the other conditions for the award of damages are met. In the second request concerning *Fosen-Linjen*, the Supreme Court of Norway asked whether this also applies where damages are claimed for the loss of profit.

485. For the division of competences between the European Commission and the Authority, a sectoral adaptation to Annex XVI to the EEA Agreement stipulates that the competence for surveillance of alleged infringements lies with the Commission if it is committed by a contracting entity in the EU, and lies with the Authority if it is committed by a contracting entity in an EFTA State.[424]

486. The general surveillance procedure foreseen in Article 31 SCA[425] is, on its own, not adequate to ensure effective compliance with the relevant public procurement rules. The general surveillance procedure does not allow for fast action at an early stage when infringements can still be corrected. Therefore, the Authority needed additional procedures to intervene at an early stage in national public procurement procedures. These additional powers (that correspond to Articles 3 and 4 of the first Remedies Directive) are entrusted to the Authority through Protocol 2 SCA.

487. According to Article 1(1) and (2) of Protocol 2 SCA, if confronted with a clear and manifest infringement, the Authority, prior to a contract being concluded, notifies the EFTA State, and the contracting authority concerned, of the reasons which it believes constitute the infringement, and requests its correction. Within twenty-one days of receipt of the notification, the State has to respond to the Authority's observations (Article 1(3) of Protocol 2 SCA). The EFTA State may either communicate to the Authority:

422. EFTA Court judgment of 1 Aug. 2019 in Case E-7/18, *Fosen-Linjen AS and AtB AS*.
423. EFTA Court judgment of 31 Oct. 2017 in Case E-16/16, *Fosen-Linjen AS and AtB AS*.
424. Sectoral adaptation 3 in Annex XVI to the EEA Agreement.
425. *See supra* Part II, Ch. 5, §1, I.

(1) its confirmation that the infringement has been corrected; or
(2) a reasoned submission as to why no correction has been made; or
(3) a notice to the effect that the contract award procedure has been suspended.

488. It follows from Article 1(5) of Protocol 2 SCA that if an EFTA State, for example, notifies the Authority that the procedure has been suspended, then it must also make known when the suspension is lifted, or another contract procedure relating, in whole or in part, to the same subject matter is begun. That notification shall confirm that the alleged infringement has been corrected or include a reasoned submission as to why no correction has been made.

489. The Authority may bring EFTA States before the EFTA Court under Article 31 SCA in case of breach of the above-mentioned obligations. The Authority can also apply to the EFTA Court for interim measures including suspension of an award procedure.[426] Concerning contracts already concluded and in breach of the public procurement rules, the Authority informed the public on 18 July 2011 of a change in its policy on pursuing infringement proceedings in the field of public procurement. Under the Authority's old policy, the Authority would, where it was of the view that the EEA rules on public procurement have been breached, invite the EFTA State concerned to recognize the breach and to express its commitment to refrain from such a breach in the future. Upon receipt of such recognition and commitment, the Authority would close the case. However, after that practice had been installed, the Court of Justice held that the adverse effect arising from an infringement of the EU/EEA procurement rules subsisted throughout the entire performance of the contract.[427] In light of this case law and the infringement policy pursued by the Commission, the Authority now in principle intends to pursue cases as long as the contract concerned continues to produce effects and the EFTA State concerned has not taken suitable corrective measures to rectify the breach.

490. Finally, review and reporting obligations for the EFTA States have been set out in Article 2 of Protocol 2 SCA. According to Article 2(1) of Protocol 2 SCA, the Authority, in conjunction with an advisory committee composed of representatives of the EFTA States, reviews the manner in which the provisions of Protocol 2 and the provisions of the Act referred to in point 5 of Annex XVI to the EEA Agreement[428] have been implemented and, if necessary, provides for proposals for amendments.

---

426. So far, the Authority has not applied for such interim measures.

427. Joined Cases C-20/01 and C-28/01 *Commission v. Germany* [2003] ECR I-3609.

428. Council Directive 89/665/EEC on the coordination of the laws, regulations and administrative provisions relating to the application of review procedures to the award of public supply and public works contracts (OJ L 395, 30.12.1989, 33); as amended by Directive 2007/66/EC of the European Parliament and the Council of 11 Dec. 2007 (OJ L 335, 20.12.2007, 31) and by Directive 2014/23/EU of the European Parliament and of the Council of 26 Feb. 2014 (OJ L 94, 28.3.2014, 1; as corrected by OJ L 114, 5.5.2015, 24).

B. Competition

491. A truly internal market requires an effective competition enforcement regime. Competition rules provide an important safeguard for undertakings, as enforcement of these rules protects them from the anticompetitive behaviour of other market players or from measures taken by States that are conducive to such behaviour, and they enable markets to work effectively for the benefit of consumers.

492. It follows from the fourth recital of the Preamble and Article 1(1) of the EEA Agreement that the establishment of equal conditions of competition is a central element of the EEA. In order to attain this objective, Article 1(2)(e) of the EEA Agreement requires the establishment of a system that ensures that competition is not distorted and that the rules thereon are equally respected. The EEA competition provisions basically serve the same purpose as the ones in the EU.

493. In the field of competition the Authority has equivalent powers and similar functions to those of the European Commission.[429] Whereas most of the Authority's activities relate to behaviour of EFTA States, the competition rules contained in Articles 53–58 and 60 of the EEA Agreement concern individual economic operators. Only Article 59 of the EEA Agreement (on public undertakings) relates to measures taken by the States. These provisions are, in practice, virtually the same as in the TFEU. The rules prohibit agreements and conduct that distort or restrict competition (Article 53 of the EEA Agreement).[430] Such conduct can, for example, include price-fixing and market-sharing arrangements, which are almost always prohibited. Other types of agreements and conduct that restrict competition are not prohibited if the restrictions are necessary to create economic improvements which benefit consumers. The competition rules also prohibit dominant undertakings from abusing their market power (Article 54 of the EEA Agreement).[431] Close cooperation between the European Commission and the Authority ensures a homogeneous interpretation and application of the competition rules in both pillars.

494. The EEA competition rules apply in the EFTA States in parallel to relevant national competition legislation. Only in the field of merger control do the Authority and the European Commission retain exclusive competence. National authorities cannot control concentrations that have an EFTA or EU dimension.

---

429. *See infra* Part II, Ch. 5, §1, II, B, 3.

430. Concerning the notion of 'restriction of competition by object', *see* EFTA Court judgment of 22 Dec. 2016 in Case E-03/16, *Ski Taxi SA, Follo Taxi SA og Ski Follo Taxidrift AS v. Staten v/Konkurransetilsynet*.

431. The EFTA Court held that a natural or legal person must be able to rely on Art. 54 of the EEA Agreement, as it is, or has been made, part of domestic law, in order to claim compensation before national courts for a violation of that provision (EFTA Court judgment of 30 May 2018 in Case E-6/17, *Fjarskipti hf. v. Síminn hf.*). Concerning the limitation period for bringing follow-on damages claims in competition law where fines have been previously imposed pursuant to Arts 53 and 54 of the EEA Agreement, *see*: EFTA Court judgment of 17 Sep. 2018 in Case E-10/17, *Nye Kystlink AS v. Color Group AS and Color Line AS*.

495. As already mentioned above, the product coverage of the EEA Agreement is limited.[432] The Authority has, consequently, no power to apply the EEA competition rules in respect of products falling outside the scope of the EEA Agreement. These cases are either governed by the national rules of the EFTA States or by the possible extraterritorial application of the EU competition rules.

496. The EEA competition rules evolve constantly in order to incorporate developments in the acquis communautaire. They changed, for example, in 2004 to reflect adjustments in anticipation of enlargement, namely the modernization of the rules implementing [ex] Articles 81 and 82 EC Treaty[433] (now Articles 101 and 102 TFEU) and the review of the EU Merger Regulation.[434] Reference to the incorporation of these changes into the EEA legal framework is made in the subsequent sections.

497. In accordance with the overall structure of the EEA Agreement, the EEA competition rules may be found in several places in the EEA Agreement, that is, in its main part, five protocols, one annex, as well as in the SCA.[435] In order to map out the situation, one could divide the rules into three categories: substantive rules, the competence/cooperation rules and procedural rules.

1. The Substantive EEA Competition Rules

498. The substantive EEA competition rules, which mirror the EU rules, to be applied by the Authority and the Commission are set out in Chapter 1 of Part IV EEA Agreement. Chapter 1 of Part IV EEA Agreement contains, *inter alia*, Articles 53 (restrictive agreements), 54 (abuse of a dominant position), 57 (mergers), 59 (public undertakings) and 60 of the EEA Agreement. Article 60 of, in conjunction with Annex XIV to, the EEA Agreement contain the specific provisions which give effect to the principles set out in Articles 53, 54, 57 and 59 of the EEA Agreement.[436] Protocols 14 (general) and 25 (competition) to the EEA Agreement refer to coal and steel.

---

432. *See supra* Part II, Ch. 2, §1, I.
433. Council Regulation (EC) No. 1/2003 of 16 Dec. 2002 on the implementation of the rules on competition laid down in [ex] Arts 81 and 82 of the Treaty (OJ L 1, 4.1.2003, 1).
434. Council Regulation (EC) No. 139/2004 of 20 Jan. 2004 on the control of concentrations between undertakings (OJ L 24, 29.1.2004, 1).
435. There are also several declarations and agreed minutes which clarify the meaning of certain provisions or the intention of the Contracting Parties.
436. For example, the EU Merger Regulation and the block exemptions which are currently applicable. Annex XIV to the EEA Agreement also lists so-called non-binding acquis, that is, the different notices issued by the Commission such as the *de minimis* Notice and the Notices on commercial agents, on subcontracting, on restrictions ancillary to mergers, etc. However, Directive 2014/104/EU of the European Parliament and of the Council of 26 Nov. 2014 on certain rules governing actions for damages under national law for infringements of the competition law provisions of the Member States and of the EU ('the Damage Directive'), OJ L 349, 5.12.2014, 1, has not yet been incorporated into Annex XIV to the EEA Agreement.

499. The three cornerstones of the EEA competition regime are laid down in Articles 53, 54 and 57 of the EEA Agreement. Article 53 of the EEA Agreement prohibits agreements or concerted practices that restrain competition between undertakings and corresponds in substance to Article 101 TFEU. When an undertaking, or a group of undertakings, has market dominance within the EEA or in a substantial part thereof, Article 54 of the EEA Agreement prohibits the abuse of such a position.[437] Article 54 of the EEA Agreement reproduces, with some minor adaptations for EEA purposes, Article 102 TFEU. Article 57 of, in conjunction with Annex XIV (Chapter A, point 1) to, the EEA Agreement regulate the control of large mergers and other concentrations of undertakings, which significantly impede effective competition in the EEA or a substantial part of it, in particular as a result of the creation or strengthening of a dominant position. Article 57 of the EEA Agreement contains both a substantive rule (on incompatible mergers) and a procedural rule (attribution of merger cases between the European Commission and the Authority). Article 57(1) of the EEA Agreement reproduces parts of the old EC Merger Regulation.[438] The whole body of the present EU Merger Regulation[439] has been taken into the EEA legal framework, with specific adaptations.[440]

500. Pursuant to Article 59 of the EEA Agreement, the Authority may also deal with cases involving anticompetitive behaviour by public undertakings, undertakings to which EFTA States have granted special or exclusive rights, or undertakings entrusted with the operation of services of general economic interest or having the character of a revenue-producing monopoly. Article 59 of the EEA Agreement reproduces most of the text of (now) Article 106 TFEU. The difference lies in Article 59(3) of the EEA Agreement, which only envisages 'appropriate measures'

437. On 14 Jul. 2010, the Authority imposed a fine of EUR 12.89 million on Posten Norge AS under Art. 54 EEA Agreement. This was the first time ever the Authority imposed a fine under the competition rules. The Decision was challenged before the EFTA Court. By judgment of 18 Apr. 2012, in Case E-15/10 *Posten Norge AS v. EFTA Surveillance Authority*, the EFTA Court dismissed the application, but reduced the fine to EUR 11.11 million. On 29 Jun. 2020, the Authority issued a decision concluding that Telenor had abused its market dominance by a pricing strategy that resulted in rivals making a loss when selling residential mobile broadband services on tablets and laptops. These margin squeeze practices prevented rival companies from competing viably from 2008 to the end of 2012 in what was an evolving and fast-growing market at the time. The Authority imposed a fine of EUR 111,951,000. The Decision was challenged before the EFTA Court. By judgment of 5 May 2022, in Case E-12/20 *Telenor ASA and Telenor Norge AS v. EFTA Surveillance Authority*, the EFTA Court dismissed the application in its entirety.

438. Council Regulation (EEC) No. 4064/89 of 21 Dec. 1989 on the control of concentrations between undertakings (OJ L 395, 30.12.1989, 1).

439. Council Regulation (EC) No. 139/2004 of 20 Jan. 2004 on the control of concentrations between undertakings (OJ L 24, 29.1.2004, 1).

440. The content of the EU Merger Regulation is reflected in Annex XIV to the EEA Agreement, Protocols 21, 22 and 24 to the EEA Agreement and Protocol 4 SCA. Council Regulation (EC) No. 139/2004 (OJ L 24, 29.1.2004, 1) has been incorporated into the EEA Agreement (Annex XIV) through the adoption of two Decisions of the EEA Joint Committee on 8 Jun. 2004. The first Decision of the EEA Joint Committee No. 78/2004 incorporated the main parts of Council Regulation (EC) No. 139/2004. The second Decision of the EEA Joint Committee No. 79/2004 incorporated Arts 13 and 22 of Council Regulation (EC) No. 139/2004.

by the European Commission or the Authority to ensure application of the provision of Article 59 of the EEA Agreement. Article 106(3) TFEU, on the other hand, gives the European Commission the power to address 'appropriate directives or decisions' to the EU Member States.[441]

2. Attribution of Competence and Cooperation Rules

501. The responsibility for handling competition cases under the EEA Agreement is shared between the Authority and the European Commission in accordance with the attribution rules contained in Article 56 of the EEA Agreement (attribution of competence for cases falling under Articles 53 and 54 of the EEA Agreement) and Article 57(2) of the EEA Agreement (attribution of merger cases). The EEA Agreement is based on the 'one-stop-shop' principle implying that either the European Commission or the Authority, but not both, is competent to handle the case. Consequently, cases dealt with by the Authority may concern undertakings located not only in the EFTA States, but also in EU Member States or third countries. Similarly, the European Commission may have jurisdiction to address the actions of undertakings located in the EFTA States.

502. The basic rule as regards the application of Article 53 of the EEA Agreement to undertakings is that the European Commission is responsible for cases falling under the competition rules of the TFEU, that is, when trade between the EU Member States is affected. The Authority handles cases where there is an effect only on trade between the EFTA States (Article 56(1)(a) of the EEA Agreement). For 'mixed cases', where trade between the EU and one or more EFTA States is affected, attribution of jurisdiction is based on the relative importance of the turnover of the undertakings concerned in the EFTA and in the EU territories (Article 56(1)(b) and (c) of the EEA Agreement).[442] The Authority is competent to handle cases where trade between EFTA States and EU States is affected and either internal EU trade or competition is not appreciably affected (Article 56(3) of the EEA Agreement).

503. The rules for attributing individual cases falling under Article 54 of the EEA Agreement are the following: cases where dominance exists only within the territory of EFTA States will be dealt with by the Authority; cases where the dominance exists only within the EU will be dealt with by the European Commission; in cases where dominance exists within both the EU and EFTA territories, the rules concerning mixed cases stated above (previous paragraph) apply (Article 56(2) and (3) of the EEA Agreement).

441. Since the Authority has no legislative powers to adopt directives, the term 'appropriate measures' was chosen.
442. With regard to the notions of 'turnover' and 'undertaking' in Art. 56(1)(b) EEA Agreement, Art. 56(4) EEA Agreement refers to the definitions in Protocol 22 to the EEA Agreement.

504. With regard to merger cases, Article 57(2)(a) of and Annex XIV (Chapter A, point 1) to the EEA Agreement provide that the European Commission has the sole competence[443] to decide on concentrations with an EU dimension.[444] The Authority is only competent to deal with applications to approve mergers if there is no EU dimension and an EFTA dimension[445] is established (Article 57(2)(b) of the EEA Agreement).

505. Where a breach of the EEA competition rules follows from measures taken by an EFTA State, the Authority has sole competence to address the matter with the State in question under Article 59 of the EEA Agreement (by virtue of Article 59(3) of the EEA Agreement).

506. If a case is submitted to the wrong authority, that authority is under an obligation to hand over the file to the competent authority. The EEA rules on the allocation of jurisdiction between the Authority and the European Commission are regularly considered in concrete instances, and a number of cases have been formally transferred from one authority to the other. According to the procedural rules of the EEA Agreement, cases may only be transferred once. For the undertakings concerned it should make no difference which of the two authorities handles a case insofar as the competition rules are the same, and they are applied in the same manner.

507. Articles 58 and 109(2) of the EEA Agreement require cooperation between the Authority and the European Commission. Article 58 of the EEA Agreement requires that the Authority and the European Commission cooperate in accordance with Protocols 23 (antitrust) and 24 (merger control) to the EEA Agreement, with a view to developing and maintaining a uniform surveillance throughout the EEA in the field of competition and to promoting a homogenous implementation, application and interpretation of the provisions of the EEA Agreement. Protocols 23 and 24 to the EEA Agreement also include procedural elements as regards cooperation between the Authority and the European Commission in so-called mixed cases involving the application of Articles 53 and/or 54 of the EEA Agreement (antitrust) or Article 57 of the EEA Agreement (merger control).

508. Based on these Protocols, the European Commission and the Authority cooperate in the handling of individual cases which affect both EFTA States and EU Member States. The EEA rules on cooperation in competition cases provide the authority, which is not handling a case, with a right to comment formally on the case at various stages, and with a right to obtain copies of the most important documents

443. The Authority also participates in referral proceedings under Art. 6 of Protocol 24 to the EEA Agreement. The Commission may, provided certain criteria are fulfilled, decide to refer a notified concentration to an EFTA State. The parties can also prior to notification of a concentration with Community dimension by way of a reasoned submission request that the concentration be examined by an EFTA State.

444. As defined in Art. 1 of Council Regulation (EC) No. 139/2004 (OJ L 24, 29.1.2004, 1).

445. An 'EFTA dimension' is established when the turnover thresholds set out in Art. 1 of Council Regulation (EC) No. 139/2004 (*supra* previous note) are met within the EFTA pillar.

lodged with, or issued by, the competent authority. Both authorities may, in such cases, take part and express views in each other's hearings and Advisory Committee meetings.[446] EEA cooperation rights are also extended to the States over which each authority has jurisdiction, so that, in mixed cases handled by the European Commission, the Authority will forward copies of documents received to the EFTA States and forward any feedback to the European Commission. In all such proceedings, the view of the Authority remains independent from those of the EFTA States.

509. Furthermore, the European Commission may request that the Authority carries out inspections on its behalf at the premises of undertakings operating within the EFTA territory.[447] The Authority has the same rights as regards the European Commission when it comes to inspections in the EU. These procedures have been applied on a number of occasions to date.

510. Pursuant to Article 15(3) of Chapter II of Protocol 4 SCA, the Authority, acting on its own initiative, may submit written observations ('amicus curiae' observations) to courts of the EFTA States where the coherent application of Article 53 or 54 so requires. With the permission of the court in question, the Authority may also make oral observations.[448]

511. The Authority and the competent authorities of the EFTA States participate in meetings of the European Competition Network (ECN)[449] to ensure effective and consistent enforcement of the EEA competition rules throughout the EEA. The Authority also cooperates with competition authorities at European level through

---

446. In accordance with the provisions in Protocol 23 to the EEA Agreement, the Authority presented, for example, in 2019 and 2018 its views in the following cases: Case AT.40436 – *Ancillary Sports Merchandise*; Case AT.40481 – *Occupants Safety Systems (II)* supplied to the Volkswagen Group and the BMW Group; Case AT.40428 – *Guess*; Case AT.40182 – *Pioneer*; Case AT.40136 – *Capacitor*; Case AT.40220 (2) – *Qualcomm* (Exclusivity Payments); and Case AT.40220 – *Qualcomm* (Exclusivity Payments). Equally, in accordance with the provisions in Protocol 24 to the EEA Agreement, the Authority presented in 2018 its views on the following merger cases: Case M.8909 – *KME/MKM*; Case M.8480 – *Praxair/Linde*; and Case M.8451 – *Tronox/Cristal*.

447. In such inspections, the Authority is empowered to enter any premises and to examine and secure documentation relating to the subject matter and purpose of the inspection. Documents may be copied from any medium and a complete archive of the seized documents will be provided to the inspected company/association at the end of the inspection. The Authority's inspection team may decide to seal certain areas of the undertaking's premises overnight. Any breach of these seals may be penalized by a fine of up to 1% of the undertaking's annual global turnover.

448. EFTA Surveillance Authority Notice on the cooperation between the Authority and the courts of the EFTA States in the application of Arts 53 and 54 of the EEA Agreement (OJ C 305, 14.12.2006, 19). Cases in which the Authority has participated so far: *The Competition Authority and Icelandic State v. Byko ehf./Norvik hf.* (Case No 42/2019); *Telenor ASA og Telenor Norge AS (Telenor)* (Case No 2019/34); *Byko ehf./Norvik hf. v. the Competition Authority and the Icelandic State and The Competition Authority v. Byko ehf./Norvik hf.* (Case No 490/2018); *The Icelandic Competition Authority v. Byko ehf/Norvik hf* (Case No. E-550/2016); *NCC AB and NCC Roads AS v. Staten v/Konkurransetilsynet* (Case No. 14-076039ASD-BORG/03); and *Bastø Fosen AS v. Color Line* (Case No. 13-178315ASD-BORG/02).

449. The ECN works on effective enforcement of the competition rules against cross-border business practices that restrict competition and damage consumers. The ECN also allows competition authorities to pool their experience and identify best practice.

the network of European Competition Authorities (ECAs),[450] and at international level through membership of the International Competition Network (ICN).[451] In addition, the Authority follows closely the work of the Competition Committee of the (OECD).[452]

3. The Procedural EEA Competition Rules

512. The procedural rules, which mirror the EU rules, are laid down in Article 55 of the EEA Agreement (grant of application powers), in Protocol 21 to the EEA Agreement (procedural and transition rules) and in Protocol 4 SCA.

513. Article 1 of Protocol 21 to the EEA Agreement states that the Authority shall, in an agreement between the EFTA States, be entrusted with equivalent powers and similar functions to those of the European Commission, at the time of signature of the EEA Agreement, for the application of the competition rules of the TFEU. This provision enables the Authority to give effect to the principles laid down in Articles 1(2)(e) and 53–60 of the EEA Agreement and in Protocol 25 thereto. The SCA lays down procedural rules to be followed by the Authority.

514. The procedural rules to be followed by the Authority, when handling competition cases, are set out in Protocol 4 SCA. These rules have been completely overhauled with a view to reflecting the changes introduced by Council Regulation (EC) No. 1/2003 on the implementation of the rules on competition laid down in [ex] Articles 81 and 82 EC Treaty (now Articles 101 and 102 TFEU).[453] Beyond the general competition law enforcement procedure, Protocol 4 SCA also contains procedural rules for transport (air, maritime and inland) in Chapters VI to XII of its Part II. Finally, Chapter XIII of Part III of Protocol 4 SCA sets out the procedural rules relating to the control of concentrations between undertakings.

515. The Authority also appointed two Hearing Officers. The main role of the Hearing Officers is to safeguard procedural rights throughout the Authority's competition investigations and to act as an independent arbiter where a dispute on the effective exercise of such procedural rights arises between the parties and the Authority's Competition and State Aid Directorate.[454] The Hearing Officers are independent of the Authority's case-handling services and play a crucial role as the

---

450. The ECA is based on informal cooperation, with meetings held at least once a year. The aim is to improve cooperation between competition authorities and to contribute to the efficient enforcement of national and European competition law.
451. The ICN is a specialized yet informal venue, which allows for a dynamic dialogue and which serves to build consensus and convergence on sound competition policy principles throughout the global antitrust community.
452. Through its Working Parties 2 (WP2) and 3 (WP3), the OECD Competition Committee promotes regular discussions and best practice sharing on a wide range of competition policy issues.
453. Decision of the EEA Joint Committee No. 130/2004 of 24 Sep. 2004.
454. EFTA Surveillance Authority Decision No. 442/12/COL of 29 Nov. 2012 on the function and terms of reference of the hearing officer in certain competition proceedings.

guardians of the procedural rights of parties in proceedings under Articles 53 and 54 of the EEA Agreement. Hearing Officers generally intervene only where a dispute on specific issues (such as the exercise of the right of access to the file, the handling of claims of legal professional privilege and requests for extensions to time limits for replies to key case documents such as statements of objections) cannot be resolved by the parties and the Authority's Competition and State Aid Directorate. The Hearing Officers also organize oral hearings and decide on applications by third parties to be heard in the proceedings.[455]

516. As regards procedures followed by the European Commission when applying the EEA Agreement, Article 1 of Protocol 21 to the EEA Agreement places an obligation on the EU to ensure that the European Commission, when applying the EEA competition rules, follows the same procedures as those used when applying the TFEU. Council Regulation (EC) No. 2894/94[456] confirms this in its Article 5, by providing that the European Commission will apply the same procedural rules when applying the EEA competition rules as it follows in an EU context.

517. According to Article 17 in Part II of Protocol 4 SCA, the Authority may carry out investigations into particular sectors of the economy or into particular types of agreements across various sectors (so-called sector enquires). A sector enquiry is essentially an information-gathering exercise that enables the Authority to gain in-depth knowledge about particular markets. Such knowledge may in turn form the basis for subsequent enforcement action under Article 53 or 54 of the EEA Agreement. Sectors that have been subject of an enquiry are financial services, energy and telecommunications.

C. State Aid

518. The task of controlling State aid is one of the most important means of ensuring that equal conditions of competition within the EEA are not distorted by actions of States. In the field of State aid, the powers to control the EFTA States are vested with the Authority.[457] Consequently, the Authority controls State aid granted by Iceland, Liechtenstein and Norway to allow fair competition and an open internal market in the EEA.[458] The powers of the Authority mirror the extended competencies of the European Commission in this area and the monitoring activities of the Authority in the field of State aid fully correspond to those of the European Commission in this field.[459] This means that the EFTA States are subject to the same

455. Final Report of the Hearing Officer in Case No. 71480 – *Telenor* (OJ C 292, 3.9.2020, 7).
456. OJ L 305, 30.11.1994, 6.
457. *See* Michael Sánchez Rydelski, 'State Aid', in *The Handbook of EEA Law* 575–603 (Carl Baudenbacher ed., Switzerland: Springer International Publishing 2015).
458. The Authority's State aid Decisions are available on the website of the Authority: www.eftasurv.int/state-aid/state-aid-register.
459. With the exception of Council Regulation (EU) 2015/1589 of 13 Jul. 2015 laying down detailed rules for the application of Art. 108 of the Treaty on the Functioning of the European Union (OJ L 248, 24.9.2015, 9), which has still not been incorporated into the EEA legal framework. Equally,

strict State aid control as the Member States in the EU. Close cooperation between the European Commission and the Authority avoids the emergence of diverging policies between the two pillars of the EEA.

519. The rules on State aid are contained in Articles 49, 59 and 61–64 of the EEA Agreement, as well as in Annexes XIII, section 1(iv) and XV, further in Protocols 9, 14, 26 and 27 to the EEA Agreement. Furthermore, the SCA contains State aid provisions in Article 24, Annex I and Protocol 3. Protocol 3 SCA contains detailed procedural provisions which are applicable to State aid cases.

1. The Substantive EEA State Aid Provisions

520. The basic substantive provisions on State aid are found in Article 61 of the EEA Agreement, which is, with some minor adaptations, identical in substance to Article 107 TFEU. The main rule in Article 61(1) of the EEA Agreement is that aid granted by EU Member States, EFTA States or through State resources, which distorts or threatens to distort competition by favouring certain undertakings or the production of certain goods, and which affects trade between the Contracting Parties, is incompatible with the functioning of the EEA Agreement. State aid is public support to economic activities. It can take many forms, for example, cash grants, tax breaks or favourable loans. As a rule, Article 61(1) of the EEA Agreement prohibits State aid to prevent negative impacts on competition and trade, but exceptions are provided for objectives such as environmental protection, regional support and research, innovation and development. These exceptions are contained in the second and third paragraphs of Article 61 of the EEA Agreement.

521. Article 61(2) of the EEA Agreement replicates the provisions of Article 107(2) TFEU and declares that the same categories of aid shall be considered automatically compatible with the functioning of the EEA Agreement. It might puzzle the reader to *see* that Article 61(2)(c) of the EEA Agreement entirely copied Article 107(2)(c) TFEU which declares State aid compatible, when it is granted to compensate for the disadvantages due to the former German division. It would be far-fetched to assume that EFTA States would grant State aid to areas in Germany affected by the former German division. However, it needs to be recalled that Article 61 of the EEA Agreement also has to be applied by the European Commission towards the Member States in the EU. Therefore, an identical wording was considered necessary.

522. Article 61(3) of the EEA Agreement basically copies the provisions of Article 107(3) TFEU, which lays down the categories of aid that may be considered

---

Regulation (EU) 2022/2560 of the European Parliament and of the Council of 14 Dec. 2022 on foreign subsidies distorting the internal market ('the Foreign Subsidies Regulation'), OJ L 330, 23.12.2022, 1, has so far not been incorporated into the EEA Agreement, due to its 'third country trade policy' dimension.

to be compatible with the functioning of the EEA Agreement. The cultural derogation in Article 107(3)(d) TFEU is not reflected in Article 61(3) of the EEA Agreement, because the cultural exception has been inserted into the EU system only after the conclusion of the EEA Agreement. The fact that Article 61(3) of the EEA Agreement does not contain a similar provision to Article 107(3)(d) TFEU has not hindered the Authority to approve State aid with a cultural dimension. Concerning the approval of cultural aid, the Authority has taken the view that such support measures might be approved on cultural grounds on the basis of Article 61(3)(c) of the EEA Agreement, provided that this approach takes the criteria developed by the European Commission sufficiently into account, and that the approach does not deviate from the European Commission's practice prior to the adoption of Article 107(3)(d) TFEU.[460]

523. Concerning derogations for aid granted to transport by rail, road and inland waterway, Article 49 of the EEA Agreement provides that '[a]id shall be compatible with this Agreement if it meets the needs of coordination of transport or if it represents reimbursement for the discharge of certain obligations inherent in the concept of a public service'. This corresponds to Article 93 TFEU.

524. With regard to the concept of public services, the Authority applies the general derogation clause in Article 59(2) of the EEA Agreement, when assessing compensation for public service obligations. Article 59(2) of the EEA Agreement corresponds to Article 106(2) TFEU.

525. Another substantive provision is Article 63 of the EEA Agreement. Article 63 of the EEA Agreement refers to Annex XV to the EEA Agreement, which contains references to secondary EU legislation.[461] In addition, it lists various frameworks, letters from the European Commission to the EU Member States, European Commission communications, and even extracts from the European Commission Annual Reports on Competition Policy. The listing puts an obligation on both the European Commission and the Authority to take due account of them in the EEA

460. *See*, for example: EFTA Surveillance Authority Decision No. 32/02/COL of 20 Feb. 2002 concerning film production and film related activities in Norway; and EFTA Surveillance Authority Decision No. 289/09/COL of 1 Jul. 2009 on the prolongation of the support schemes to audiovisual productions, film related activities and film production companies.

461. Such as the General Block Exemption Regulation (GBER), i.e., Commission Regulation (EU) No. 651/2014 of 17 Jun. 2014 declaring certain categories of aid compatible with the internal market in application of Arts 107 and 108 TFEU (OJ L 187, 26.6.2014, 1), as amended; the *de minimis* Regulations (general), i.e., Commission Regulation (EU) No. 1407/2013 of 18 Dec. 2013 on the application of Arts 107 and 108 TFEU to *de minimis* aid (OJ L 352, 24.12.2013, 1); and Services of General Economic Interest (SGEI), i.e., Commission Regulation (EU) No. 360/2012 of 25 Apr. 2012 on the application of Arts 107 and 108 TFEU to *de minimis* aid granted to undertakings providing services of general economic interest (OJ L 114, 26.4.2012, 8); the SGEI Decision, i.e., Commission Decision of 20 Dec. 2011 on the application of Art. 106(2) TFEU to State aid in the form of public service compensation granted to certain undertakings entrusted with operation of services of general economic interest (OJ L 7, 11.1.2012, 3); and the Transparency Directive, i.e., Commission Directive 2006/111/EC of 16 Nov. 2006 on the transparency of financial relations between Member States and public undertakings as well as financial transparency within certain undertakings (OJ L 318, 17.11.2006, 17).

context and thus ensures that the acquis in the field of State aid is interpreted identically by both surveillance authorities. It has also placed an obligation on the Authority to adopt acts corresponding to those adopted by the European Commission.[462] Consequently, the Authority has adopted, after consultation with the European Commission and the EFTA States, a number of procedural and substantive rules in the field of State aid (so-called State Aid Guidelines),[463] incorporating most of the principles, as well as guidelines and frameworks, developed in the context of the EU State aid rules.

2. The Procedural EEA State Aid Provisions

526. Article 62(1) of the EEA Agreement provides that all existing systems of State aid in the territory of the Contracting Parties, as well as any plans to grant or alter State aid, shall be subject to constant review as to their compatibility with Article 61 of the EEA Agreement. According to Article 62(1) of the EEA Agreement, this review shall be carried out by the European Commission as regards the EU Member States and by the Authority as regards the EFTA States. Both surveillance authorities have therefore their own decision-making autonomy. The attribution of cases depends on the State which is proposing the aid measure.

527. Article 62(1)(b) of the EEA Agreement further specifies that the Authority is entrusted with the powers and functions laid down in Protocol 26 to the EEA Agreement. Article 1 of Protocol 26 reads as follows:

> The EFTA Surveillance Authority shall, in an agreement between the EFTA States, be entrusted with equivalent powers and similar functions to those of the EC Commission, at the time of the signature of the Agreement, for the application of the competition rules applicable to State aid of the Treaty establishing the European Economic Community, enabling the EFTA Surveillance Authority to give effect to the principles expressed in Articles 1(2)(e), 49 and 61 to 63 of the Agreement. The EFTA Surveillance Authority shall also have such powers to give effect to the competition rules applicable to State aid relating to products falling under the Treaty establishing the European Coal and Steel Community as referred to in Protocol 14.

528. Article 2 of Protocol 26 further mentions that in addition to the acts listed in Annex XV to the EEA Agreement, Council Regulation (EC) No. 659/1999 of 22 March 1999 laying down detailed rules for the application of Article 93 of the EC

462. *See* the General Note No. II in Annex XV to the EEA Agreement.
463. Procedural and Substantive Rules in the Field of State Aid. Adopted and issued by the Authority on 19 Jan. 1994 (OJ L 231, 3.9.1994, 1; EEA Supplement No. 32, 3.9.1999, 1). The State Aid Guidelines are constantly updated and can be obtained via the website of the Authority: www.eftasurv.int/state-aid/state-aid-guidelines.

Treaty[464] reflects the powers and functions of the European Commission for the application of the competition rules in the area of State aid.[465]

529. Concerning the Authority's competence in the field of State aid, Article 24(1) SCA contains an enumeration of the provisions on State aid of the EEA Agreement, the application of which the Authority is to ensure. It is drafted in a similar way as Protocol 26 to the EEA Agreement, specifying not only the general State aid provisions in Article 61 of the EEA Agreement, but also provisions related to specific fields, including Article 49 of the EEA Agreement (transport sector) and Protocol 14 to the EEA Agreement (ECSC steel industry). Article 24(2) SCA further states that '[i]n application of Article 5(2)(b) [of the SCA], the EFTA Surveillance Authority shall, in particular, upon the entry into force of this Agreement, adopt acts corresponding to those in Annex I'. Based on Articles 5(2)(b) and 24 SCA, the Authority has adopted a number of procedural and substantive rules in the field of State aid, incorporating most of the principles, as well as guidelines and frameworks, developed in the context of the EU State aid rules. For this purpose, the Authority has made a certain number of adaptations to the text of the non-binding acts which have been, in principle, only of a technical nature, as it could not, due to the homogeneity requirements, change the substance of the rules contained in the acts. The Authority initially issued these Guidelines in January 1994. They have since then been updated regularly.[466]

530. The primary procedural rules are set out in Article 1 in Part I of Protocol 3 SCA. It sets out the procedures for the examination of new and existing aid.[467] These provisions are comparable to Article 108 TFEU. Furthermore, the full text, with some technical adaptations, of the EU Procedural Regulation[468] was incorporated into Protocol 3 SCA as Part II.[469] Further implementing provisions to Part II

---

464. OJ L 83, 27.3.1999, 1, as amended.
465. However, bearing in mind that Council Regulation (EU) 2015/1589 of 13 Jul. 2015 laying down detailed rules for the application of Art. 108 of the Treaty on the Functioning of the European Union (OJ L 248, 24.9.2015, 9) has still not been incorporated into the EEA legal framework.
466. Procedural and Substantive Rules in the Field of State Aid. Adopted and issued by the Authority on 19 Jan. 1994 (OJ L 231, 3.9.1994, 1; EEA Supplement No. 32, 3.9.1994, 1). The State Aid Guidelines are constantly updated and can be obtained via the website of the Authority: www.eftasurv.int/state-aid/state-aid-guidelines.
467. Concerning the delimitation between new and existing aid, *see*, for example: Joined Cases E-5/04, E-6/04 and E-7/04 *Fesil and others v. EFTA Surveillance Authority* [2005] Report of the EFTA Court, 121; Joined Cases E-4/10, E-6/10 and E-7/10 *Liechtenstein, REASSUR Aktiengesellschaft and Swisscom RE Aktiengesellschaft v. EFTA Surveillance Authority* [2011] Report of the EFTA Court, 22; Case E-14/10 *Konkurrenten AS v. EFTA Surveillance Authority* [2011] Report of the EFTA Court, 268; and EFTA Court judgment of 24 Jan. 2023 in Case E-1/22, *G. Modiano Limited and Standard Wool (UK) Limited v. EFTA Surveillance Authority.*
468. Council Regulation (EC) No. 659/1999 of 22 Mar. 1999 laying down detailed rules for the application of [ex] Art. 93 [now Art. 108 TFEU] of the EC Treaty (OJ L 83, 27.3.1999, 1).
469. Agreement between the EFTA States of 10 Dec. 2001, amending Protocol 3 to the Surveillance and Court Agreement.

of Protocol 3 SCA have been adopted by the EFTA Surveillance Authority's Decision No. 195/04/COL of 14 July 2004.[470]

531. The last sentence of Article 1(3) in Part I of Protocol 3 SCA provides that Contracting Parties may not implement new State aid measures before they have been approved by the Authority ('the standstill clause').[471] Any new State aid put into effect without the Authority's authorization is unlawful. Parties affected by unlawful State aid can bring direct actions before national courts for damages, recovery and/or injunctive measures. The Authority's guidelines on the enforcement of State aid law by national courts ('the Enforcement Guidelines')[472] underline the key role of national courts in enforcing EEA State aid law and underline the Authority's availability to assist national courts when confronted with such case.[473]

532. Article 1 in Part III of Protocol 3 SCA lays down the principles concerning the establishment and functions of an EFTA Advisory Committee on aid granted for transport by rail, road, and inland waterway, a Committee that also exists on the EU side.

3. Cooperation Between the European Commission and the EFTA Surveillance Authority

533. As already mentioned above, both the European Commission and the Authority have their own decision-making autonomy. With a view to ensuring a uniform surveillance in the field of State aid throughout the territory covered by the EEA Agreement, Article 62(2) of the EEA Agreement obliges the European Commission and the Authority to cooperate in accordance with the provisions set out in Protocol 27 to the EEA Agreement. According to this Protocol, the European Commission and the Authority have, *inter alia*, an obligation to exchange information and views on general policy issues and inform each other on all decisions as soon as they have been taken. For cases where one of the surveillance authorities considers that the other does not correctly apply the State aid rules, Article 64 of the EEA Agreement contains a special dispute settlement procedure.[474]

---

470. This Decision of the Authority reflects Commission Regulation (EC) No. 794/2004 (OJ L 140, 30.4.2004, 1).
471. Using the General Block Exemption Regulation (GBER), EFTA States can implement aid measures without having to follow the notification process. Instead, the EFTA States can simply submit information to the Authority by using the GBER information sheet template, available on: www.eftasurv.int/state-aid/gber-information-sheets.
472. The Enforcement Guidelines are available on the Authority's website: www.eftasurv.int/state-aid/state-aid-guidelines.
473. On 15 Mar. 2023, the Authority submitted for the first time written pleadings in a State aid case, which was pending before the Norwegian Supreme Court in Case 22-135401SIV-HRET *Oslo kommune v. Grønnegata 21 AS.*
474. *See infra* Part II, Ch. 6, §2.

4. State Aid to Fisheries

534. The product coverage of the EEA Agreement is limited.[475] There will most likely be State aid cases which will concern, at the same time, products both covered and not covered by the EEA Agreement. In these cases, the Authority will examine only that part of the aid which supports products covered by the EEA Agreement.[476] The dividing line is to be found in a case-by-case approach, taking into consideration all specific elements related to the aid measure in question. In this context, the question whether the Authority's competence covers the assessment of State aid to the fisheries sector has been an issue of frequent dispute.[477] State aid provisions applicable under the EEA Agreement to the fisheries sector are exhaustively set out in Protocol 9 to the EEA Agreement. Although Article 4(1) of Protocol 9 to the EEA Agreement states that State aid to the fisheries sector that distorts competition shall be abolished, the Authority has consistently taken the position that it is for the Contracting Parties themselves to interpret and enforce Article 4 of Protocol 9 to the EEA Agreement.[478] Protocol 9 to the EEA Agreement is a derogation from the general rules of the EEA Agreement governing State aid, as it does not envisage a continuous surveillance and monitoring function, with, for example, advance notification obligations regarding aid plans. On the contrary, only an ex-post system of assessment has been envisaged. Furthermore, Protocol 26 to the EEA Agreement and Article 24 SCA do not confer upon the Authority the powers to assess State aid under Protocol 9 to the EEA Agreement. Such power does also not follow directly from Protocol 9 to the EEA Agreement. Consequently, the Authority lacks competence to assess State aid to the fisheries sector.[479]

D. The Role of EU Agencies and Other Bodies: Deviations from the Two-Pillar Structure

535. Institutional developments in EU law that were not foreseen at the time of conclusion of the EEA Agreement increasingly require deviations from the

475. *See supra* Part II, Ch. 2, §1, I.
476. *See* in this context: EFTA Court judgment of 15 Dec. 2016 in Case E-1/16 *Synnøve Finden AS v. The Norwegian Government*.
477. *See* Case E-2/94, *Scottish Salmon Growers Association Limited v. EFTA Surveillance Authority* [1 Jan. 1994–30 Jun. 1995] Report of the EFTA Court, 59.
478. EFTA Surveillance Authority's Decisions of 30 Oct. 1996 (Dec. No. 195/96/COL), of 15 Jul. 2005 (Dec. No. 176/05/COL), of 26 Nov. 2008 (Dec. No. 729/08/COL) and of 27 Jul. 2016 (Case No. 79116). The EFTA Surveillance Authority's Decision of 27 Jul. 2016 was challenged before the EFTA Court. In the judgment of 27 Nov. 2017 in Case E-12/16, *Marine Harvest ASA v. EFTA Surveillance Authority*, the EFTA Court followed the EFTA Surveillance Authority's position.
479. *See* the Authority's Decision No. 95/96/COL of 30 Oct. 1996 (and others mentioned *supra*) and, *similarly*, O. Gjems-Onstad, *EØS-avtalen og EØS-loven* (Oslo, Gyldendal, 2000), 73, but compare S.M. Stefánsson, 'The EEA Agreement and Fish and Other Marine Products', in *Fiskeripolitikken i EØS* 7 (21–23) (Eisenreich ed., Copenhagen: Norfeir, 1996), who argues that the Authority should be competent. *See* in this context also the EFTA Court judgment of 27 Nov. 2017 in Case E-12/16, *Marine Harvest ASA v. EFTA Surveillance Authority*, in which the EFTA Court confirmed that the Authority lacks the competence to carry out State aid surveillance in the fisheries sector.

traditional two-pillar structure. The increasing delegation of tasks to EU regulatory agencies and bodies in the EU pillar gives rise to the practical issue that it would be difficult or unnecessarily burdensome to mirror fully the system established in the EU in the EFTA pillar by establishing equivalent EFTA-pillar agencies and bodies. In such cases, the Contracting Parties to the Agreement have on a number of occasions agreed to deviate from the two-pillar system by agreeing on a 'one-pillar solution', where the EFTA States allocate tasks to be performed by a body in the EU pillar. Whenever that solution is chosen, any power of such EU bodies to adopt binding decisions, to grant authorizations or to issue fines are particularly problematic for the institutional set-up underpinning the EEA Agreement.

536. Decentralized agencies and bodies have gradually been given more powers to adopt legally binding decisions. Agencies have been given competence to take decisions addressed to individual undertakings, to individual EU Member States or to the EU Member States in general. The European Union Aviation Safety Agency (EASA), the European Union Intellectual Property Office (EUIPO) and the Agency for the Cooperation of Energy Regulators (ACER) have all been granted the competence to adopt binding decisions on certain matters. The European Financial Supervisory Authorities (European Banking Authority (EBA), European Securities and Markets Authority (ESMA) and European Insurance and Occupational Pensions Authority (EIOPA), collectively known as European Supervisory Authorities (ESAs)) are other examples of agencies having extensive competences, with the power to adopt legally binding decisions addressed to private undertakings.

537. If the agencies or bodies are given the competence to issue individual decisions towards private market participants, the inclusion of an adaptation text upon incorporation of the act into the EEA Agreement is in most cases necessary to maintain the sovereignty of the EFTA States and their constitutions. A core issue consists in determining whether, and how, binding decisions are to apply to the EFTA States or undertakings/persons based in the EFTA States. A related problem is providing for avenues of judicial review of such decisions as challenges to acts of EU bodies normally lie only before the EU courts and the Board of Appeal of the agency, but not the EFTA Court.

538. In view of the constitutional constraints of the EFTA States, the power to impose binding decision or sanctions on market participants based in an EFTA State must normally be vested with a body in the EFTA pillar. Different options are available to achieve this. For example, in the regulation of medicinal products, the power to issue decisions on fines addressed to market authorization holders based in the EFTA States was previously vested in the EFTA States themselves, but is now with the EFTA Surveillance Authority.[480] The EFTA Surveillance Authority ('the Authority') has been also given the competence to issue such decisions in the field of financial markets.

480. See Decision of the EEA Joint Committee No 92/2017 of 5 May 2017 (OJ L 36, 7.2.2019, 41).

539. The establishment of the three ESAs,[481] which are equipped with sweeping powers, has given rise to particular challenges. The ESAs are, for example, competent to take decisions to (i) temporarily prohibit or restrict certain financial activities that threaten the orderly functioning and integrity of the financial markets or their stability; (ii) adopt individual decisions addressed to financial institutions/ market participants requiring the necessary action to comply with their obligations under EU law; (iii) adopt individual decisions in emergency situations requiring competent national authorities to take necessary action; and (iv) settle disagreements between competent national authorities in cross-border situations. Natural or legal persons may appeal against binding decisions of the ESAs to a Board of Appeal. Appeals against decisions of the Board of Appeal can be brought before the General Court of the European Union. The fundamental EEA challenge related to the incorporation of the ESAs into the EEA Agreement has been how to preserve the key advantages of supervision by a single authority whilst respecting the two-pillar structure of the EEA Agreement.

540. As to the power to issue decisions towards market participants in the EFTA pillar, the adaptation texts attribute competence to the Authority, thus preserving the two-pillar structure. In order to meet concerns regarding the homogeneity of supervision in the extended internal market, the adaptation texts require that the decisions of the Authority are to be based on a draft from the relevant ESA.[482]

As regards acts of a non-binding nature, it is the ESAs that are competent, also vis-à-vis EEA-EFTA competent authorities and market operators, that includes the adoption of recommendations and non-binding mediation. Action on either side will be preceded by, as appropriate, consultation, coordination or exchange of information between the ESAs and the Authority. A new Protocol 8 to the Surveillance and Court Agreement (SCA) was concluded, setting out the powers and functions of the Authority in the field of financial services.

A final point to note here is that the EEA Agreement does not contain any rules on participation in regulatory agencies or similar decentralized and independent bodies, be that by the EFTA States themselves or the Authority. An important recurring challenge arising in the context of regulatory agencies and bodies concerns the participation in the management boards of these bodies. The lack of legal basis in the EEA Agreement for such participation means that an adaptation text is necessary upon incorporation of the relevant acts into the EEA Agreement. Participation in management boards provides an opportunity to influence the decision-shaping and decision-making of the agencies, as well as to monitor the work they carry out. Such influence is important in two particular ways. On the one hand, the decentralized agencies in some instances assist the European Commission in the preparatory work for the updating and development of Union legislation, which may ultimately

481. The European Banking Authority (EBA) established by Regulation (EU) No. 1093/2010 (OJ L 331, 15.12.2010, 12), the European Insurance and Occupational Pensions Authority (EIOPA) established by Regulation (EU) No. 1094/2010 (OJ L 331, 15.12.2010, 48) and the European Securities and Markets Authority (ESMA) Regulation (EU) No. 1095/2010 (OJ L 331, 15.12.2010, 84).

482. A similar solution was found concerning decisions the Authority adopts in the area of energy (electricity), which are based on drafts from ACER.

be incorporated into the EEA Agreement and the EFTA States usually seek a solution where they have the right to participate in the management boards of bodies and agencies, albeit without the right to vote. This solution was agreed upon *inter alia* with regard to the European Medicines Agency and EASA. On the other hand, the Authority sees participation in the management boards as important in the context of its market surveillance and enforcement duties in order to obtain information at an early stage, foster a good working relationship with the agencies, enhance accountability of the agencies and increase homogeneity within the EEA.

§2. Judicial Control

541. The EFTA States have endeavoured to equip the EFTA Court with largely the same competence as the CJEU, thereby giving the EFTA Court the necessary basis for securing homogeneity in the application of the EEA Agreement. There are, however, several differences to the EU legal system. Most of those differences are due to the particular institutional set-up of the EEA, serving to preserve the sovereignty of the EFTA States and keeping the EEA Agreement as an instrument of public international law, and have not played a major practical role in the Court's work.

The coordination between the EFTA Court and the CJEU still works on an informal basis. Article 106 of the EEA Agreement, which provides for a system to safeguard homogeneous interpretation was never implemented. Nevertheless, there were barely any problems with regard to the homogenous interpretation between the two courts.[483]

I. The Infringement Procedure

542. According to Article 31 SCA, the EFTA Surveillance Authority may bring an EFTA State before the EFTA Court if it considers that the State has failed to fulfil an obligation under the EEA Agreement or the SCA.[484] The provision has its counterpart in Article 258 TFEU. There is, however, a minor difference between the two provisions in that Article 31 SCA provides that a reasoned opinion shall be given only 'unless otherwise provided for in this agreement'. This proviso refers to the particular procedures, which may apply, for example, with regard to public procurement, CSA.[485]

543. The reference to the EEA Agreement does not imply that the EFTA Court cannot rule on the conformity of national measures with acts corresponding to directives, decisions or regulations. According to Article 119 of the EEA Agreement, the legal acts included in the annexes to the EEA Agreement constitute an integral part

483. *See* Baur, G. 'Preliminary Rulings in the EEA: Bridging (Institutional) Homogeneity and Procedural Autonomy by Exchange of Information'. In The EEA and the EFTA Court, edited by Baudenbacher. Oxford: Hart, 2014.

484. *See supra* Part II, Ch. 5, §1, I, A.

485. *See supra* Part II, Ch. 5, §1, II, A and II, C, as well as Case E-2/05 *EFTA Surveillance Authority v. Iceland* [2005] EFTA Court Report, 202.

of the Agreement. Moreover, as stated in Article 42 SCA, the protocols and annexes thereto form an integral part of the SCA. Therefore, also the EFTA States' obligations under those legal instruments can be subject to an infringement procedure under Article 31 SCA.

544. In contrast, the legal texts contained in the annexes to the EEA Agreement under the headings 'Acts of which the Contracting Parties shall take note' or acts of which the European Commission and the EFTA Surveillance Authority 'shall take due account' do not form part of the Agreement in the sense that they cannot form the basis of infringement procedures under Article 31 SCA. Finally, other agreements made in connection with the EEA cannot, although they may give rise to obligations on the part of the EFTA States, form the basis of a procedure under Article 31 SCA. For instance, the Agreement on the Standing Committee is not mentioned among the legal acts that can form the basis of an infringement action brought by the EFTA Surveillance Authority. The reason is probably that the Standing Committee is an internal cooperation organ as between the EFTA States. The EFTA States did not, therefore, find that conflicts as to the interpretation of this Agreement should be a matter that fell within the competence of the Authority.[486]

545. The procedural steps before an infringement case can be submitted to the EFTA Court (informal discussions on civil servant level, letter of formal notice and reasoned opinion) are similar to the ones found in EU law. Moreover, the EFTA Court has sought to apply the same procedural rules concerning the infringement procedure as the ones developed by the CJEU.[487]

546. The SCA does not contain a provision on sanctions against EFTA States that fail to comply with the judgments of the EFTA Court. Article 33 SCA merely provides that the EFTA State concerned shall take the necessary measures to comply with the judgments of the EFTA Court. In this respect, the rules differ from the ones applicable to EU Member States where Article 260 TFEU provides for the possibility of pecuniary sanctions being imposed on EU Member States, a rule that incidentally also applies in relation to judgments relating to an EU Member State's obligations under EEA law. This difference does not, of course, entail that the

486. *See* M. Magnussen, 'Traktatbruddsøksmål ved EFTA-domstolen', *Lov og Rett* (2002): 131 (155).

487. *See inter alia*, with regard to the relevant time for assessing whether a State has failed to fulfil its obligation under the Agreement, *see* Case E-10/97 *EFTA Surveillance v. Norway* [1998] EFTA Court Report, 135; Case E-3/00 *EFTA Surveillance Authority v. Norway* [2000–2001] EFTA Court Report, 73; Case E-3/10 *EFTA Surveillance Authority v. Iceland* [2009–2010] EFTA Court Report, 188; Case E-11/10 *EFTA Surveillance Authority v. Liechtenstein* [2009–2010] EFTA Court Report, 368 and the EFTA Court judgment of 12 Jul. 2023 in Case E-15/22 *EFTA Surveillance Authority v. Norway*. *See also* Case E-13/10 *Aleris Ungplan*, Order of 31.1.2011, with regard to the inadmissibility of actions against decisions of the Authority not to commence infringement actions against an EFTA State.

obligation on EFTA States to comply with the judgments of the EFTA Court is less strict than the equivalent obligation on EU Member States to comply with the judgments of the CJEU.[488]

II. Disputes Between EFTA States

547. According to Article 32 SCA, the EFTA Court has jurisdiction in actions concerning the settlement of disputes between two or more EFTA States regarding the interpretation or application of the EEA Agreement, the Agreement on a Standing Committee of the EFTA States or the SCA. Until now, no case has been brought under this provision. Having in mind that the corresponding provision in Article 259 TFEU has only very rarely been used, this is not surprising.

548. Article 32 SCA also covers disputes concerning the Agreement on the Standing Committee. The reason is that EFTA States under that agreement not only coordinate the positions to be taken in the EEA but also take certain decisions for the implementation of the EEA Agreement that, in the EU, are taken by the Commission or the Council. Indeed, it is important to avoid a deadlock in these matters, as this could negatively affect the functioning of the EEA Agreement. Since the Agreement on the Standing Committee is not mentioned among the legal acts that can form the basis of an infringement action brought by the EFTA Surveillance Authority, Article 32 SCA is broader than Article 31 SCA in this respect.

549. As mentioned, the provision in Article 32 SCA has its counterpart in Article 259 TFEU. Article 32 SCA, however, differs from the corresponding provision in the EU law in two respects. First, there is no obligation for an EFTA State to bring the matter before the EFTA Surveillance Authority before it is referred to the EFTA Court. On the other hand, nothing prevents an EFTA State from bringing the matter to the attention of the Authority. Indeed, for political reasons it might often be preferable that proceedings are brought by the Authority and not by an EFTA State under Article 32 SCA.

550. Second, the SCA contains no provision corresponding to Article 344 TFEU according to which EU Member States undertake not to submit a dispute concerning the interpretation or application of the EU Treaties to any method of settlement other than those provided for in those Treaties. Thus, Article 32 SCA only establishes a competence for the EFTA Court, but does not prevent the EFTA States from settling a dispute between them by other means, for example, by raising the issue in the EEA Joint Committee.[489]

---

488. *See* Case E-18/10 *EFTA Surveillance Authority v. Norway* [2011] EFTA Court Report, 204 and the EFTA Court judgment of 12 Jul. 2023 in Case E-15/22 *EFTA Surveillance Authority v. Norway.*

489. *See* L. Sevón, 'The EEA Judicial System and the Supreme Courts of the EFTA States', in *Accord EEE, Commentaires et réflexions* 603 (609) (Jacot-Guillarmod ed., Zürich: Schulthess 1992).

551. Article 32 SCA is only applicable in relation to disputes between the Contracting Parties of the EFTA pillar and cannot be used cross-pillar. Should a disagreement arise between one or several EFTA States on the one hand, and the EU or EU Member States, on the other hand, the problem would be dealt with in accordance with the provisions concerning cross-pillar dispute settlement.[490] If a conflict concerning the interpretation and application of EEA rules were to arise between EU Member States – an unlikely scenario since in the relations between these States EU rules are applied – the conflict would be settled through internal EU procedures and, in the last instance, by the CJEU.

III. Advisory Opinions

552. As is the case for the EU law, the SCA does not contain provisions enabling a natural or legal person to bring an action against an EFTA State before the EFTA Court.[491] Instead, the SCA has opted for a preliminary reference procedure broadly similar to the one found in Article 267 TFEU. Thus, according to Article 34 SCA, the EFTA Court shall have jurisdiction to give advisory opinions on the interpretation of the EEA Agreement. Where such a question is raised before any court or tribunal in an EFTA State, that court or tribunal may, if it considers it necessary to enable it to give judgment, request the EFTA Court to give such an opinion.[492] The purpose of Article 34 SCA is to establish cooperation between the Court and the national courts and tribunals. It is intended to be a means of ensuring a homogeneous interpretation of EEA law and to provide assistance to the courts and tribunals in the EFTA States in cases which they have to apply provisions of EEA law.[493]

553. If the question of EEA law arises before a national court in an EU Member State, that court will not be able to refer the matter to the EFTA Court but can instead use the ordinary procedure in Article 267 TFEU so that the CJEU, in accordance with the two-pillar structure, can give the needed interpretation of the relevant EEA provision.

A. *Differences with Article 267 TFEU*

554. Although Article 34 SCA resembles Article 267 TFEU, there are a number of differences between these provisions.

490. *See infra* Part II, Ch. 6, §1.
491. *See* Case E-3/94 *Friedmann* [1994–1995] EFTA Court Report, 83.
492. Article 107 and Protocol 34 to the EEA Agreement provide for the possibility that an EFTA State may allow its court and tribunals to ask the ECJ to decide on the interpretation of an EEA rule. As this solution, however, causes constitutional and political difficulties for the EFTA States, the possibility has not been utilized.
493. *See* EFTA Court judgment of 15 Jul. 2021 in Case E-11/20 *Sverrisson*, para. 33 and EFTA Court judgment of 19 Apr. 2023 in Case E-9/22, para. 22.

555. The first difference is that Article 34 SCA does not provide for any mandatory references for national courts or tribunals whose decisions are final. Thus, even national courts or tribunals whose decisions are final are not under an obligation to refer question concerning the interpretation of EEA law to the EFTA Court.[494] Moreover, Article 34 SCA provides that an EFTA State may limit references to courts whose decisions are final. Of all the original EEA-EFTA States, only Austria made use of that possibility. After Austria joined the EU, the possibility has not had any implications in practice.

556. The second difference is that the rulings of the EFTA Court under Article 34 SCA are merely advisory to the national court. The EFTA States chose not to give the EFTA Court competence to give binding interpretations on the Agreement. Although formally of importance, the practical implications of this difference to the EU legal system should not be overestimated. A national court that has requested an advisory opinion would normally be reluctant to disregard that opinion. It has, moreover, been argued that should the referring court disregard an opinion of the EFTA Court that finds part of an EFTA State's legislation incompatible with EEA law that would amount to a violation of the EEA Agreement by the EFTA State concerned.[495] This view might, at first sight, seem surprising, as the national court has no obligation to follow the advisory opinion of the EFTA Court. The reasoning would be that the infringement concerned would not stem from the fact that the

---

494. It has been argued that it follows from the principles of judicial protection and loyalty laid down in Art. 3 EEA that national courts of last instance are not free to the decide whether or not to refer, but that similar criteria as those found in Art. 267(3) TFEU should apply by analogy to the national courts in the EFTA countries, *see* S. Magnusson, 'On the Authority of Advisory Opinions, Reflections on the Functions and the Normativity of Advisory Opinions of the EFTA Court', *Europarättslig Tidskrift* (2010): 528, and, broadly along the same lines, Baudenbacher, *The EFTA Court in Action* 21–22 (Stuttgart: German Law Publishers 2010). This view is irreconcilable with the clear wording of Art. 34 SCA and the deliberate will of the EFTA States not to copy Art. 267 TFEU in full. According to Magnusson (*supra* at footnote 489), where a court of last instance refuses to make a reference to the EFTA Court the result is that a party to the main proceeding 'has been denied the opportunity (and the procedural right) to have its case (or the EEA part of its case) resolved by the competent judicial institution'. However, even under EU law the preliminary reference procedure does not constitute a means of redress available to the parties to the main proceedings, cf. Case 283/81 *CILFIT* [1982] ECR 3415. Moreover, it is hardly appropriate to characterize the national Supreme Courts of the three EEA-EFTA States as anything less than 'competent judicial institution[s]'. That being said, relatively speaking the national courts of the EFTA Countries have been slightly more reluctant in making preliminary references than have their EU counterparts. On this aspect *see* H. Haukeland Fredriksen, 'Om mangelen på tolkningsspørsmål fra norske domstoler til EFTA-domstolen', *Jussens Venner* (2006): 372; H. Haukeland Fredriksen, 'EU/EØS-rett i norske domstoler', 90–95; H.P. Graver, 'The Effect of EFTA Court Jurisprudence on the Legal Orders of the EFTA States', in *The EFTA Court Ten Years On*, Baudenbacher, Tresselt & Orlygsson eds, 79 (82–86) and Davíd Thór Björgvinsson, 'Application of Article 34 of the ESA/Court Agreement by the Icelandic Courts', in *Economic Law and Justice in Times of Globalisation*, 37 (Monti et al. eds, Festschrift for Carl Baudenbacher).

495. *See* C. Baudenbacher, 'The Legal Nature of EEA Law in the Course of Time', in *Afmælisrit Thor Vilhjálmsson* 39 (46) (Björgvinsson ed., Reykjavik: Bókaútgáfá Orators 2000). According to S. Magnusson, 'On the Authority of Advisory Opinions, Reflections on the Functions and the Normativity of Advisory Opinions of the EFTA Court', *Europarättslig Tidskrift* (2010): 528 (541–546), 'most probably' a national court will breach its obligation under Art. 3 EEA if it does not follow an advisory opinion of the EFTA Court.

national court did not follow the advisory opinion, but rather from the fact that the national court, by arriving at another result than the EFTA Court, had applied the EEA Agreement incorrectly. Therefore, the EFTA Surveillance Authority should be able to bring an infringement case against the State concerned for having failed to fulfil its obligation to a correct administration of EEA law, and the EFTA Court would find in favour of the Authority sticking to its view on the law as expressed in the preliminary advisory opinion.[496] In the *STX* case,[497] the Norwegian Supreme Court questioned the conclusion arrived at in the advisory opinion delivered by the EFTA Court but refrained from concluding on the point of difference and solved the case on another ground. This has led to a lively debate as to the desirable level of judicial dialogue within the EFTA pillar.[498]

557. The third difference is that the jurisdiction of the EFTA Court under Article 34 SCA does not, as Article 267 TFEU, extend to the validity of what would, in EU law, be labelled as secondary legislation. As already explained, EEA law is generated by way of amending the EEA Agreement. The EFTA Court is not competent to review the legality of such legislative acts and therefore cannot, in the same manner as the CJEU, annul secondary legislation, if that legislation does not conform with the EEA Agreement and general principles of a constitutional nature. As *CIBA*[499] demonstrates, there is, however, a fine line between decisions on validity and decisions on interpretation. In that case, the referring court had asked whether the EEA Joint Committee was empowered to decide that an EFTA State could adopt derogations from existing Community acquis. Arguing that the competence of the EFTA Court was exhaustively listed in the SCA, the Norwegian Government contended that the Court could not rule on the validity of a decision of the EEA Joint Committee. The EFTA Court dismissed that argument by stating that the question related to the interpretation of the provisions of the EEA Agreement concerning the competences of the EEA Joint Committee and to the interpretation of provisions that the EEA Joint Committee had agreed to insert in an annex to the Agreement. According to Article 34 SCA, the Court has jurisdiction to give advisory opinions on the interpretation of the 'EEA Agreement' and, pursuant to Article 1(a) SCA, that term included both the main part of the EEA Agreement and its Protocols and Annexes, as well as the acts referred to therein. Since there was no relevant legal source to suggest that any provision governing the function of the EEA Joint Committee should be excluded from the jurisdiction of the Court under Article 34 SCA, the Court declared itself competent to answer the question, notwithstanding that it related to the competence of the EEA Joint Committee.

558. This judgment illustrates that the EFTA Court, in the same manner as the CJEU, seeks to construe the preliminary procedure in the spirit of cooperation which should rule the relationship between, on the one hand, these two courts and,

496. *See* L. Sevón, in *The Fifth Nordic Conference on EFTA and the European Union* 46 and 48 (Sundström ed., Helsinki: Yliopistopaino, 1994).
497. Case E-2/11 *STX Norway Offshore AS and Others v. Norway* [2013] EFTA Court Report, 258.
498. *See*, for example, Ahlberg, K., 'The EFTA court clashes with Norway's Supreme Court', *Nordic Labour Journal* (7 Nov. 2013).
499. Case E-6/01 [2002] EFTA Court Report, 281.

on the other, the national courts and tribunals. When a national court in an EFTA State is in doubt as to the solution of a question of EEA law, the EFTA Court will do its utmost to give guidance to the national court. Had the EFTA Court declined to answer the question referred in the *CIBA* case, the national courts would have been alone in ruling upon the validity of acts of the EEA Joint Committee and the EFTA Surveillance Authority. As consequence of this, and of the fact that a national court can hardly have the competence to declare such acts invalid erga omnes, a national court's decision not to apply such an act would endanger the uniform application of EEA law. A similar reasoning has led the CJEU in *Foto Frost*[500] to hold that national courts have an obligation to refer questions on the validity of secondary EU acts if they are inclined to find the relevant acts illegal. Whether a parallel obligation can be imposed on national courts of an EFTA State is, in the light of wording of the SCA, doubtful.[501]

559. The judgment in *CIBA* concerned an indirect validity assessment of decisions of the EEA Joint Committee. It can hardly be imagined that the EFTA Court will stretch its jurisdiction even further and open up for an indirect validity assessment of the EU rule that the EEA Joint Committee takes into the EEA Agreement. Such an assessment would interfere with the CJEU's monopoly on ruling on the validity of secondary EU law as laid down in the above-mentioned *Foto Frost* case. It has been argued that this means that the EFTA Court cannot rule on the 'constitutional' validity of secondary EU law that is incorporated into the EEA Agreement but only on the validity of the adaptations to the EU act that the EEA Joint Committee should make. To the extent that such a limitation excludes a substantial part of the protection of individual rights, which is offered by the EU legal order, this is a logical consequence of the whole EEA set-up.[502] At the same time, it should be possible for the EFTA Court to ensure the protection of fundamental rights by ruling on the applicability or enforceability, within the EFTA States, of provisions of secondary legislation incorporated into the EEA Agreement.

B. Different Questions of Competence and Procedure

560. The EFTA Court is competent under Article 34 SCA to interpret the Protocols to the EEA Agreement unless another result clearly follows from the provisions of the Agreement. In this respect, the EFTA Court's jurisdiction regarding Protocol 9 to the EEA Agreement caused discussion. It has sometimes been argued

500. Case 314/85 [1987] ECR-4199.

501. *See*, in this respect, H. Graver, 'The EFTA Court and the Court of Justice of the EC: Legal Homogeneity at Stake?', in *EEA-EU Relations* 31 (40–43) (Müller-Graff & Selvig eds, Berlin: Berlin Verlag 1999), who argues against such an obligation.

502. *See* O. Due, 'The EFTA Court and Its Relationship to the European Court of Justice', in *The Fifth Nordic Conference on EFTA and the European Union* 52 (61) (Sundström ed., Helsinki: Yliopistopaino, 1994). *See* further, as regards the similar issue in annulment proceedings, *infra* Part II, Ch. 5, §2, IV, A. Also the – never used – possibility in Art. 107 of the EEA Agreement and Protocol 34 to the EEA Agreement restricts itself to allowing references concerning the interpretation of EEA rules.

that this protocol constitutes a *lex specialis* in EEA law and that this should imply that the EFTA Court does not have competence to interpret Protocol 9 to the EEA Agreement at all.[503] However, in *Ásgeirsson*,[504] the Court held that no provision of relevant law concerning its jurisdiction prevented it from interpreting Article 7 of Protocol 9 to the EEA Agreement. In addition, the EFTA Court did not comment on the suggestion by the EFTA Surveillance Authority that certain provisions in Protocol 9 to the EEA Agreement, other than the one relevant for the case, were covered by separate dispute settlement mechanisms and, therefore, outside the competence of the EFTA Court.[505]

561. As a point of departure, the EFTA Court does not have jurisdiction over the application or interpretation of the different bilateral FTAs, which still exist between the EFTA States and the EU.[506] However, exceptions to the general rule of separation between the EEA Agreement and the bilateral FTAs exist in the form of clauses connecting both sets of law. Thus, where the relevant provision of the EEA Agreement is phrased in a way that explicitly calls for an assessment of which of two trade regimes is more favourable in a given factual situation, this is to be distinguished from an interpretation of the FTA.[507]

562. The EFTA Court has held that the expression 'court or tribunal' in Article 34 SCA must, like in Article 267 TFEU, be given an autonomous interpretation. In this interpretation, it is not decisive how the body has been labelled under national law. The EFTA Court further noted that the purpose of Article 34 SCA is to establish cooperation between the EFTA Court and the courts and tribunals in the EFTA States. It is intended as a means of ensuring a uniform interpretation of the EEA Agreement and to provide assistance to the courts and tribunals in the EFTA States in cases in which they have to apply provisions of the EEA Agreement. Building on this, from an EU point of view, well known aim, the EFTA Court applied the same criteria as are known from the case law of the CJEU in relation to Article 267 TFEU, namely whether the body requesting an advisory opinion had been established by law, had a permanent existence, exercised binding jurisdiction, was bound by rules of adversary procedure, applied the rule of law and could be considered independent.[508] In view of the fact that in particular in Norway and Iceland, it is common for disputes concerning some subject matters to be directed to specialist complaint

503. *See supra* Part II, Ch. 2, §1, I.
504. Case E-2/03 [2003] EFTA Court Report, 185.
505. *See also* EFTA Court judgment of 27 Nov. 2017 in Case E-12/16 *Marine Harvest ASA v. EFTA Surveillance Authority*.
506. *See supra* Part I, Chs 1 and 3.
507. Case E-2/03 *Ásgeirsson* [2003] EFTA Court Report, 185.
508. Case E-1/94 *Restamark* [1994] EFTA Court Report, 15; Joined Cases E-8/94 and E-9/94 *Mattel* [1994–1995] EFTA Court Report, 113; Case E-4/04 *Pedicel* [2005] EFTA Court Report, 1; Case E-4/09 *Inconsult Anstalt* [2009–2010] EFTA Court Report, 86; and Case E-1/11 *Dr A* [2011] EFTA Court Report, 484.

boards, references from such bodies have generally been accepted without all the requirements posited by the CJEU being scrutinized in detail.[509]

563. The EFTA Court has also sought to apply the principles concerning the distribution of competence between the national court and the court giving the preliminary judgment developed by the CJEU in relation to Article 267 TFEU. Thus, the EFTA Court has held that it does not have competence to rule on the interpretation of provisions of national legislation, nor to ascertain to what extent provisions of EEA law have been properly transposed into national law.[510] Likewise, it has recalled that the procedure provided for in Article 34 SCA is an instrument of cooperation between the EFTA Court and the national courts. In this respect, it is a matter for the national court to examine and evaluate evidence and to make factual findings, and then apply the EEA law (as construed by the EFTA Court) to the facts of the case.[511]

564. Once again drawing an analogy with Article 267 TFEU, the EFTA Court has held that under Article 34 SCA it is for the national court to assess whether an interpretation of the EEA Agreement is necessary for it to give judgment.[512] A party to the main proceedings cannot make the EFTA Court extend the subject matter of a preliminary reference. Since the issues before the EFTA Court are determined by the preliminary reference, the role of the parties in the proceedings before the EFTA Court is limited to making suggestions to the Court as to how the reference should be interpreted and the questions answered.[513] Inspiration from the case law concerning Article 267 TFEU has also led the EFTA Court to hold that it can decline to answer a request for an advisory opinion if the question is hypothetical or has no connection with the circumstances or purpose of the main proceedings.[514] The Court has moreover reiterated the case law of the CJEU according to which, in order to provide a useful interpretation in the context of a preliminary ruling, it is necessary that the referring national court gives an explanation of the factual circumstances on which the submitted questions are based. The EFTA Court furthermore referred to case law of the CJEU that this information must not only enable the Court to give a reply to the national court, but must also give the Governments of the Contracting

509. *See*, e.g., EFTA Court judgment of 16 Jul. 2020 in Case E-8/19 *Scanteam* for a reference from the Norwegian Complaints Board for Public Procurement and Case E-5/16 [2017] EFTA Court Report, 52 ('*Angry Boy*') for a reference from the Norwegian Board of Appeal for Industrial Property Rights.

510. Case E-2/95 *Eidesund* [1995–1996] EFTA Court Report, 1; Case E-3/95 *Langeland* [1995–1996] EFTA Court Report, 36; Case E-1/01 *Einarsson* [2002] EFTA Court Report, 1, and Case E-1/10 *Periscopus* [2009–2010] EFTA Court Report, 198.

511. Case E-8/00 *LO* [2002] EFTA Court Report, 114.

512. Case E-1/95 *Samuelsson* [1994–1995] EFTA Court Report, 145; Case E-5/96 *Ullensaker Kommune* [1997] EFTA Court Report, 30; Case E-7/01 *Hegelstad* [2002] EFTA Court Report, 310; Case E-2/03 *Ásgeirsson* [2003] EFTA Court Report, 185, and Case E-5/10 *Kottke* [2009–2010] EFTA Court Report, 320.

513. Case E-6/96 *Wilhelmsen* [1997] EFTA Court Report, 53.

514. Case E-1/95 *Samuelsson* [1994–1995] EFTA Court Report, 145; Case E-6/96 *Wilhelmsen* [1997] EFTA Court Report, 53; Case E-2/03 *Ásgeirsson* [2003] EFTA Court Report, 185, and Case E-10/04 *Piazza* [2005] EFTA Court Report, 76.

Parties and other interested parties the opportunity to submit observations pursuant to the Statute of the EFTA Court.[515] In this respect, Article 88 of the Court's Rules of Procedure lays down that a request for an advisory opinion shall be accompanied by a description of the facts of the case as well as a presentation of the provision in issue in relation to the national legal order. According to Article 95 of the Rules of Procedure, the EFTA Court may further ask the national court for clarification.[516]

565. In *CIBA*[517] the question arose whether a request for an advisory opinion could be declared inadmissible due to the fact that the same national court had already received an advisory opinion relating to the same dispute before it. The EFTA Court referred to the case law of the CJEU according to which a further reference to that court may be justified, *inter alia*, when the national court encounters difficulties in understanding and applying the preliminary judgment, when it refers a fresh question of law, or when it submits new considerations which might lead to a different answer to a question submitted earlier. In contrast, it is not permissible to use the right to refer a question as a means of contesting the validity of the earlier judgment. The EFTA Court found that the same reasoning should apply in relation to the advisory opinion procedure under Article 34 SCA.

566. Finally, with reference to case law of the CJEU, the EFTA Court has in several cases found that where domestic legislation, in regulating purely internal situations not governed by EEA law, adopts the same or similar solutions as those adopted in EEA law, it is in the interest of the EEA to forestall future differences of interpretation. Provisions or concepts taken from EEA law should thus be interpreted uniformly, irrespective of the circumstances in which they are to apply.[518]

IV. The Annulment Procedure

A. *Jurisdiction*

567. According to Article 36 SCA, the EFTA Court has jurisdiction in actions brought by an EFTA State against a decision of the EFTA Surveillance Authority on grounds of lack of competence, infringement of an essential procedural requirement, or infringement of the SCA, of the EEA Agreement or of any rule of law relating to their application, or misuse of powers. According to the second paragraph of

515. Case E-4/01 *Karlsson* [2002] EFTA Court Report, 240. The influence of the case law of the ECJ can also be seen when the EFTA Court answers a request for advisory opinion with reference to other EEA provisions than the ones mentioned by the national court in its question, *see*, for example, Case E-4/07 *Þorkelsson* [2008] EFTA Court Report, 3.

516. This possibility was used in Joined Cases C-8/94 and E-9/94 *Mattel* [1995] EFTA Court Report, 113.

517. Case E-6/01 [2002] EFTA Court Report, 281.

518. Case E-17/11 *Aresbank* [2012] EFTA Court Report, 916, para. 45 and judgment of the EFTA Court of 19 Apr. 2023 in Case E-9/22 *Verkfræðingafélag Íslands, Stéttarfélag tölvunarfræðinga and Lyfjafræðingafélag Íslands v. Iceland*, para. 25.

Article 36 SCA, any natural or legal person may, under the same conditions, institute proceedings before the EFTA Court against a decision of the EFTA Surveillance Authority addressed to that person or against a decision addressed to another person, if it is of direct and individual concern to the former. According to the third paragraph of Article 36 SCA, the annulment proceedings must be instituted within two months of the publication of the measure, or of the day on which it came to the knowledge of the applicant, as the case may be.

568. The SCA does not contain any provision giving the EFTA Court competence to hear challenges against other legal acts than decisions. The reason is presumably that the EFTA Surveillance Authority was not supposed to have competence to issue binding rules of a general character, just as there exists no body corresponding to that of the EU Council.[519]

569. In contrast to the CJEU, the EFTA Court does not have exclusive jurisdiction in staff cases. According to the Staff Regulations of the EFTA Surveillance Authority, EFTA Secretariat and EFTA Court, such disputes are dealt with by the Administrative Tribunal of the ILO. At the same time, it is not clear how the Staff Regulations could oust the jurisdiction of the EFTA Court over disputes arising out of a decision of the EFTA Surveillance Authority (e.g., terminating employment). It is in any event conceivable that cases concerning staff matters might reach the EFTA Court if, for some reason, they are not covered by the jurisdiction of the ILO Administrative Tribunal. Such a situation might, for example, arise where the claimant is not a member of staff or the issue relates to a matter not falling under the appeal procedure laid down in the Staff Regulations.

570. One of the main differences to Article 263 TFEU is that Article 36 SCA is limited to decisions taken by the Authority. Thus, other bodies of the EFTA (such as the Standing Committee) and of the EEA (such as the EEA Joint Committee) fall outside the competence of the EFTA Court.

571. Specific rules enabling affected parties to appeal against the Authority's decisions in the field of competition can be found in Article 35 SCA and in Protocol 4 thereto. Those provisions prescribe that the EFTA Court shall have unlimited jurisdiction with regard to penalties imposed by the Authority.

572. Finally, according to Article 39 SCA, save as otherwise provided for in Protocol 7 SCA, the EFTA Court shall have jurisdiction in actions against the EFTA Surveillance Authority relating to compensation for damages provided for in Article 46(2) SCA.

519. *See* S. Norberg, 'The EFTA Court and Its Relations to the European Court of Justice', in *The Fifth Nordic Conference on EFTA and the European Union* 233 (261) (Sundström ed., Helsinki: Yliopistopaino 1994). In fact, the Authority has, although very rarely, been delegated such powers.

B. Procedural Questions

573. The EFTA Court has found that the reasons which led the CJEU to its interpretations of expressions of EU law are relevant for the EFTA Court when applying expressions in the SCA that are identical in substance to those which the CJEU has interpreted. This interpretative principle must also govern issues such as to what constitutes a decision of the EFTA Surveillance Authority, whether a measure is reviewable and who has locus standi to bring an action for annulment of a decision for the purposes of Article 36 SCA. Thus, CJEU's case law on direct and individual concern has had an influence also on EEA law,[520] and it remains to be seen whether, and if so to what extent, the EFTA Court will change its case law on locus standi as a consequence of the widening of those rules in EU law with the Lisbon Treaty and the new Article 263 TFEU. Similarly, the EFTA Court has referred to the case law of the CJEU in order to decide whether a decision by the EFTA Surveillance Authority constituted a reviewable act within the meaning of Article 36 SCA.[521]

C. Intensity in Control

574. The EFTA Court has also followed the jurisprudence of the CJEU concerning judicial control of the Commission and held that the EFTA Court could not substitute its own assessment for that of the EFTA Surveillance Authority in cases which involve assessments of an economic and social nature which must be made in an EEA context. In reviewing the substantive issues in such situations, the EFTA Court will therefore confine itself to verifying whether the facts, on which the contested finding was based, have been accurately stated by the EFTA Surveillance Authority and whether there has been any manifest error in assessment or a misuse of powers.[522] Thus, reticence should be expected in relation to the Authority's assessment of whether a given State aid is compatible with the EEA Agreement under Article 61(2) and (3) of the EEA Agreement. Conversely, where the question is whether a given measure constitutes aid at all within the meaning of Article 61(1) of the EEA Agreement, a lesser margin of discretion is offered to the EFTA Surveillance Authority.[523]

---

520. Case E-2/94 *Scottish Salmon Growers* [1994–1995] EFTA Court Report, 59; Case E-4/97 *Norwegian Bankers' Association* [1998], EFTA Court Report, 38; Case E-2/02 *TBW and Bellona* [2003] EFTA Court Report, 52; Joined Cases E-5/04, E-6/04 and E-7/04 *Fesil and others* [2005] EFTA Court Report, 117; Case E-9/04 *The Bankers' and Securities Dealers' Association of Iceland* [2006] EFTA Court Report, 42; Case E-5/07 *Private Barnehagers Landsforbund* [2008] EFTA Court Report, 62, and Case E-6/09 *Magasin- og Ukepresseforeningen* [2009–2010] EFTA Court Report, 144.
521. Case E-4/97 *Norwegian Bankers' Association* [1998] EFTA Court Report, 38. *See also* Case E-13/10 *Aleris Ungplan AS*, Order of 31 Jan. 2011, with regard to the inadmissibility of actions against decisions of the Authority not to commence infringement actions against an EFTA State.
522. Case E-4/97 *Norwegian Bankers' Association* [1999] EFTA Court Report, 1.
523. Case E-6/98 *Norway v. EFTA Surveillance Authority* [1999] EFTA Court Report, 74; Joined Cases E-5/04, E-6/04 and E-7/04 *Fesil and others* [2005] EFTA Court Report, 117, and Joined Cases E-4/10, E-6/10 and E-7/10 *Liechtenstein, REASSUR Aktiengesellschaft and Swisscom RE Aktiengesellschaft v. EFTA Surveillance Authority*, judgment of 10 May 2011.

V. Actions for Failure to Act

575. Should the EFTA Surveillance Authority, in infringement of the SCA or the EEA Agreement, fail to act, an EFTA State may bring an action before the EFTA Court to have the infringement established. According to Article 37(2) SCA, the action is admissible only if the EFTA Surveillance Authority has first been called upon to act. If, within two months of being called upon to act, the EFTA Surveillance Authority has not defined its position, the action may be brought within a further period of two months. According to Article 37(3) SCA, the same applies to any natural or legal person to whom the EFTA Surveillance Authority has failed to address any decision.

576. The provision is modelled on Article 265 TFEU. In *Hansen*,[524] the EFTA Court drew upon jurisprudence of the CJEU concerning the corresponding provision in the then applicable Article 232 EC Treaty and held that it followed from the scheme of Article 37 SCA that an application for failure to act must be preceded by a formal notice calling upon the EFTA Surveillance Authority to act. Furthermore, the subject matter of that notice must be set out in a manner as to make it clear what decision the EFTA Surveillance Authority should have taken under EEA law.

VI. Interim Measures

577. Pursuant to Article 40 SCA, actions before the EFTA Court do not have suspensory effect. The Court may, however, if it considers that circumstances so require, order that the application of the contested act be suspended. Also in this context the EFTA Court has chosen to take into account the jurisprudence of the CJEU, although not being required to do so by Article 3 SCA. In *Norway v. EFTA Surveillance Authority*[525] the Court, however, decided to suspend the application of a decision of the Authority whereby Norway was ordered to stop granting a particular kind of State aid, but not to require repayment of aid already given. Notwithstanding that the EFTA Court itself stated that it found inspiration in case law of the CJEU, it seems difficult to image that the EU courts would have come to the same result.

524. Case E-7/96 [1997] EFTA Court Report, 100. *See also* Case E-5/08 *Bergling* [2009–2010] EFTA Court Report, 316, and Case E-6/09 *Magasin- og Ukepresseforeningen* [2009–2010] EFTA Court Report, 144.

525. Case E-6/98 *R* [1998] EFTA Court Report, 244.

Chapter 6. Cross-Pillar Dispute Settlement

578. The issue of the dispute settlement procedures was one of the more difficult issues during the negotiations for the EEA Agreement. The initial solution, foreseen by the Contracting Parties, comprised an EEA Court, which was to settle disputes between the Community, as it then was, and one or more EFTA States, as well as between EFTA States.[526] However, in its Opinion 1/91,[527] the CJEU considered that system incompatible with the EC Treaty. As the Opinion was of a binding nature, the Contracting Parties had to renegotiate the judicial system of the EEA. They agreed on what was to become Article 111 of the EEA Agreement on the settlement of disputes. Accordingly, the provisions on the settlement of disputes were clearly only the second best option for the Contracting Parties.

579. In the EEA, three kinds of disputes between the EEA States can arise. Disputes can arise between EU Member States, between the EFTA States and between one or more EU Member State or the EU on the one hand and one or more EFTA States on the other hand. Since the two first mentioned kinds of disputes are of an intra-pillar nature, they did not need to be dealt with within the EEA Agreement, whose essence it is to link the two pillars. Only the last mentioned disputes needed to be dealt with therein. Article 111 of the EEA Agreement is the most important, though not the only relevant, provision of the EEA Agreement regarding dispute settlement.[528]

§1. Dispute Settlement Procedure under Article 111 of the EEA Agreement

I. Parties to the Dispute

580. Article 111(1) of the EEA Agreement defines locus standi in the EEA dispute settlement procedure. The EU or an EFTA State may bring a matter under dispute, which concerns the interpretation or application of the EEA Agreement, before the EEA Joint Committee. EFTA as such is not entitled to start the procedure, as it is the EFTA States and not EFTA that are the Contracting Parties to the EEA Agreement. The EU, in turn, is a Contracting Party and may, as such, bring a matter under dispute to the EEA Joint Committee. The EU Member States, although being Contracting Parties seem not to enjoy this right. At first sight surprising, this solution is in line with the fact that the EEA Joint Committee would anyway take its decision by agreement between the EU and the EFTA States, speaking with one voice.[529]

526. *See supra* Part II, Ch. 1, §2, IV.
527. Opinion 1/91 [1991] ECR I-6079. *See also* H. Fredriksen, in Arnesen et al. (eds), *Agreement on the European Economic Area, A Commentary* (2018): 867.
528. Article 111(1) of the EEA Agreement is reported to have been invoked twice, in matters involving the heavy vehicle fee as well as the supplementary protection certificates. *See* H. Fredriksen, in Arnesen et al. (eds), *Agreement on the European Economic Area, A Commentary* (2018): 872.
529. *See supra* Part II, Ch. 3, §2, II, B. The EU Member States act as observers in the EEA Joint Committee.

581. Although Article 111 of the EEA Agreement does not regulate explicitly the situation of respondents, logic demands that the same parties who can bring a matter under dispute before the EEA Joint Committee could also be respondents in such a dispute. Accordingly, although the dispute may oppose an EFTA State to an EU Member State, the dispute would be dealt with in the EEA Joint Committee as a dispute between an EFTA State and the EU. This solution is all the more appropriate as it cannot be expected that the EFTA States would know when they would have to designate the EU as the respondent, or one or more of its Member States.[530]

582. The fact that an EU Member State can be neither a complainant nor a respondent in the dispute settlement procedures does not mean that it is not involved in resolving the dispute. Council Regulation (EC) No. 2894/94 provides that the Council formulates the EU position in all cases where the Decision of the EEA Joint Committee would not merely extend EU legislation to the EFTA States.[531]

583. The question also arises whether the EFTA Surveillance Authority and the Commission can become a party to a dispute on the basis of Article 109(5) of the EEA Agreement, which states that in case of disagreement between the two surveillance authorities, either of them may refer the matter to the EEA Joint Committee, which shall deal with it in accordance with Article 111 of the EEA Agreement. It is clear that the Commission could bring the matter before the EEA Joint Committee under Article 109(5) of the EEA Agreement. In such a situation, the Commission will be able to act both as a representative of a Contracting Party as well as a surveillance authority. The EFTA Surveillance Authority can also bring the matter to the EEA Joint Committee under Article 109(5) of the EEA Agreement but will only be entitled to express its views. It cannot, however, raise a matter as a dispute, as only the EFTA States can do so.[532]

II. Dispute Settlement Procedure

584. The dispute settlement procedure depends to a large extent on the subject matter. However, every dispute must relate to the application or interpretation of the EEA Agreement. Although this provision should not be interpreted too strictly, it results from the general principles of law and the structure of the EEA Agreement that the EEA Joint Committee cannot interfere with procedures pending before the EFTA Surveillance Authority or the CJEU. It would not be acceptable that the EEA Joint Committee reversed the case law of a court.[533]

530. *See also* Art. 2(c) EEA Agreement, which remains very general when it comes to defining the term 'Contracting Parties' concerning the Community and the EC Member States.
531. It can be assumed that the EEA Joint Committee would have to take a formal decision with a view to resolve the dispute.
532. *See* S. Norberg et al., *The European Economic Area, EEA Law, A Commentary on the EEA Agreement* 225 et seq. (Stockholm: Fritzes 1993).
533. *See* S. Norberg et al., *The European Economic Area, EEA Law, A Commentary on the EEA Agreement* 279 (Stockholm: Fritzes 1993).

585. Every dispute that is to be dealt with in accordance with Article 111 of the EEA Agreement will first be submitted to the EEA Joint Committee, which tries to settle the dispute after having received the information which might be of use. The EEA Joint Committee is not expected to find the legally correct solution to the dispute. It only needs to find a solution that is acceptable to all the parties to the dispute, its main goal being to maintain the good functioning of the EEA Agreement. This indicates that the first stage of the dispute settlement procedure is of a political, rather than a legal nature.[534] If the EEA Joint Committee succeeds in finding an acceptable solution, it must be assumed that it will terminate the dispute by adopting a Decision of the EEA Joint Committee. It is only if the EEA Joint Committee has not found a solution within three months after the dispute has been submitted to it, that the dispute settlement enters its next stage.

586. At the following stages of the dispute settlement procedure, the subject matter of the dispute becomes important with a view to determining the right procedure to be followed. Either the dispute concerns the interpretation of a provision of the EEA Agreement which is identical in substance to the corresponding rules in EU law (*see* Article 111(3) of the EEA Agreement), or it concerns the scope or duration of safeguard measures taken in accordance with Article 111(3) or 112 of the EEA Agreement or the proportionality of rebalancing measures taken in accordance with Article 114 of the EEA Agreement (*see* Article 111(4) of the EEA Agreement). A third category of disputes is not dealt with in the EEA Agreement: if the dispute concerns a provision that is not identical in substance to the corresponding rule in EU law, concerns a provision that has no counterpart in EU law, and does not concern safeguard or rebalancing measures, neither Article 111(3) nor Article 111(4) of the EEA Agreement would apply.

A. *Disputes Concerning the Interpretation of Provisions of the EEA Agreement Which Are Identical in Substance to the Corresponding Rules in EU Law*

587. In cases where the dispute concerns the interpretation of provisions of the EEA Agreement, which are identical in substance to the corresponding rules of EU law, the second phase of the dispute settlement procedure is started, after either three or six months, depending on whether or not the parties to the dispute agreed to submit it to the CJEU.[535] If the parties to the dispute have done so, the CJEU will give a ruling on the interpretation of the relevant rules of the EEA Agreement.

588. Two aspects of this process merit being highlighted. First, it is not the EEA Joint Committee that has to agree to request a ruling by the CJEU. It is enough if the parties to the dispute agree to do so.[536] In the light of the fact that EU Member

534. *See also* H. Fredriksen, in Arnesen et al. (eds), *Agreement on the European Economic Area, A Commentary* (2018): 873.
535. So far, there are no examples of the parties agreeing to submit a dispute to the CJEU.
536. *See* H. Fredriksen, in Arnesen et al. (eds), *Agreement on the European Economic Area, A Commentary* (2018): 876.

States are not formally party to a dispute during the political stage of the dispute settlement procedure, one could argue that the agreement will necessarily be between one or more EFTA States on the one hand and the EU on the other hand. However, it has been argued that whether or not an individual EU Member State is competent to agree to request the CJEU to give a ruling would have to be assessed in the light of Article 2 of the EEA Agreement, which defines the term 'Contracting Party' on the EU side by referring to the respective fields of competences of the Community, which will now have to be understood as meaning EU, and its Member States under EU law.[537]

589. Second, the CJEU will not settle the dispute once and for all. It merely rules on the interpretation of the relevant rules of the EEA Agreement. This means that once the CJEU has given its binding and authoritative ruling[538] on such an interpretation, the EEA Joint Committee will have to formally close the matter. The fact that the CJEU does not settle the dispute as such, can be explained by the fact that once the EEA Joint Committee has been entrusted with solving the dispute pursuant to Article 111(1) of the EEA Agreement, it should not be up to two Contracting Parties alone to take the dispute off its agenda. Indeed, as the EEA Joint Committee has the task of 'maintaining the good functioning of the [EEA] Agreement' (*see* Article 111(2) of the EEA Agreement in fine), the dispute has become a matter of interest to all the Contracting Parties.

590. If the parties to the dispute have not requested the CJEU to deliver a ruling on the interpretation of the EEA Agreement, either of the Contracting Parties to the dispute may take safeguard measures in accordance with Article 112(2) of the EEA Agreement, following the procedure of Article 113. This means in particular that the safeguard measures cannot be applied before the lapse of seven months after the matter under dispute has been submitted to the EEA Joint Committee.[539] It also means that the safeguard measure can be taken against one of the Contracting Parties only.[540] The other option that the Contracting Parties to a dispute has, in case they cannot agree on submitting the issue to the CJEU, is to suspend the affected part of the Annex to the EEA Agreement concerned by the dispute. The Contracting Parties can freely choose between the options offered by Article 111(3) of the EEA Agreement.

591. The exercise of the options referred to in Article 111(3) of the EEA Agreement is, however, subject to the condition that such measures are necessary in order

537. *See* S. Norberg et al., *The European Economic Area, EEA Law, A Commentary on the EEA Agreement* 280 (Stockholm: Fritzes 1993).
538. *See* S. Norberg et al., *The European Economic Area, EEA Law, A Commentary on the EEA Agreement* 281 (Stockholm: Fritzes 1993).
539. *See* Art. 113(3) EEA Agreement: 'A Contracting Party may not take safeguard measures until one month has elapsed after the date of notification under paragraph 1.'
540. Article 111(3) of the EEA Agreement only refers to Art. 112(2), thereby excluding the application of Art. 112(3).

to remedy possible imbalances stemming from the dispute. Whether such an imbalance exists, is to be determined by the Contracting Party that resorts to the measures in question. In its assessment, the Contracting Party invoking an imbalance is not entirely free: first, there must be a causal link between the dispute and the imbalance and, second, the Contracting Party must substantiate its claim that there is such an imbalance.[541] If the Contracting Party, against which these measures are taken, contests the fulfilment of this condition, it can always submit the issue to the arbitration tribunal under Article 111(4) of the EEA Agreement. Accordingly, it can be assumed that no surveillance authority is competent to assess whether the condition concerning the imbalance of rights and obligations is fulfilled.[542]

B. Disputes Concerning the Scope or Duration of Safeguard Measures Taken in Accordance with Article 111(3) or 112 of the EEA Agreement or the Proportionality of Rebalancing Measures Taken in Accordance with Article 114 of the EEA Agreement

592. In these cases, any Contracting Party may refer a dispute to an arbitration tribunal pursuant to Article 111(4) of the EEA Agreement and Protocol 33 to the EEA Agreement, which are based on a two party arbitration concept even if there may be two or several participants on either side.[543] The arbitration tribunal takes its decisions by majority and the arbitration award shall be binding upon the Contracting Parties. However, the jurisdiction of the arbitration tribunal is very limited: Article 111(4) of the EEA Agreement requires that both some substantive and some procedural conditions be met before the arbitration procedure can be started.

593. Among the substantive conditions, positive and negative conditions can be distinguished. The former require that the dispute must concern the scope or duration of safeguard measures taken in accordance with Article 111(3) or 112 of the EEA Agreement or the proportionality of rebalancing measures taken in accordance with Article 114 of the EEA Agreement. The fact that disputes regarding safeguard measures or rebalancing measures may be referred to an arbitration tribunal can be explained by the risk of abuse by one Contracting Party in the taking of safeguard and rebalancing measures: The arbitration mechanism allows a Contracting Party to call upon an independent arbitration tribunal when it considers that another Contracting Party has gone too far as regards the scope and duration of a safeguard measure or the proportionality of the ensuing rebalancing measures.[544]

541. *See* S. Norberg et al., *The European Economic Area, EEA Law, A Commentary on the EEA Agreement* 281 (Stockholm: Fritzes 1993).
542. Note that if the surveillance authorities were competent to assess whether the condition concerning the imbalance of rights and obligations is fulfilled, that condition would not be effectively monitored on the EU side, as it would be the Commission that would both invoke the condition and monitor its fulfilment.
543. *See* L. Sevón, 'The EEA Judicial System and the Supreme Courts of the EFTA States', in *Accord EEE – Commentaires et réflexions* 607 (O. Jacot-Guillarmod ed., Zürich: Schulthess 1992).
544. *See* S. Norberg et al., *The European Economic Area, EEA Law, A Commentary on the EEA Agreement* 283 (Stockholm: Fritzes 1993).

594. It has been argued that the actual taking of safeguard measures or rebalancing measures cannot be subject to arbitration.[545] However, that view must be questioned.[546] Indeed, any assessment on the scope, duration or proportionality of a measure always needs to be made based on a point of departure, which is either the threat of serious economic, societal or environmental difficulties of a sectoral or regional nature liable to persist (in the case of safeguard measures) or an imbalance between the rights and obligations created by safeguard measures (in the case of rebalancing measures). If the arbitration tribunal were to find that that point of departure simply did not exist in reality, it could do nothing but consider the measures to be too far-reaching.

595. The negative condition requires that the dispute does not concern a question of interpretation of the provisions of the EEA Agreement referred to in Article 111(3) of the EEA Agreement. This condition is crucial. Indeed, the CJEU has considered that it has been granted the monopoly to interpret EU law.[547] Therefore, and with a view to ensuring that the CJEU would consider the EEA Agreement compatible with the EC Treaty (and now the EU Treaties), it was necessary to exclude from the jurisdiction of the arbitration tribunal any competence that could, even indirectly, affect the CJEU's monopoly.

596. The procedural conditions provided for by the EEA Agreement ensure that the arbitration tribunal is only called upon as a last resort.[548] First, three months must have passed since the dispute has originally been submitted to the EEA Joint Committee. Second, the EEA Joint Committee has not succeeded in resolving the dispute.

597. As it has been indicated above, any Contracting Party may submit a dispute that fulfils all the substantive and procedural conditions to the arbitration tribunal. Contrary to Article 111(3) of the EEA Agreement, there is no need that the Contracting Party that calls upon Article 111(4) of the EEA Agreement be a party to the dispute. If the original dispute opposed an EFTA State to the EU, and the former would take safeguard measures, another EFTA State could submit the dispute to the arbitration tribunal. This being said, if the EU takes safeguard measures against the EFTA States, the EU Member States are not entitled to invoke Article 111(4) of the EEA Agreement. If they could, they could circumvent the provision according to which it is the European Commission that takes the safeguard measures for the EU (Article 113 of the EEA Agreement). Accordingly, as it is the case in Article 111(1)–(3) of the EEA Agreement, the dispute is always dealt with between one or more EFTA States and the EU.

---

545. *Ibid.*

546. *See* H. Fredriksen, in Arnesen et al. (eds), *Agreement on the European Economic Area, A Commentary* (2018): 880.

547. *See* Opinion 1/91 [1991] ECR I-6079, para. 35.

548. So far, this procedure has indeed never been used.

C. Other Disputes

598. It cannot be excluded that a dispute between one or more EFTA States and the EU does not concern the interpretation of provisions of the EEA Agreement, which are identical in substance to the corresponding rules of EU law, and does not concern safeguard or rebalancing measures. Such disputes could, for instance, arise regarding the interpretation of some provisions contained in Part V (Horizontal provisions relevant to the four freedoms) or Part VII (Institutional provisions) of the EEA Agreement or in connection with the interpretation of any act, the substance of which has been adapted for the purposes of the EEA Agreement.

599. As already indicated, the EEA Agreement does not contain a special procedure for settling this kind of disputes. The only provision that could be invoked in this context, is Article 5 of the EEA Agreement on the droit d'évocation.[549] The procedure set out therein is of an essentially political nature. Indeed, if the Contracting Parties do not find an agreement either at the level of the EEA Joint Committee or the EEA Council, the dispute will simply not be resolved. It is only if the dispute concerns the amendment of one of the Annexes to the EEA Agreement that a procedure with an additional incentive for resolving the dispute applies.[550]

§2. Other Relevant Provisions of the EEA Agreement

600. As indicated above, Article 111 of the EEA Agreement is the most important, though not the only, provision of the EEA Agreement regarding dispute settlement. Other provisions also contain rules on how to deal with situations, in which different views on the EEA Agreement prevail in the two pillars. However, all these procedures are of an essentially political nature. Neither of them provides for a procedure leading to a final and authoritative solution.

601. Paragraph III of the sectoral adaptations in Annex XIII (Transport) to the EEA Agreement contains particular rules for disputes that arise between the EFTA States, or between one or more EFTA State and an EU Member State. The disputes that are covered by this *lex specialis*[551] are those for which the acts referred to in the Annex contain special procedures for the settlement of disputes between the EU Member States. However, the provisions of Annex XIII do not set out a dispute settlement procedure in great detail. They merely provide that a dispute that opposes an EFTA State to an EU Member State will be submitted to the EEA Joint Committee for settlement applying equivalent procedures.

602. Article 64 of the EEA Agreement provides for a special procedure where one of the surveillance authorities considers that the other surveillance authority

549. *See infra* Part II, Ch. 6, §2.
550. *See* Art. 102 of the EEA Agreement, *infra* Part II, Ch. 4, §3, II, B, 2.
551. *See* S. Norberg et al., *The European Economic Area, EEA Law, A Commentary on the EEA Agreement* 487 (Stockholm: Fritzes 1993).

does not apply the rules on State aid in conformity with the EEA Agreement.[552] If the two surveillance authorities do not find an agreement on the matter, the competent authority of the affected Contracting Party may take interim measures and consultations shall be held in the EEA Joint Committee. If these consultations fail to lead to a conclusion within three months, the interim measures may be replaced by permanent measures.

603. Another provision, which provides for a political process designed to settle disputes, is the droit d'évocation. The droit d'évocation was a major claim of the EFTA States during negotiation. The importance of the droit d'évocation is illustrated by the fact that it is not only referred to in Articles 89(2) and 92(2) of the EEA Agreement, but also in general terms in Article 5 of the EEA Agreement in Part I (Objectives and principles).[553] The reason for the importance of the droit d'évocation is twofold. First, it could be used by the EFTA States to obtain the opportunity to get involved at least in the decision-shaping of the EU acts at an early stage; second, it allows the EFTA States to suggest common solutions to problems encountered in the implementation of the EEA Agreement.[554] While the former has not really materialized, the latter reason of importance of the droit d'évocation has proved to be very much used by the EFTA States.

604. In substance, the droit d'évocation consists of the right of each Contracting Party to raise a problem at any time in the EEA Joint Committee or the EEA Council. Pursuant to Article 5 of the EEA Agreement, that right is to be exercised in accordance with the modalities laid down in Articles 92(2) and 89(2) of the EEA Agreement, respectively. While Article 92(2) of the EEA Agreement provides that the Contracting Parties shall hold consultations in the EEA Joint Committee on any point of relevance to the EEA Agreement giving rise to a difficulty and raised by one of them, Article 89(2) of the EEA Agreement stipulates that the Contracting Parties may, after having discussed it in the EEA Joint Committee, or directly in exceptionally urgent cases, raise in the EEA Council any issue giving rise to a difficulty.

605. The droit d'évocation set out in the provisions referred to in the previous paragraph merits clarifications on two points. On the one hand, the Contracting Parties may raise any matter giving rise to a difficulty. Hence, they may raise questions concerning not only interpretation, implementation or application of the rules of the EEA Agreement, but also questions in the context of the decision-making procedure under the Agreement.[555] The matters that could be raised under the droit d'évocation are virtually unlimited, as long as they in some way concern the EEA

552. *See* C. Jordal & G. Mathisen, in Arnesen et al. (eds), *Agreement on the European Economic Area, A Commentary* (2018): 610–612.

553. *See* D. Tynes, in Arnesen et al. (eds), *Agreement on the European Economic Area, A Commentary* (2018): 209.

554. *See* O. Jacot-Guillarmod, 'Préambule, objectifs et principes', in *Accord EEE – Commentaires et réflexions* 63 (O. Jacot-Guillarmod ed., Zürich: Schulthess, 1992), and the discussions in the EEA Council on the Community agencies.

555. *See* S. Norberg et al., *The European Economic Area, EEA Law, A Commentary on the EEA Agreement* 103 (Stockholm: Fritzes 1993).

Agreement. On the other hand, the use of the words 'at any time' in Article 5 of the EEA Agreement implies that any matter raised under the droit d'évocation should be discussed without delay, depending on how urgent the matter is in the opinion of the Contracting Parties raising it.[556]

556. *See* S. Norberg et al., *The European Economic Area, EEA Law, A Commentary on the EEA Agreement* 104 (Stockholm: Fritzes 1993).

Chapter 7. Finance

§1. Financing of EFTA Participation in EU Activities

606. As it has been explained before, the costs incurred by the EFTA Secretariat in connection with the provision of services for EEA matters are reflected in the budget of the EFTA Secretariat.[557] What is not covered by the EFTA Secretariat's budget is the EFTA States' contribution for their participation in EU activities. These contributions are determined in the so-called EEA budget and are to be transferred by the EFTA States directly into the EU budget, without transiting through EFTA. The contributions of the EFTA States are additional to the funds already foreseen by the EU budget, that is, the total budget for the EU activity is increased due to the EFTA participation.[558]

607. The principles governing the EEA budget are set out in Article 82 and Protocol 32 to the EEA Agreement and distinguish contributions to the operational and administrative budgets of the activities concerned. The level of the contributions to the operational budgets is based on a proportion of the GDP figures in the EFTA States compared to that of the EC. Contributions to the administrative budgets are negotiated individually for each activity and may include contributions in kind by the provision of staff.

608. The procedure of the EEA budget is, to a large extent, dependent on the budgetary procedure on the EU side. A first set of discussions between the EFTA and EU side regarding the EEA budget normally takes place at the end of the second semester of the year preceding the financial year in question, after the Commission has presented a proposal for the EU budget. At this time, a preliminary draft EEA budget is drawn up. This preliminary draft EEA budget is subsequently scrutinized within each pillar and discussed again in a second meeting between the two pillars.

609. Once the EU budget has been adopted, the draft EEA budget can be finalized and cleared within the EFTA pillar. This happens normally in January or February of the financial year concerned. The draft budget is then handed over to the Commission, which is responsible for clearing the budget in the EU pillar. The common goal of the EFTA and EU pillar is to adopt the EEA budget as early as possible in the year, if possible no later than February.

610. The EEA budget adopted early each financial year may sometimes include activities entered sous réserve. This concerns activities, in which the EFTA States are expected to participate on the basis of a Decision of the EEA Joint Committee yet to be adopted. If that Decision of the EEA Joint Committee is, however, not

557. *See supra* Part I, Ch. 5.
558. The EFTA States' contributions to the reduction of economic and social disparities through the so-called EFTA funds are not included in the EEA budget.

adopted in the first half of the financial year in question, the relevant budget line may be deleted by the EEA Joint Committee, when adopting the final adjusted EEA budget in June.

§2. Financing the EFTA Surveillance Authority and the EFTA Court

611. According to Article 47 SCA, the Governments of the EFTA States shall, on a proposal from the Authority and after consulting a committee consisting of members of Parliament of the EFTA States, who are members of the EEA Joint Parliamentary Committee, each year before 1 January by common accord establish a budget for the coming year and the apportionment of those expenses between the EFTA States. The Authority shall be consulted before a decision modifying or amending its proposal for a budget is adopted. As it was seen most correct that independence from the EFTA States should also pertain to administrative and financial matters, the Governments of the EFTA States have decided that they should only decide on the approval of the budget of the Authority. The Governments have, moreover, decided to exercise this role within the framework of the so-called ESA/EFTA Court Committee. The Governments are represented in this Committee via their ambassadors to the EU in Brussels.

612. For the same reasons, namely independence of the EFTA Court from the EFTA States, the Governments of the EFTA States have similarly decided that they should only decide on the approval of the budget of the EFTA Court. Thus, according to Article 48 SCA, the Governments shall, on a proposal from the EFTA Court, each year before 1 January by common accord establish a budget for the EFTA Court for the coming year and the apportionment of those expenses between them. As it is the case for the budget of the Authority, the Governments have decided to exercise this task within the framework of the so-called ESA/EFTA Court Committee.

Chapter 8. Publications and Addresses

§1. PUBLICATIONS

613. The EFTA Secretariat, the EFTA Surveillance Authority and the EFTA Court each have their own internet addresses, which are the following: www.efta.int, www.eftasurv.int and www.eftacourt.int. All three websites contain detailed information on the day-to-day developments in the fields of operations of the bodies concerned and include unofficial versions of the underlying legal texts and, when appropriate, unofficial consolidated versions thereof.

614. The EFTA Surveillance Authority publishes an annual report on its activities pursuant to an obligation imposed on it by Article 21 SCA. Of particular note are also biannual publications of the Internal Market Scoreboard containing an up-to-date snapshot of its enforcement efforts in the internal market area, supplemented by a wealth of statistical data, as well as an Annual Report. The Authority's website also hosts a Public Document Database through which all formal decisions adopted can be accessed, including usually the full-text versions of letters of formal notice and reasoned opinions issued to the EFTA States in the exercise of the Authority's enforcement powers.

615. The website of the EFTA Secretariat contains also electronic versions of the publications of EFTA. Among these publications is the Annual Report, which describes each year the activities of EFTA and the EFTA Secretariat.

The EFTA Secretariat, in cooperation with the Publication Office of the European Union, also publishes the EEA Supplement to the Official Journal of the European Union. This publication serves as the official journal for any matter of EEA relevance in the Icelandic and Norwegian languages.

§2. ADDRESSES

616. The EFTA Secretariat's three offices are located at the following addresses:

In Geneva (Headquarters):

EFTA Secretariat

9-11, Rue Varembé
CH-1211 Geneva 20
Switzerland
Tel: 41 22 332 2600
E-mail: mail.gva@efta.int

In Brussels:

EFTA Secretariat

Avenue des Arts 19H
B-1000 Brussels
Belgium
Tel: 32 2 286 17 11
E-mail: mail.bxl@efta.int

Financial Mechanism Office

Postal address:
Avenue des Arts 19H
B-1000 Brussels
Belgium
Tel: 32 2 286 17 01
E-mail: info-fmo@efta.int

In Luxemburg:

EFTA Statistical Adviser's Office

Postal address:
European Commission, Eurostat Bech F2/908 L-2920 Luxembourg
Luxembourg
Visiting address:
Bâtiment BECH
Rue Alphonse Weicker 5
L-2721 Luxembourg
Luxembourg
Tel: 352 4301 37775
E-mail: efta-lux@ec.europa.eu

The EFTA Surveillance Authority's offices are located at the following address:

EFTA Surveillance Authority

Avenue des Arts 19H
B-1000 Brussels
Belgium
Tel: 32 2 286 18 11
E-mail: registry@eftasurv.int

The EFTA Court's offices are located at the following address:

EFTA Court

1, Rue du Fort Thüngen
L-1499 Luxembourg
Luxembourg

Tel: 352 42 1081
E-mail: eftacourt@eftacourt.int

Selected Bibliography

Arnesen, F. *Statslig Styring og EØS-retlige skranker.* Oslo: Universitetsforlaget, 1996.

Arnesen, et al. 'Agreement of the European Economic Area – A Commentary'. Baden-Baden: Nomos, C.H. Beck and Hart, 2018.

Arnesen, F. et al. *Oversikt over EØS-retten.* Oslo: Universitetsforlaget, 2022.

Barents, R. 'The Court of Justice and the EEA Agreement: Between Constitutional Values and Political Realities'. In *The European Economic Area EC-EFTA*, edited by Stuyck & Looijestijn-Clearie. Dordrecht: Kluwer, 2000.

Baudenbacher, C. 'The EFTA Court – An Example of the Judicialisation of International Economic Law'. *European Law Review* (2003): 880.

Baudenbacher, C. 'The Legal Nature of EEA Law in the Course of Time'. In *Afmælisrit Tor Vilhjálmsson*, edited by Björgvinsson. Reykjavik: Bókaútgáfá Orators, 2000.

Baudenbacher, C., Tresselt P. & T. Orlygsson. *The EFTA Court Ten Years On.* Oregon: Oxford and Portland, 2005.

Baudenbacher, C. *The EFTA Court in Action.* Stuttgart: German Law Publishers, 2010.

Baudenbacher, C. (ed.). *The Handbook of EEA Law.* Cham, Heidelberg: Springer, 2016.

Baur, G. 'Preliminary Rulings in the EEA: Bridging (Institutional) Homogeneity and Procedural Autonomy by Exchange of Information'. In *The EEA and the EFTA Court*, edited by Baudenbacher. Oxford: Hart, 2014.

Bergmann, E. 'Iceland and the EEA 1994–2011'. *Europautredningen.* Utvalget for utredning av Norges avtaler med EU, Rapport no. 7., Oslo, 2011.

Bernitz, U. 'Om EEA-avtalet – Backgrund, utformning och tolkning'. In *EEA-avtalet i svensk ret*, edited by Bernitz, et al. Stockholm: Juristförlaget, 1993.

Bieber, R. 'EWR-Abkommen und parlamentarische Zusammenarbeit'. In *Accord EEE – Commentaires et réflexions*, edited by Jacot-Guillarmod. Zürich: Schulthess, 1992.

Björgvinsson, D.T. 'Application of Article 34 of the ESA/Court Agreement by the Icelandic Court'. In *Economic Law and Justice in Times of Globalisation*, edited by Monti, et al. Festschrift for Carl Baudenbacher. Baden-Baden: Nomos 2007, 37.

Broberg, M. & N. Fenger. *Preliminary References to the European Court of Justice.* Oxford: Oxford University Press, 2010.

Børde, K. 'The European Economic Area, Norway and the European Union: Achievements, Possibilities and Limitations'. In *The European Economic Area – Norway's Basic Status in the Legal Construction of Europe*, edited by Müller-Graff & Selvig. Berlin: Berlin Verlag A. Spitz, 1997.

Bright, C. & K. Williams. 'Understanding the European Economic Area: Context, Institutions, and Legal Systems'. In *Business Law in the European Economic Area.* Oxford: Oxford Press Oxford, 1994.

Bruha, T. 'Is the EEA an Internal Market?'. In *EEA-EU Relations*, edited by Müller-Graff & Selvig. Berlin: Berlin Verlag, 1999.

Bull, H. 'EØS-avtalen – litt om avtalens struktur og om prinsippene for gjennemføring i norsk rett'. *Lov og Rett* (1992): 583.

Christiansen, P. 'The EFTA Court'. *European Law Review* (1997): 539.

Due, O. 'The EFTA Court and Its Relationship to the European Court of Justice'. In *The Fifth Nordic Conference on EFTA and the European Union*, edited by Sundström. Helsinki: Yliopistopaino, 1994.

Due, O. 'The EFTA Court and Its Responsibility to the European Court of Justice'. In *The Fifth Nordic Conference on EFTA and the European Union*, edited by Sundström. Helsinki: Yliopistopaino, 1994.

Everson, M., M. Vahl & S. Woolcock. *Navigating by the Stars.* Brussels: Centre for European Policy Studies, 2002.

Felder, D. 'Structure institutionnelle et procédure décisionnelle de l'EEE'. In *Accord EEE – Commentaires et réflexions*, edited by Jacot-Guillarmod. Zürich: Schulthess, 1992.

Fenger, N. 'Limits to a Dynamic Homogeneity between EC Law and EEA Law'. In *Liber Amicorum Claus Gulmann*, edited by Fenger, Hagel-Sørensen & Vesterdorf. Copenhagen: Thomson, 2006.

Forman, J. 'The EEA Agreement Five Years on: Dynamic Homogeneity in Practice and its Implementation by the two EEA Courts'. *Common Market Law Review* (1999): 751.

Foss, T. 'Fiskeri'. In *EØS-håndboken, EØS-Avtalen – innhold og praktisering*, edited by Gjønnes, Knudtzon. Oslo: Universitetsforlaget, 1998.

Gjems-Onstad, O. *EØS-afvtalen og EØS-loven.* Oslo: Gyldendal, 2000.

Gjønnes, K. *EØS-håndboken, EØS-Avtalen – innhold og praktisering.* Oslo: Universitetsforlaget, 1998.

Gormley, L. 'The European Economic Area and the Europe Agreements'. In *The European Economic Area EC-EFTA*, edited by Stuyck & Looijestijn-Clearie. Dordrecht: Kluwer, 2000.

Graver, H.P. & U. Sverdrup. *ESA og Norge.* Oslo: Arena, 2002.

Graver, H.P. 'The EFTA Court and the Court of Justice of the EC: Legal Homogeneity at Stake?'. In *EEA-EU Relations*, *EEA-EU Relations*, edited by Müller-Graff & Selvig. Berlin: Berlin Verlag, 1999.

Haas, G. & V. Zellweger. 'Allgemeine und Schlussbestimmungen'. In *Accord EEE – Commentaires et réflexions*, edited by Jacot-Guillarmod. Zürich: Schulthess, 1992.

Haukeland Fredriksen, H. 'Om mangelen på tolkningsspørsmål fra norske domstoler til EFTA-domstolen'. *Jussens Venner* (2006): 372.

Haukeland Fredriksen, H. 'Er EFTA-domstolen mer katolsk enn paven? Noen betraktninger om EFTA-domstolens dynamiske utvikling av EØS-retten og streben etter dialog med EF-domstolen'. *Tidsskrift for Rettsvitenskap* (2009): 507.

Haukeland Fredriksen, H. 'EU/EØS-rett i norske domstoler'. Europautredningen, Rapport No. 3: Oslo, https://bora.uib.no/bora-xmlui/bitstream/handle/1956/8056/E%c3%98S-rett%20i%20norske%20domstoler.pdf?sequence=1&isAllowed=y.

Haukeland Fredriksen, H. 'Hvem avgjør tolkningen af EØS-avtalen'. *Tidsskrift for Rettsvitenskap* (2010): 247.

Haukeland Fredriksen, H. & Mathisen G. '*EØS-rett*' 4. utgave. Oslo: Fagbokforlaget, 2022.

Hayes, E. 'The Internal Market and EFTA As Viewed from Bruxelles'. In *EFTA and the EC: Implications of 1992*, edited by Laursen. Maastricht: European Institute of Public Administration, 1990.

Hettne, J. & M. Fritz. *Sverige möter EG-rätten – EES-avtalet och dess införlivande med svensk rätt.* Stockholm: Nerenius & Santérus, 1994.

Jacot-Guillarmod, O. 'Préambule, objectifs et principes'. In *Accord EEE – Commentaires et réflexions*, edited by Jacot-Guillarmod. Zürich: Schulthess, 1992.

Jerwell, S.L. *Lovgivningen i EØS – Beslutningsprosessen, gjennomføringen og konsekvensene.* Oslo: Capellen Akademisk Forlag, 2002.

Johansson, M. & S. Norberg. 'EFTA-Domstolen – Garant för det homogena EES – Reflektioner i ljuset av 17 års tillämpning av EES-avtalet'. *Europarättslig Tidskrift* (2011): 379.

Laursen, F. 'EC-EFTA Relations: A Game-Theory Perspective'. In *The Political Economy of European Integration*, edited by Laursen. Maastricht: European Institute of Public Administration, 1995.

Magnussen, M. 'Traktatbruddsøksmål ved EFTA-domstolen'. *LoR* (2002): 131.

Magnusson, S. 'On the Authority of Advisory Opinions, Reflections on the Functions and the Normativity of Advisory Opinions of the EFTA Court'. *Europarättslig Tidskrift* (2010): 528.

Mathisen, G. 'Om EFTA Domstolen'. *Europarättslig Tidskrift* (2010): 13.

Müller A. & Schroeder W. (eds). '*25 Jahre Europäischer Wirtschaftsraum*'. Baden-Baden: Nomos, 2020.

Müller-Graff, P.C. 'EEA-Agreement and EC Law: A comparison in Scope and Content'. In *The European Economic Area – Norway's Basic Status in the Legal Construction of Europe*, edited by Müller-Graff & Selvig. Berlin: Berlin Verlag, 1997.

Norberg, S. 'Perspectives on the Future Development of the EEA'. In *Afmælisrit Tor Vilhjálmsson*, edited by Björgvinsson. Reykjavik: Bókaútgáfa Orators, 2000.

Norberg, S. 'The Dynamic and Homogeneous European Economic Area – Challenges for the EFTA Court'. *European Business Law Review* (1994): 191.

Norberg, S. 'The EFTA Court and Its Relations to the European Court of Justice'. In *The Fifth Nordic Conference on EFTA and the European Union*, edited by Sundström. Helsinki: Yliopistopaino, 1994.

Norberg, S. 'The EFTA Court, One of the Two Main Components of the EEA Judicial Mechanism'. In *The European Economic Area EC-EFTA*, edited by Stuyck & Looijestijn-Clearie. Dordrecht: Kluwer, 2000.

Norberg, S. 'The EFTA Court'. In *European Courts, Practice and Precedents*, edited by Plender. London: Sweet & Maxwell, 1997.

Norberg, S., et al. *The European Economic Area, EEA Law, A Commentary on the EEA Agreement.* Stockholm: Fritzes, 1993.

Reymond, C. 'Institutions, Decision-making Procedure and Settlement of Disputes in the European Economic Area'. *Common Market Law Review* (1993): 449.

Sánchez Rydelski, M. 'Private Enforcement of EEA Law in Liechtenstein', *Liechtensteinische Juristen-Zeitung*, LJZ 3/23 (2023).

Sejersted, F. 'Between Sovereignty and Supranationalism in the EEA Context – On the Legal Dynamics of the EEA Agreement'. In *The European Economic Area – Norway's Basic Status in the Legal Construction of Europe*, edited by Müller-Graff & Selvig. Berlin: Berlin Verlag A. Spitz, 1997.

Sevón, L. 'The EFTA Court and Its Relations to the European Court of Justice'. In *The Fifth Nordic Conference on EFTA and the European Union*, edited by Sundström. Helsinki: Yliopistopaino, 1994.

Sevón, L. 'The ECJ, the EFTA Court and the National Courts of the EFTA Countries'. In *Rettsteori og Rettsliv – Festskrift til Carsten Smith*, edited by Lødrup, et al. Oslo: Universitetsforlaget, 2002.

Sevón, L. 'The EEA Judicial System and the Supreme Courts of the EFTA States'. In *Accord EEE, Commentaires et réflexions*, edited by Jacot-Guillarmod. Zürich: Schulthess, 1992.

Sevón, L. & M. Johansson. 'The Protection of the Rights of Individuals under the EEA Agreement'. *European Law Review* (1999): 373.

Skouris, V. 'The ECJ and the EFTA Court under the EEA Agreement: A Paradigm for International Cooperation between Judicial Institutions'. In *The EFTA Court Ten Years On*, edited by Baudenbacher, Tresselt & Orlygsson. Oregon: Oxford and Portland, 2005.

Stefánsson, S.M. 'The EEA Agreement and Fish and Other Marine Products'. In *Fiskeripolitikken i EØS*, edited by Eisenreich. Copenhagen: Nordisk Råd for Forskning i Europæisk Integrationsret, 1996.

Svedman, S.E. *Prosperity.* In *The Fundamental Principles of EEA Law*, edited by Baudenbacher, Springer, 2017.

van Gerven, W. 'The Genesis of EEA Law and the Principles of Primacy and Direct Effect'. *Fordham International Law Journal* 3 (1992): 955.

van Stiphout, T. 'Achieving Legal Homogeneity in the Field of Free Movement of Capital'. In *Rit Lagadeildar (Faculty of Law's Collection).* Bifröst School of Business, 2006.

van Stiphout, T. 'Homogeneity vs. Decision-Making Autonomy in the EEA Agreement'. *European Journal of Law Reform* 3. Eleven International Publishing (2007): 431.

van Stiphout, T. 'The l'Oreal Cases – Some Thoughts on the Role of the EFTA Court in the EEA Legal Framework: Because It's Worth It!'. *Jus & News* (2009), 1.

Vilhjálmsson, T. 'EFTA-domstolen'. In *Rettsteori og Rettsliv – Festskrift til Carsten Smith*, edited by Lødrup, et al. Oslo: Universitetsforlaget, 2002.

Wahl, N. 'Relevanta avgöranden av EG-domstolen'. In: *EES-avtalet i svensk rätt*, edited by Bernitz, et al. Stockholm: Juristförlaget, 1993.

Wallis, D. *Forgotten Enlargement.* London: Centre for Reform, 2002.

Weiss, F. 'The European Economic Area Agreement – A Legal Still Life'. *Yearbook of European Law*, 1992.
Wijkman, P.M. 'The Winding Voyage to and beyond the EEA'. In *35 Years of Free Trade in Europe*, edited by Ems. Geneva: EFTA, 1995.
Zatschler, C. 'Priority'. In *The Fundamental Principles of EEA Law*, edited by Baudenbacher, Springer, 2017.

Index

The numbers here refer to paragraph numbers.

Index

www.ingramcontent.com/pod-product-compliance
Lightning Source LLC
Chambersburg PA
CBHW071444230926
51846CB00001B/333
* 9 7 8 9 4 0 3 5 3 3 9 8 8 *